# FRAGILE
# EDEN

# FRAGILE EDEN

*A Ride Through New Zealand*

Robin Hanbury-Tenison

Salem House Publishers

Topsfield, Massachusetts

First published in the United States by Salem House Publishers, 1989
462 Boston Street, Topsfield, Massachusetts, 01983

*Library of Congress Cataloging in Publication Data*
Hanbury-Tenison, Robin.
Fragile Eden: a ride through New Zealand /
by Robin Hanbury-Tenison.
p.   cm.
Includes index.
ISBN 0-88162-413-6: $19.95
1. New Zealand—Description and travel—1981–
2. Hanbury-Tenison, Robin—Journeys—New Zealand.
3. New Zealand—Economic conditions—1945–
I. Title.
DU413.H36 1989
919.31′0437—dc 19
88-31127
CIP

ISBN: 0 88162 413 6

Printed and bound in Great Britain

# Contents

Toitu he kainga, whatunga rongaro he tangata.

The land will remain long after the people have vanished from the earth.

*Maori proverb*

# *Acknowledgements*

As always with a long journey, there are far too many people who helped us in innumerable ways for it to be possible to mention them all. There were those New Zealanders who gave advice freely both before and after the ride; many will be disappointed to see that we did not always take it. In particular we are grateful to His Excellency Mr Bryce Harland, the New Zealand High Commissioner to the Court of St James, for his encouragement, and to Glynn Christian, the New Zealand writer, for his advice.

There were farmers throughout both islands, especially those of the high country, who let us ride across their land, use their musterers' huts and shearers' quarters. They did not have to do so and were generous to trust us. We would like to assure them that we always left gates as we found them.

But there are invariably one or two people whose help makes the difference between success and failure. Robyn and Kitt Grigg gave the initial impetus to make us believe it was possible; Bernard Pinney showed us the way and told us what to do; above all Clyde and Carol Langford took the trouble to set it up, get the horses, find Jacky and lend us their truck. To them all we are especially indebted.

Louella once again receives only scant praise for her courage and fortitude, for smoothing our way by charming those we met and never complaining. She and I would both like to dedicate this book to our three horses, Manaaki, Wahini (One Whinney) and Star, but chiefly to Jacky who made it all such fun.

# Introduction

Noel Coward spent a couple of months in New Zealand once. On his return to England he was asked how he had found it.

'Closed' he replied. And this is how most Europeans still think of New Zealand. A beautiful place certainly, inhabited by splendid farmers and peaceful natives, but definitely boring. Innumerable coffee table books written by New Zealanders about their country do not help to dispel this image. They extol the scenery and the human energy to be found there but, however breathtaking the photography and impressive the achievements, the result is bland and one begins to wonder if there is much beneath the surface.

This book is an attempt to see behind the façade of a country I expected to like but did not think I would grow to be moved and excited by. The inevitability of a visit to New Zealand had been growing on me for some time. Our hill farm in Cornwall has been under strong New Zealand influence ever since Hugh Fullerton-Smith, known to all as Pancho, came into my life. In 1974 he began a thorough reorganization of what was then a rundown and un-economic enterprise. He used gangs of his compatriots, often highly qualified in other fields such as accountancy or architecture, but mostly from farming backgrounds and taking some time off to see the world. They came and went, cheerfully farming, digging, building in all weathers without making a fuss or expecting any special favours. I grew to admire their self reliance and steady good humour, to recognize as national characteristics their trustworthiness and stead-fastness. They all assumed we would come to their country and look them up one day.

More recently we had forged closer farming ties with the country. Pancho, now share farming with me, was awarded a Nuffield scholarship for agriculture in 1985 in order to study angora goat farming and mohair production in New Zealand. As a result of his three-month visit we became pioneers of this virtually unknown type of farming in Britain. He also returned full of enthusiasm for deer farming as a promising form of agriculture with a great future, so we sold all our cows and began bringing in magnificent stags and hinds to our newly fenced enclosures. Both these enterprises were started in partnership with innovative New Zealand farmers who had long-term experience of goat and deer husbandry, which has for more than a decade been a familiar part of the agricultural scene over there.

My wife Louella's father was born in New Zealand and she had scores of relatives there; she had visited it seventeen years before and loved it. The time had clearly come for her to show me somewhere for a change.

We chose to ride through the two main islands on horses because that is the best way to see a country and because it seemed especially appropriate to do so through one the size of England and Wales but with only one-sixteenth of our population. Our first long ride together had been across France and had come about because we needed new horses for the farm and had fallen in love with the wild white horses of the Camargue. Having bought two we naturally rode them home, and that ride became an idyll of autumnal French orchards, inns with mouth-watering food and long, deserted, cross-country paths through forests and meadows.

Next we survived a hard and exhausting 1,000 miles through China, largely on the edge of the Gobi Desert where we suffered ordeal by heat and filth, which can be quite stimulating, and by incomprehension and obdurate bureaucracy, which are dispiriting. As we rode we talked of making another ride together but promised ourselves that this time it would be through an English-speaking democracy for a change, where we could look forward to a hot bath sometimes. Days spent in the saddle from dawn to dusk do make the prospect of occasional moments of luxury peculiarly appealing.

In New Zealand we wanted to avoid roads completely and with all our good contacts we were optimistic we would be allowed to ride across country for most of the way. It was a glorious journey and we enjoyed it hugely; but it was full of surprises.

Instead of stolid, unimaginative farmers, concerned only with material survival, we found thoughtful and often cultured and sensitive people facing a series of economic crises which were rocking the foundations of their lives. Instead of the fat, green, fertile land we had expected, much of the country we rode through was young and fragile, threatened by noxious, introduced pests and in places in danger of collapse from over use. And instead of docile Maori, cheerfully accepting their role as second-class citizens, we learned that through the new Waitangi Tribunal they are demanding the return of much of their land and actively asserting their rights to a separate culture, language and identity.

It is these very real but, I believe, not insuperable problems which make New Zealand an exciting place; because the New Zealanders will overcome them in time and with luck, thus making their country a true Eden. Perhaps their difficulty the first time around was that there were no serpents in their garden and so they have had first to create and then learn to exorcise their own devils in order to become a whole people.

We came to see this small, underpopulated and generally success-ful country as a microcosm of the problems besetting many other nations today. On the surface the people were confident and robust, grasping the challenges they face enthusiastically and overcoming each difficulty with the resourcefulness for which they are renowned. Yet underneath we found a rapidly growing questioning of the conventional wisdoms which brought with it fear and uncertainty. New Zealand is a country undergoing profound changes environ-mentally, socially and agriculturally; the rest of the world will have a lot to learn from watching how they deal with them.

# Chapter One

# Farms and Fires

The mountains looked brown and parched, bare of all vegetation, monochrome and empty. We could have been over northern China and I half expected to see the line of the Great Wall following the ridges. Instead there were zig-zag tracks occasionally revealing the steepness of the slopes and, in the background, the snow-capped peaks of the southern Alps, which might just as well have been the Himalayas. From these, great braided rivers could be seen bringing snow melt down from the glaciers to make a smudge of cloudy water at the top end of the still, azure lakes into which they flowed. It was strangely comforting to see a form of apparent pollution which was for once not attributable to man.

This was the country we would be riding through and it looked hard and uncompromising. Apparently it was once covered in forests, but I could see none from the air. What have we done to our poor planet? Like a dog with mange, we seem to have scratched it bare. Even here, in a part which had previously escaped man's depredations, it appeared he had worked twice as hard to catch up. I began to wonder if coming to New Zealand was a mistake. It was the last time I did so.

We had arrived in Auckland jet-lagged and exhausted from different sides of the world, and had taken an onward flight to Invercargill. Louella had been left to cope with last-minute arrangements at home and with packing and transporting all our luggage. There was far less than we had needed when we rode on horses along the Great Wall of China but it still made a formidable pile of cases which, thanks to Air New Zealand's efficiency, had all arrived safely in Auckland.

Louella's journey from Cornwall to Auckland took thirty-four hours and she arrived early in the morning with plenty of time to catch the connection on to Invercargill at 9.00 a.m. My flight from Kuala Lumpur was late and touched down at 8.40 a.m. I had resigned myself to missing the connection and having to make new plans, but my name was called out and an elegant stewardess took me in hand and raced me through immigration and customs before pointing me in the direction of the taxis. I had five minutes to get to the other terminal where more staff would be waiting to rush me on to the internal flight on which Louella, who had arranged all this, would be waiting. 'I'll send your suitcase on, don't worry!', she shouted after me and I realized that for once I was in a country where I could reasonably believe that she would. A few moments later, I burst into the cabin of Louella's plane to find her calmly expecting me to make it; and to hear the pilot saying, 'Welcome aboard, boys and girls. We plan this flight to be good as gold so just sit back and relax.'

On the way out to New Zealand I had spent a week in Malaysia as the leader of an international fact-finding mission looking into deforestation in Borneo and the arrests of environmentalists who had dared to question their government's policies. It had been a profoundly depressing experience, during which we had come up against a cynical disregard on the part of ministers both for human rights and for sound scientific evidence of the disastrous course they were taking. The plundering of Sarawak's remaining forests is one of the worst examples of the greedy demolition of the world's richest ecosystem in order to line a few politicians' pockets.

As a result my environmental hat was firmly in place as we flew down the South Island of New Zealand on a baking cloudless day in mid-January. I wear several hats and they sometimes sit a touch uneasily together on my head. As a practical farmer, I am concerned with earning a good living from the rather poor land we farm at 800 feet on Bodmin Moor. This often involves working the land hard, as well as the application of some fertilizers and pesticides. However, over the years I have also become increasingly committed to conservation, both on my own farm, where I have planted quite large areas with indigenous hardwoods, as well as bringing back wild-flower water-meadows, and in tropical rain forests and deserts all over the world, where I have taken part in scientific expeditions. So it was with particular interest that I peered down at the dramatic landscape below.

Man only came to New Zealand a thousand or so years ago. The earliest Polynesian ocean travellers discovered the previously unin-habited islands some time before AD 1000, but the main Maori arrivals did not happen until a few hundred years later, perhaps around 1350, which was in turn only 300 years before Abel Tasman became the first European to sight New Zealand. By contrast the Australian aborigines are now thought to have crossed from New Guinea via land bridges as much as 40,000 years ago.

Unlike the aborigines, the Maori cultivated the land from the beginning, growing crops of taro, yams, gourds, fernroot and the sweet potato, the kumara, which they had brought with them in their canoes. Early Europeans noted how meticulously these gardens were prepared and dug, with light fences to protect the young plants from the wind, and careful weeding of the neat rows. Ironically, however, these horticultural skills were largely forgotten or ignored by the early British settlers, who were determined to impose their own systems of agriculture on this new land, which bore so many superficial resemblances to their homeland, but was in reality so very different.

For a century or so after serious colonization by Europeans began, the land was rich enough to support their exploitation of it, which largely consisted of removing its gold and timber, while converting as much as possible to grass. This produced mutton, wool and dairy products, which became the mainstay of the country's economy, Britain's consumption of all three being apparently limitless, so that New Zealand was sometimes described as 'an offshore farm for Britain'. Then came the Common Market and the need for change. Alternative markets for these products were not easy to find and it became necessary to start doing something different.

What New Zealand has achieved in the last fifteen years or so is quite remarkable. The almost total economic dependence on grass has gone, to be replaced by horticulture with some of the most advanced and high-quality fruit production in the world and vineyards where excellent wine is made in large quantities and by the most modern methods. These changes have brought with them, too, a transformation of the people's character and behaviour. The need to compete in a complex world has given them a new confidence, confirmed by their success not just in commercial enterprises but also in sport and in the arts. The case of wine is indicative of this impact; not long ago, we were told, pubs where no 'sheilas' would be seen, were packed with urgent beer drinkers in the evening for what was known as 'the 6 o'clock swill'. Now most households serve and appreciate wine, as well as beer, and a change in the law has removed the necessity of putting away as much beer as possible by 6.00 p.m.

Though there is much to be learnt from the example set by New Zealand in how to adapt to changing conditions and to overcome what may seem like insuperable difficulties, the environmental and social costs of New Zealand's past mistakes have been high. These interested me just as much as the agricultural changes which we hoped to see on our journey.

★     ★     ★

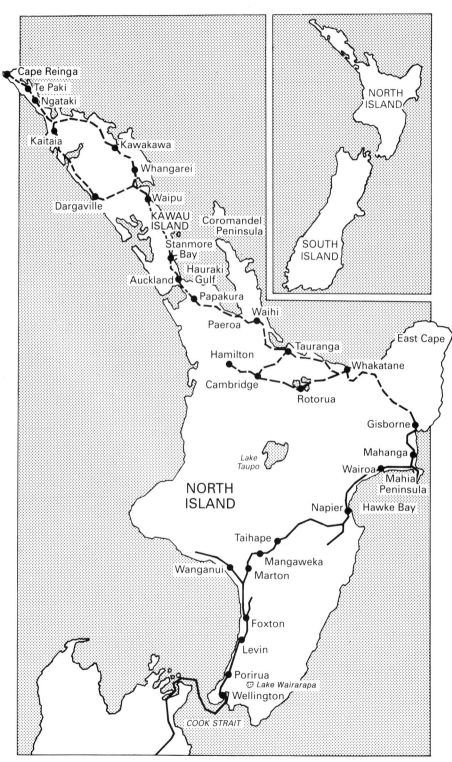

The North Island, Maui's fish to the Maori. Turn the map on its side and it does indeed become a leaping fish.

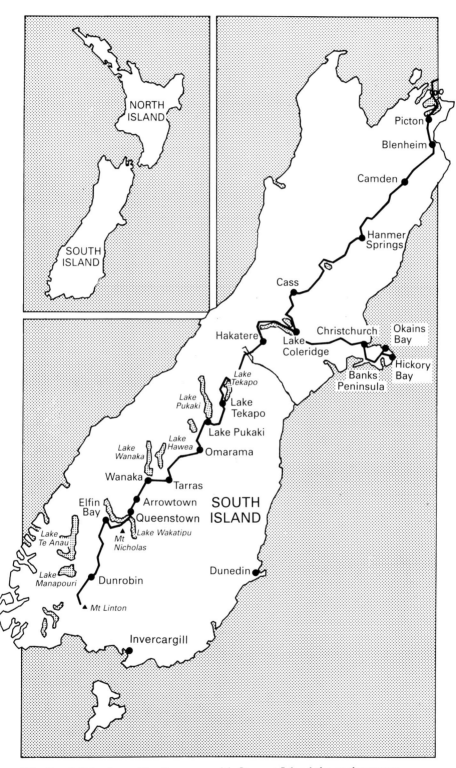

The South Island was Maui's canoe, with Stewart Island the anchor stone.

At Invercargill Clyde and Carol Langford, our partners in the angora goat enterprise, met us in the truck which was to be our support vehicle for the next eight weeks. They had driven down in it from Gisborne, taking four days over the 750 mile (1,200 km) journey which we were about to retrace more slowly on horseback. They had brought three horses, so that we should have one as a spare, and they had also found someone to drive the truck and be our 'minder'. Her name was Jacky Fitzgerald and she was employed by Riding for the Disabled in Gisborne, where she taught physically and mentally handicapped children and adults, and also socially deprived and maladjusted teenagers, to find a new confidence and self-respect through learning to ride horses.

She and the horses had been dropped off at Mount Linton Station, just north of Invercargill, and we now set off in the truck to drive there. This was Clyde's farm truck, but he had had it cleverly modified for our journey. In spite of being relatively small it could still carry three horses, had room for three passengers in the cab and had a large compartment behind that for transporting feed and baggage in which we could, if necessary, camp.

We had offered to raise money for charity through our ride and Jacky's employers had sensibly grabbed their opportunity for some publicity by nailing a large sign to each side of the truck which read 'Robin and Louella Hanbury-Tenison / Riding through New Zealand / Support Riding for the Disabled'. We were some weeks into our ride before it occurred to us that some of the strange looks we received from passersby when we rejoined Jacky and the truck from time to time were directed at assessing which particular disablement we suffered from ourselves.

The cab had been painted bright yellow and Carol told us that they called the truck Kowhai, after the native tree (*Sophora microphylla*) whose golden yellow blossoms have sometimes been used as a national emblem. It is also the Maori word for yellow.

Kowhai was to give us much greater freedom of action than we would have enjoyed without her. We could travel much lighter than if we had had to carry everything in our saddlebags or on a pack horse; we could canter freely across country when the mood took us, without becoming preoccupied about covering a particular distance in order to reach our journey's end; and we could skip sections which would involve roadwork or, later in the North Island, countryside where there were too many fences and restrictions to make cross-country riding a pleasure. Our rides have always been intended as interesting and pleasurable ways of seeing a country rather than feats of endurance and so we are free of the need to prove anything through religiously travelling between two particular points. To have ridden all the way from Bluff, near Invercargill, at the southern tip of the

Our support truck carried our spare horse. We met up with it every few days which gave us much more freedom to travel across country.

South Island to North Cape at the top of the North Island would not only have taken far longer than we could spare, but would also have involved long distances on roads. We also felt it would be presumptuous for a couple of 'poms' to go to New Zealand and do something which we were sure must have already been done by a Kiwi, although I have so far failed to find a book recording such a ride.

At Mount Linton it was a time for introductions. Jacky, for the first and last time in our friendship, looked stern and formidable. Perhaps, we thought, she was worried about whether she would like this couple she had been landed with for two months. Perhaps she doubted our competence with horses, an area in which fortunately she excelled. Perhaps she was missing her children, whom she would not see again until we reached Gisborne. Perhaps she was just shy.

Then it was the turn of the horses. Clyde had found us two excellent stock horses, which we had bought on his recommendation without ever seeing them. On the way up in the truck we asked him to describe them.

'They are actually a mixture of breeds', he said. 'Arab with a lot of thoroughbred influence; also Cleveland Bay for the bone and strength; and a bit of draft-horse like Clydesdale. This combination has been modified over the years to become what we call a station hack. Now your two have been bred further to produce an extra pace. To do this a pacing stallion has been mated to a New Zealand hack and this introduces an amble into its gait. This gives it the ability to move round the station faster and keep up a good speed all day.'

Our 'amblers' were a gelding for Louella and a mare for me. Like many New Zealand horses they had no names and we had to think what to call them. Clyde and Carol's farm is called Manaaki, which means 'blessing' or 'abundance' in Maori and Louella chose that name for hers. Mine was to be the first mare I had ever owned and so I called her Wahine, the Maori for 'woman'. It was also the name of a famous ferry between the two islands which sank in a great storm in February 1968 with the loss of many lives. We hoped the name would not be a bad omen, particularly as we planned to cross the Cook Strait

Wahine and Manaaki relaxing at the seaside. They always rolled at the end of the day.

on one of the ferry's successors in five weeks' time, almost exactly twenty years to the day later.

They were good-looking horses, much finer boned than I had expected and with intelligent heads. Both had grey faces and dark roan bodies faintly dappled with grey spots. They were friendly and easy to catch, which was a relief. The third horse, which turned out to be Wahine's full brother but was a bay, was already called Star, and proved invaluable. In the end he was to be ridden just as much as the other two and, although not such a comfortable ambler, he was probably the strongest of the three.

We unpacked our clean new Camargue saddles which we had had made by one of the remaining great saddle makers of the Camargue. We had been forced into this by the chemical treatment given to second-hand saddles imported into New Zealand to kill any resident ticks or bugs – our battered old saddles would probably not have survived it. The Camargue saddle is a work of art which should last for several generations if properly treated. More important still it is supremely comfortable for rider and horse, allowing them to cover great distances together as painlessly as possible. It is a good deal larger and heavier than a normal saddle having a high cantle and pommel and the big iron stirrups as used by medieval knights which give protection when kicking one's way through undergrowth. It is ridden long, like a Western saddle, so that one does not rise to the trot. Although heavier, it has a larger bearing area on the horse and so in the end is easier on the horse's back. However, Jacky looked doubtful.

Clyde had bought some thick pure wool saddle cloths in Gisborne which were said to be excellent for preventing saddle sores, always the biggest worry on a long ride. These were selected in preference to our new expensive felt ones from the Camargue and the saddles were tried on. The only thing about horses I ever had to show Jacky, and then only once, was how to tie the special quick-release knots by which these saddles are attached to the girth. Luckily they both fitted the horses well and seemed comfortable for them.

Suddenly Jacky smiled, a big, open grin which changed her completely. From that moment on we both loved her and never had the least cause to revise our opinion. She was the most relaxed and easy-going yet capable and trustworthy person imaginable. Everyone loved her and she became our perfect ambassadress through the diplomatic minefield we faced among the isolated and independent farmers of the South Island. Children instantly attach-ed themselves to her wherever she stayed, helping her with the horses and hero-worshipping her. There was no escaping the greater affection the horses had for her than for us, their owners and constant riders. If they played up she spoke sharply to them and they responded at once. Her care of them was constant and immaculate, maintaining always the highest Pony Club standards, below which we were forever slipping and having to be corrected like naughty children. I never did learn the correct way to take off a horse blanket . . .

Dear Jacky, her initial coolness had arisen from worries that our famous saddles, of which she had been forewarned, would hurt the horses and that we, unfeelingly, would insist on using them.

We rode Manaaki and Wahine for the first time that evening and, under Clyde's instruction soon had the knack of getting them to hold an amble. It was a wonderfully comfortable sensation, like sitting on a log in a choppy sea. The secret was to let ourselves relax into the unfamiliar rhythm and roll a little from side to side with the horse. Seen in action, the gait looks strange as both front and back legs on the same side move together, giving an impression a bit like the wheels of a steam engine. It was a great relief for us to find that the combination of Camargue saddles and our amblers seemed to work for both horse and rider so that we could look forward to a happy time together.

Twenty-four hours later we were riding through one of the most beautiful and satisfying landscapes I have ever seen. One of the many delights of New Zealand is the way in which it constantly surprises you with sudden contrasts. The weather is liable to change in minutes from scorching to freezing, from calm to gale, from sunshine to downpour; the landscape too, on a grand, sweeping scale, is full of surprises. One moment it is rugged, primitive and harsh, the next soft and welcoming.

Now lush green hills, liberally sprinkled with patches of park-like woodland, rolled away towards impressive mountains with alpine meadows, while beyond them the formidable Alps themselves stood in high white ranges. To one side we could see our first tussock grassland, the shimmering golden native vegetation of the high country. Large copses of untouched dark green original bush filled the gullies and far below us were fertile cultivated valleys where the land had been ploughed and seeded with fresh green grasses.

It was a scene of bucolic perfection and as a farmer I was deeply impressed. Better still, everything seemed to be admirably organized so that there was a pervading sense of competence. The gates opened and shut easily, even from our horses, which boded well since many hundreds of gate openings lay ahead of us. They even had the names or numbers of the paddocks on them, neatly painted on metal plates. Sleek brown Hereford cows grazed contentedly, each with a big pure bred calf at her side and, of course, there were sheep as far as the eye could see.

This was Mount Linton Station, the property where we had been advised to start the ride. It is an exceptional place, an example of high country farming at its best but, as we were to find out, hardly typical of the problems faced by those less well favoured.

At 28,000 acres (11,000 hectares) it is almost small compared to many of the great sheep stations which dominate the whole of the eastern side of the southern Alps from one end of the South Island to the other. But the land is rich, the enterprise financially secure and a great deal of money and effort has been invested to make the operation run smoothly and efficiently.

In the *Guinness Book of Records*, the largest sheep station in the world is given as Commonwealth Hill, in the north west of South Australia. There between 60,000 and 70,000 sheep are grazed on 4,080 square miles (10,567 square km) – 2,611,200 acres (1,056,753 hectares). On Mount Linton there are about 80,000 sheep on little over one per cent of that acreage, which just goes to show how much more fertile New Zealand can be than Australia. Allan Armitage, the young, fair, capable head shepherd, the first and one of the most impressive of many such men we were to meet in New Zealand, had greeted us the day before and shown us round enthusiastically. He told us there were about 1,000 miles (1,600 km) of fences to maintain and 100 miles (160 km) of metal roads on the farm (in New Zealand this means gravel rather than tarmac, which is referred to as tar seal).

On Mount Linton they kill twenty sheep a week to feed the dozen or so employees and their families, plus a further ninety every two weeks to feed the eighty sheepdogs. These were kept in a long straight row of 'dog motels', raised kennels each with a small enclosed run, the first but also the longest of many such streets of dogs we were to see. Elsewhere their accommodation was often much simpler, oil drums sunk horizontally into the hillside being often all they had. Yet the dogs usually looked well and fit, if raggle-taggle in the extreme as regards their breeding. They were there to work and it was in everyone's interests to keep them strong. Each shepherd would own up to a dozen dogs, selecting which ones should work each day and always feeding them himself.

Allan proudly pointed out the airstrip and the modern woolsheds where twelve shearers could work side by side. The property even had a resident pilot who flew both a helicopter and fixed wing aircraft. 'It's probably the best run property in New Zealand,' Allan said, with gentle conceit.

This pride in the land, the stock and their management was a common feature we were to find in both owners and managers in New Zealand. Defensiveness about their country, combined with an innate suspicion of foreigners (especially 'poms'), made them touchy sometimes about discussing the mistakes of the past and differing attitudes to their environment. On arrival in New Zealand I was for a time obsessed with the country's origins. So much has been changed through man's influence that I was constantly asking how it had been before, whether the remaining forest had once covered the land, whether moas had grazed where now there were sheep, whether the screes and landslides were natural or man made. These questions seemed irrelevant to those faced with earning a living from the land on which they lived and I had later to hunt through New Zealand's copious literature to find some of the answers.

The truth is that New Zealand has been hugely changed by man, perhaps more so than anywhere else on earth. There is no other comparable environment with which to compare it, but recent excavations in the barren country over which we had flown have confirmed that years ago it was all rainforest. In a cave, well-preserved fragments of tropical birds, some still with skin and tufts of feathers, were found next to remains of tree ferns, lance woods and other rainforest plants. It is now generally believed that these forests were first destroyed about a thousand years ago by early Polynesian hunters lighting fires to drive out the moas. These flightless birds seem not, as was originally thought, to have roamed the great tussock grasslands of the South Island, like ostriches on the African veldt, rheas on the pampass of South America or emus in Australia, but instead to have inhabited mixed shrubland and forests. Most of the dozen or so species of moa were not very big, but the largest (*Dinornis maximus*) was the tallest bird ever to live on earth, standing well over 3.5 metres (12 feet), and would have browsed like an elephant or a giraffe on leaves, branches and seeds. To help digest this diet it had stones in its gizzard weighing a total of almost $6\frac{1}{2}$ lb (3 kg). Later, in the mid-nineteenth century, European farmers used fire as virtually their only management tool in the South Island, taking advantage of the forest clearing already accomplished by the Maori. At first burning simply to remove the thorn scrub through which it was difficult to drive stock, they soon found, as they would have suspected from similar British practices such as the swaling still carried out on Bodmin Moor, that the regrowth of freshly burnt tussock was far more palatable to stock than the old growth.

There is a lively description of this ecologically disastrous process in *Station Life in New Zealand*, one of the charming books written by Lady Barker about her time in New Zealand between 1865 and 1868. Although experiencing all the rigours and hardships of an early settler, she seems to have regarded it all as a jolly picnic and to have enjoyed herself hugely. In December 1867 she writes of the 'exceeding joy of "Burning" ':

I am quite sorry that the season for setting fire to the long grass, or, as it is technically called, 'burning the run', is fairly over at last . . . It is useless to

New Zealand has been hugely changed by man. Traces of old landslips and fresh ones scar a terrain lacking vegetation to bind the soil.

think of setting out on a burning expedition unless there is a pretty strong nor'-wester blowing; but it must not be too violent, or the flames will fly over the grass, just scorching it instead of making a 'clean burn'. But when F---- pronounces the wind to be just right, and proposes that we should go to some place where the grass is of two, or, still better, three years' growth, then I am indeed happy. I am obliged to be careful not to have on any inflammable petticoats, even if it is quite a warm day, as they are very dangerous; the wind will shift suddenly perhaps as I am in the very act of setting a tussock a-blaze, and for half a second I find myself in the middle of the flames. F---- generally gets his beard well singed, and I have nearly lost my eyelashes more than once. We each provide ourselves with a good supply of matches, and on the way we look out for the last year's tall blossom of those horrid prickly bushes called 'Spaniards', or a bundle of flax-sticks, or, better than all, the top of a dead and dry Ti-ti palm. As soon as we come to the proper spot, and F---- has ascertained that no sheep are in danger of being made into roast mutton before their time, we begin to light our line of fire, setting one large tussock blazing, lighting our impromptu torches at it, and then starting from this 'head-centre', one to the right and the other to the left, dragging the blazing sticks along the grass. It is a very exciting amusement, I assure you, and the effect is beautiful, especially as it grows dusk and the fires are racing up the hills all round us. Every now and then they meet with a puff of wind, which will perhaps strike a great wall of fire rushing up-hill as straight as a line, and divide it into two fiery horns like a crescent; then as the breeze changes again, the tips of flame will gradually approach each other till they meet, and go on again in a solid mass of fire . . .

On the whole, I like burning the hill-sides better than the swamp – you get a more satisfactory blaze with less trouble; but I sigh over these degenerate days when the grass is kept short, and a third part of a run is burned regularly every spring, and long for the good old times of a dozen years ago, when the tussocks were six feet high. What a blaze they must have made! The immediate results of our expeditions are vast tracts of perfectly black and barren country, looking desolate and hideous to a degree hardly to be imagined; but after the first spring showers a beautiful tender green tint steals over the bare hill-sides, and by and by they are a mass of delicious young grass, and the especial favourite feeding-place of the ewes and lambs . . .

In the height of the burning season last month I had Alice S---- to stay with me for two or three weeks, and to my great delight I found our tastes about fires agreed exactly, and we both had the same grievance – that we never were allowed to have half enough of it; so we organized the most delightful expeditions together . . . Alice said that what made it so fascinating to her was a certain sense of its being mischief, and a dim feeling that we might get into a scrape. I don't think I ever stopped to analyse my sensations; fright was the only one I was conscious of, and yet I liked it so much.

Clearly they were both potentially lethal pyromaniacs, who must have gleefully done untold damage to the environment. And yet she writes so vividly and entertainingly that she is easy to forgive.

At Mount Linton we were seeing the better side of man's influence. It was hard to argue with the premise that the land had been made more, much more, productive since his arrival. With an interest by the owner, Alistair McGregor, in planting native trees, preserving and even extending the areas of indigenous bush, as well as growing some fine stands of commercial forestry in suitable places, the prospect was enhanced. As I had stood with Allan and looked out over the great expanse of productive country for which he was responsible, I had to agree that landscape at its finest is usually attributable, at least in part, to man's influence.

# CHAPTER TWO

# Tussocks and Transplants

New Zealand is one of the very few snake-free countries in the world. This is due to its separation by the deep Tasman Sea from Australia for at least 80 million years. Land snakes only crossed temporary land bridges from South East Asia into New Guinea and Australia some 15–20 million years ago. By then it was far too late for them to reach New Zealand.

In fact some snakes, among them the most poisonous of all, do quite frequently cross the Tasman. They are all sea-snakes, however, and although two of the species found do climb out of the sea and up cliffs, they always return to their natural habitat.

The absence of snakes, and indeed of virtually any venomous reptiles or insects, gives a curiously bland atmosphere to the New Zealand environment. Nature here has few weapons with which to fight man's onslaught and I believe this has had a profound influence on the relationship between the two. As a species we have an apparently uncontrollable urge to push our physical frontiers to the limit, to essay the barriers which nature has evolved, like children testing their parents to see how far they can go before there is an explosion.

Where nature's defences have been strong, a sort of mutual respect has grown up, animistic gods have been worshipped, taboos have been imposed and man has learnt to live within natural laws. Only when technology combined with greed have made it possible for us to dominate nature easily have we done so, but there has always been a lingering sense of respect for our perceived adversary, and that is one of the bases of modern conservation. From it has grown the modern approach which recognizes the interdependency of all life.

In New Zealand it was, in a sense, always too easy and consequently that respect seems to have been lacking. Without snakes the bush was a safer and less frightening place which could be dominated merely by means of a lot of hard work. Lady Barker would not have been allowed to frolic so freely around the countryside, with or without petticoats, if the tussocks had teemed with snakes. Even in England, where snakes are scarce enough to pose no real cause for fear, many people hesitate to walk where adders have been seen, while in most of the rest of the world people are loath to sleep out alone in the bush for fear of dangerous wild animals, particularly snakes. In New Zealand this instinctive reluctance seems to have been absent and the annals of the early pioneers are full of stories of solitary travellers and bush men.

For us it was good to know, as we rode through our first day, that the wildlife posed no danger. It was the physical challenge ahead that was a bit more daunting. The high country of the South Island is a region of legendary toughness. The only book I was able to get hold of describing a similar journey to the one we proposed was *High Country Journey* by Peter Newton. During January and February 1950, he had ridden what he describes as 'the whole length of the Canterbury back country' from Glen Lyon to Molesworth. 'The opportunity for such a trip', he wrote, 'is given to few'. I had pored over his descriptions of one sheep station after another, trying to reconcile their positions with maps and becoming thoroughly confused by his reports of stock numbers, acreages and changing ownerships. The 1 in 50,000 scale maps I bought, though clear and accurate, were not as much help as I had hoped, since we planned to travel across country and those routes could only be plotted properly once we were talking to the people on the ground. They, having granted us permission to cross their land (we hoped), would be able to tell us where there were gates to be found and whether the intervening country was passable by horse. As Peter Newton wrote, 'throughout the length of my trip I would be dependent on the hospitality of the runholders and as it was my intention to write of the stations along the route, I had some doubts as to how my scheme might be received.' He was a hard man, much of whose life had been spent among the people he was to visit. We were strangers and, worse still, we were English. 'That's only one better than being Aussies!' a friend told us cheerfully. Peter Newton also wrote, 'Five or six hundred miles in hard country is a pretty solid trip for a horse.' We had started some 150 miles (240 km) south of Glen Lyon and intended riding north of Molesworth and so had at least as far ahead of us. But by making less detours to visit stations off the route and with Jacky and Kowhai to back us up we hoped to cover the ground rather quicker.

The exciting prospect was that the country seemed by all accounts to have changed little in the almost forty years since *High Country Journey* was written. Many of the runholders were the sons or nephews of those with whom our predecessor had stayed. Before leaving home I had sent off a round robin to every address we had in

New Zealand saying what we intended to do and asking for advice. Many of the South Island names came from Kit and Robyn Grigg, owners of a property on the Banks Peninsula near Christchurch whom we had met skiing in France the year before, and it was their enthusiasm and advice which encouraged us to plot our original route. Later a chance meeting in Cornwall with a cousin of theirs, Bernard Pinney, changed everything.

Bernard is not a man with whom it is easy to argue. Once he had decided to take us in hand there was no stopping him. With incredible energy and kindness, on his return to New Zealand he wrote to, telephoned, or called on everyone he knew along the route, checking what was possible and warning them that we were coming. His father, Robert Pinney, was the author of the classic *Early South Canterbury Runs*, the present Pinney property, Dunrobin, was to be our first night's stop, and Bernard had recently become the independent chairman of the committee appointed to supervise the running of Molesworth, the government-owned property which is the largest in New Zealand. It would have been impossible to find anyone better able to help us and he did so unstintingly.

The first piece of advice that Bernard gave us was that the best cure for jet lag was a long day's ride – so it was thanks to him that twenty-four hours after setting foot in Auckland, we found ourselves in the saddle riding out from Mount Linton. Clyde rode with us on Star for the first day, while Carol and Jacky drove round to Dunrobin by road. We had already made plans to spend the last week of our journey in two months' time riding together from Manaaki, Clyde and Carol's farm near Gisborne, out to our final destination at East Cape on the North Island.

It had rained hard in the night and another shower fell at dawn. This was only to be expected as, however long the preceding drought, all our rides have begun in the rain. This time we were told that New Zealand had just endured the driest two months for thirty-eight years. We took the opportunity before leaving of taking some publicity photographs for our only sponsor. In New Zealand the brand name which is used generically for all sorts of chequered woollen waterproof coats is Swandri; we would have been much less conspicuous if we had worn these, as many people had suggested. In Britain the eponymous mackintosh – a word never heard in New Zealand, incidentally – is being replaced by the Barbour. This has a very upmarket image, being the essential outer garment of the upper middle classes and the upwardly mobile, who now wear them spotless to the City. In a facetious moment we wrote to Barbours saying that our old farm coats were pretty scruffy and that we had seen that they had recently brought out a beautiful, new, but quite expensive riding coat, the Burleigh. Perhaps they would like us to show them off in New Zealand. To our great surprise two coats arrived by return of post. We were extremely glad of their protection on many occasions and we never rode without them.

The rest of our riding gear consisted of our old and faithful leather chaps, now worn shiny and smooth after their previous two 1,000 mile (1,600 km) journeys, and our big black Camargue hats which were considered much less unusual in New Zealand, where many stock men wore something similar.

After the rain it became a sparkling, sunny, spring-like morning with birdsong and a clear view to the dazzling horizons. The horses strode out eagerly side by side and tackled hills with gusto. Remembering the reluctant animals we had ridden across China, it all seemed too good to be true.

Soon the day began to heat up and we took off our sweaters (generally called jerseys or jumpers in New Zealand) and put them in our saddle bags with our Barbours. For the first four hours or so we followed a Mount Linton farm track, although we were often able to cut across open country when we could see it winding ahead.

Gnarled broadleaf trees (*Griselina littoralis*) grew in some of the enclosures, which are never called fields, always paddocks. Under-grazed by the stock, so that they stood alone, these trees reminded us of the scrub oaks of Cornwall. In the gullies the bush was often dense and ungrazed. Here and there a red flowering creeper had spread over the crowns of trees, giving a fiery splash of colour to the landscape. This was the scarlet mistletoe (*Elytranthe colensoi*), which we were told was spreading fast and was regarded as a pest, since it was thought to strangle and kill the trees over which it grew. The Maori call it pikirangi, which means 'climb to the sky'. Tane, the creator of life, had a basket from which he drew out all the trees and plants of the forest. When there was only one left, the pikirangi, he said, 'I cannot let my youngest child lie on the ground,' and so he put it up on the tops of the trees, near the sky.

All life on the land is descended from Tane and is part of him still. Great trees were especially identified with him and there were many rituals to be observed when one was to be cut down, such as fasting beforehand and burning the first chips of timber to remove the tapu (taboo). It was seen as a serious thing to fell a forest giant; Tane himself fell with it. Even the least imaginative of us must feel an echo of this when we see a mighty oak crash to the ground.

When the time came to cross the boundary on to the next property we rode to the point where the fence reached the Wairaki River. The horses jumped into the deep water easily, while we teetered on the rocks trying not to fall in and then remounting once they had found their feet. The river bottom was uneven and slippery, full of round boulders, but the horses were sure-footed and sensible so that we

Louella and Manaaki in the Wairaki River on our first day's ride.

were able to ride along quite easily for a few hundred yards until there was a suitable spot to jump them up the bank and on to dry land again. We were now on the outer edge of a much less well-run property and the contrast in the condition of the cattle was immediately noticeable. We even saw some dead cows which had been left to rot, something we were sure would never be allowed on Mount Linton. The country also became wilder with large stands of indigenous bush beginning to close in on us on either side of the valley as we headed north towards a ridge. There we abruptly left the open tussock country and entered for the first time a wonderful ancient beech wood.

The southern beech (*Nothofagus*) is of the same family as the European beech and the botanical differences between them are relatively minor. However, the New Zealand beeches look very different, being evergreen like virtually all the other native trees and having tiny leaves, some even smaller than those of box. What the advantage of these is to the tree has been a matter of much speculation. The conclusion, we were told, was that they are a defence against the tremendous gales of up to 120 mph (200 kph) which occasionally occur throughout the South Island; larger leaves would blow off.

The beeches we were riding through were big and impressive trees. Further away they carpeted the steep valley sides, starting and stopping with abrupt lines caused on the lower slopes by grazing, on the top by the timber line. My eye was drawn to the eroded slopes above, where the mountains seemed to break through the soil, exposing bare rock and the first of the endless succession of screes with which we were to become all too familiar. Again I found myself wondering how much was natural and how much due to man's influence. This is a subject which has been hotly debated in New Zealand for many years and the issue is still far from clear. Over the weeks ahead we were to hear a wide variety of views ranging between the extremes of those who claimed that grazing had no influence whatever on erosion, which had been going on for millenia, to those who believed there should be no stock at all in the high mountains, including the introduced wild game animals, which should be exterminated.

All are agreed that these high grasslands are very rich in all kinds of vegetation and deserve special study. It is in the treatment that disagreement occurs. Already in 1865, while Lady Barker was enjoying herself so much, a botanist named Buchanan was protesting at the burning:

Nothing can show greater ignorance of grass conservation than the repeated burning of pasture . . . The finer species of grass, having fine fibrous roots ramifying near the surface, are either destroyed by the fire or afterwards by sun or frost; while . . . many plants worthless as pasture, having large succulent roots, strike deep in the soil and are preserved . . . It is a fallacy to suppose that grass country requires repeated burning to clear the surface of the excess of plants, as the old and withered grass forms shelter to the young shoots, protecting them from parching winds, sun and frosts.

This was written just before the disastrous impact of the rabbit began to take effect, but at a time when large numbers of sheep were being introduced. The pasture Buchanan was defending was not, itself, the original cover of the land. It had been created by occasional burning by the Maori. Even the beech woods were probably not original, but ones which had been burned and then allowed to regrow. The great open expanses of grassland we saw above and below the beech forests were the result of another hundred years of modification. None the less these tussock grasslands are a wonderful sight and they stir strong emotions in those who know them.

Riding through an ancient beech wood on the South Island. Unlike the
European species, the southern beeches (*Nothofagus*) are evergreen. Most of the
original forests were cleared when the first settlers moved into the high country.

It was the South Island which was settled first in any major way by
Europeans. They came mainly through the church: good Scottish
members of the breakaway Free Church hoping to escape the
bitterness of their breaks with the Established Kirk; and staunch
Anglicans escaping the corruption and destruction they foresaw
coming to the northern hemisphere. At first they tried to copy
faithfully British mixed farming, but there was no market in the small
new country for their produce. It was only when they turned to sheep
that things began to look up for a time.

For the first twenty years or so after settlement in the mid-
nineteenth century, the tussock grasslands seemed like a big natural
farm to be exploited to the hilt. All that was needed was to burn and
fresh grass would appear indefinitely. The first signs of environmental damage were masked by the huge explosion of the rabbit
population in the 1870s, which was seen, understandably, as the
main problem. Whether the settlers would otherwise have recog-

nized how grossly they were abusing the land and changed their ways to develop better management techniques is doubtful. They were strangers in a land which seemed bounteous but was in truth extremely fragile, both geologically and biologically. Applying the farming techniques of England, even those of Scotland, to the mountain country of the South Island was a catastrophe.

Colossal numbers of rabbits moved into the tempting dry hills where 'the burning and heavy grazing by sheep had created conditions ideal for them. They had no natural predators and they became a plague of giant proportions. Catching them and selling their skins and meat became a major industry, so profitable indeed that full-time rabbiters began to pay farmers for the right to clear out their properties – only they always took care to leave a breeding stock behind to keep the trade going. By 1919 annual rabbit exports were worth one million pounds, representing over twenty million skins as well as a thriving industry in frozen carcasses. The greatest numbers, however, were killed by using poisoned bait consisting of carrots and strychnine. Yet they still increased and they had a devastating effect on the land, especially during droughts, when they throve while the sheep and cattle died. Where luxuriant tussocks had once flourished they bared the ground, encouraging thistles to take over. These too were, ironically, an alien import which had arrived accidentally in sacks of grass and grain seed, especially oats, and they soon became a major pest, spreading as rapidly as the rabbits. In some places hundreds of acres of thistles 6 feet (2 m) high formed impenetrable barriers through which a man on a horse could not pass.

An even great irony was that for a time the only effective enemy of the thistle was yet another import, the house sparrow. Walter Buller, author of *A History of the Birds of New Zealand* (1873), wrote of the variegated Scotch thistle:

This formidable weed threatened at one time to overrun the whole colony. Where it has once fairly established itself it seemed well nigh impossible to eradicate it, and it was spreading with alarming rapidity, forming a dense growth which nothing could face. In this state of affairs the sparrows took to eating the ripe seeds. In tens of thousands they lived on the thistle, always giving it the preference to wheat or barley. They have succeeded in conquering the weed. In all directions it is dying out.

Unfortunately he spoke too soon; thistles, both the Scotch and the Californian, are still a serious pest in both islands. Sparrows in their turn came to be seen as a menace and a bounty of about a penny a head was paid for them. Hundreds of thousands were shot, trapped and poisoned without any apparent effect on their population.

Ferrets, developed originally by the Romans through selective breeding of the wild polecat, and long known as effective rabbit killers, were first brought into New Zealand in 1867 and within twenty years 4,000 had been liberated on the South Island. In Britain and Europe escaped ferrets have never done very well in the wild, probably because of their tameness and the many dangers to be faced from predators. However, in New Zealand, like so much else, they prospered exceedingly and today the largest population of wild ferrets in the world is to be found there. Stoats and weasels came next and did well, too, until the poisoning programmes began when many died after eating rabbits that were weak or already dead from strychnine or the more modern poison 1080, both of which linger in the body. The survivors, now short of rabbits to prey on, turned to birds, especially the defenceless native ones, which were already suffering the depredations of the cats that had also been released in large numbers.

Thus one mistaken cure inevitably led to another and nothing seemed able to delay for long the relentless population growth of the rabbits. Prizes were offered and advertised internationally for anyone who could invent a successful method for killing them. One of the more outrageous entries suggested that a strong buck rabbit should be caught alive and have a long sharp spike strapped to its belly before being released again. Female rabbits would then be impaled and killed in large numbers while mating. As a contemporary writer put it 'their laxity of morality was to be punished by a death wound dealt to them by the exotic weapons affixed to the bucks'.

For the next seventy-five years there was a gradual deterioration. Sheep numbers halved, the land became impoverished, erosion increased and in places the land was even abandoned to the rabbits. In spite of all the desperate efforts of the Rabbit Boards, little progress was made until the end of the Second World War, when there was a revolution.

Many New Zealanders had trained as pilots with the RAF and on their return to their native country they found new uses for their flying skills. At first the planes, usually Tiger Moths, were simply hired to deliver materials to the remote areas where the rabbiters were working, saving weeks of travel on foot leading pack horses. Then someone had the idea of spreading the poisoned bait from the air. While his assistant poured the bait through a spout in the floor of the plane, the pilot controlled the rate of application by varying his altitude and speed. Though crude it was effective, proved much cheaper than spreading by hand and was the start of a whole new era of aerial farming.

Once the rabbits disappeared, the character of the land changed and new plants began to grow. The first of these was sorrel, which gave the ground a red brown tinge visible to pilots from a long way away, but natural regeneration of the better grasses was slow. Using the sorrel as a nurse crop to protect the seeds from being blown or washed away, experiments were conducted in aerial sowing with spectacular success. Soon thousands of acres were being sown with grass seed, much of the pioneering work being done at the vast state-owned property of Molesworth, where the legendary manager Bill Chisholm was in his innovative prime.

Later, even more dramatic results were achieved when aerial topdressing of the land with superphosphates began. This has been described as the biggest revolution ever to hit New Zealand's agriculture. Throughout both islands we came on short grass runways in the most remote and unlikely places. While they themselves make little impact on the landscape, the inevitable 'super' huts in which the fertilizer (superphosphate of lime) is stored out of the rain until it is convenient for the plane to spread it are nearly always an eyesore. In the sweeping scenery of the tussock grasslands these huts are a particularly irritating intrusion and they are often placed with an apparently aggressive disregard for aesthetics. Perhaps this is just another sign of the pragmatism of the farmers which makes them shy away from compromising with nature. They recognize the beauty of their land but seem to think it should stand up on its own without any help or concessions from them. This is an attitude which is coming under increasing attack within the country. With the rapid growth of tourism, and the nation's mounting dependence on it as a source of foreign currency, there is a sudden interest in landscape conservation. Some South Islanders also identify strongly with tussock grassland, which symbolizes for many their relationship with the land. Recently a spate of studies and papers on the visual and ecological significance of the high country has appeared, and there has been a growing awareness of its beauty, richness and potential value.

New Zealand farmers have a reputation for being the best. Ever since the first settlers arrived from Britain they have had to adapt in order to survive. They brought out with them good quality sheep, cattle, horses and dogs, the product of the British agricultural revolution, and they found a sort of Eden where their animals could thrive. With immense labour they 'broke the country in' and made farms out of the wilderness, only to find that there was no market for the produce of the farming systems for which the animals had been developed. Without large cities to feed there was no need for large quantities of meat and so they sent wool and tallow for export instead. Only with the arrival of refrigeration was there a sudden boom. In return for, among other things, promising to stop exporting whisky, Britain granted New Zealand unlimited access for the sale of meat and dairy products. That happy state of affairs was to last until Britain entered the EEC in 1972.

At the same time every effort was made to transform New Zealand

New Zealand farmers have a reputation for being the best. They are also great improvisers.

so that it was as much like Britain as possible. Shiploads of animals, birds and plants were sent out, often in such appalling conditions that they died in large numbers on the way. Many of those that did arrive failed to acclimatize but those that survived tended to flourish to the extent that they supplanted native species.

Darwin, who visited New Zealand in 1835 before this process was underway, later wrote prophetically:

From the extraordinary manner in which European productions have recently spread over New Zealand, and have seized on places which must have been previously occupied by the indigenes, we must believe that if all the animals and plants of Great Britain were set free in New Zealand, a multitude of British forms would in the course of time become thoroughly naturalized there, and would exterminate many of the natives.

Not only the rabbit but also some thirty other introduced mammals survive in the wild. Prior to man's arrival there were only two, and those were both bats. Mammals evolved far too late to cross the land bridges in time. The same number of introduced birds now make a confusing ornithological blend with the locals. The original small birds of New Zealand were described in 1770 by the British botanist and explorer Joseph Banks as singing 'more melodiously than any I have heard'. Their numbers were 'very great' and their song audible a quarter of a mile offshore. Sadly they were silenced, either shot or banished by the clearance of the land and competition from sheep which altered their habitat.

The introduction of British birds was originally intended mainly to combat the plagues of insects, caterpillars, slugs and snails, themselves accidental imports. Before their arrival the soil and vegetation had been largely free of insect life and this meant there were few, if any, predators with the result that the newcomers bred uncontrollably. In 1907 a train was stopped near Wanganui by an 'army' of caterpillars, which prevented the wheels gripping and then swarmed all over the engine and carriages. On the whole the birds did their job well, although many, such as sparrows and larks, came to be regarded as pests themselves in time. However, the introduced birds probably do as much to combat the introduced insect pests as any application of pesticides could, and their songs have replaced the 'music' of the indigenous birds with the familiar melodies of an English garden.

With well over 500 foreign plants being brought in, often accidentally, it was inevitable that many would prosper as weeds. Currently sixty-five are classified as 'noxious' and huge efforts are made annually to control them, yet they continue to spread. Gorse and broom can take over whole hillsides if not checked, while brambles (called blackberry in New Zealand) and a species of rose, the eglantine (known now as sweetbriar), escaped from early gardens to make hazardous tangles in which sheep are caught by the sharp thorns concealed behind the sweet-smelling pink flowers and aromatic leaves. At first there were virtually no restrictions on settlers bringing in any garden or farm plants or seeds. Often they were wrapped in moss or soil for the journey, which was how many of the insects and slugs arrived.

House flies, fleas, flukes and tapeworms, all probably unknown to the Maori before the arrival of the Europeans, were soon added to the list of hyperactive pests with which the settlers had to contend. Yet still they remained preoccupied with importation, and for a variety of different reasons. One of the greatest desires of the early settlers was to introduce the game which they had usually been forbidden to hunt as tenants or farm labourers at home. The deer which were traditionally kept in parks around the stately homes of England were coveted in particular, the idea being that they could then be hunted freely by all. In 1847 Colonel William Wakefield, the first agent of the

Red deer were first introduced to New Zealand in the 1850s. Now deer farming is a major industry.

New Zealand Company, which was formed by his brother Edward Gibbon Wakefield, wrote: 'The sport of hunting them would be highly attractive and would conduce to the breed of horses, and afford a manly amusement to the young colonists, fitting them for the more serious life of stock-keeping and wool-growing.'

Some of the first red deer were sent out by Prince Albert, who had also sent deer to Australia, from the Windsor Deer Parks strain. Those that survived acclimatized easily and bred rapidly. By the 1930s they had reached epidemic numbers and were recognized as a threat to the native forests, where they were doing irreparable damage by preventing the regeneration of young trees. Hundreds of thousands were culled each year with little effect on population numbers and, due to the trophy hunters' constant pursuit of the stags with the finest antlers, with a gradual deterioration in the quality of the stock.

At first the greatest numbers were killed by professional hunters, who usually left the carcasses to rot. Then in the 1960s some enterprising people started using helicopters to kill and collect deer, exporting the meat to Europe. It was a highly successful business and for the first time since their introduction deer numbers started to drop to a level where they were becoming hard to find. This led directly to the idea of farming deer, since a profitable export market had been created, the commodity was becoming scarce in the wild and helicopter costs were rising. The first deer farm permit was issued in 1970, and in 1973 Bernard Pinney started one of the country's first herds at Dunrobin, building up to over 1,000 head. Now stock is being imported into New Zealand to improve their degraded wild blood lines and it was through our involvement in that business that we came to start our own deer enterprise in Cornwall.

Today there are large and small deer farms all over New Zealand and a deer unit is a familiar addition to many others whose main operation may be sheep or cattle, dairying or even fruit farming. This is because it has been found that with the right facilities deer are easy and cheap to rear, and at present they represent the most profitable type of farming in the country.

Bernard Pinney, who met us later that afternoon and took Clyde's place to ride with us for the last few hours, told us more about tussock grass:

There is a great art in retaining the tussocks. If you get rid of them you are greatly increasing the fragility of the mountainside because they have a very strong root system which holds the soil together. Once you open up this soil, either by making a track or by overgrazing it before heavy rainfall, it takes centuries to restore it; in fact usually you can't. So it is very important to keep the top cover on and the tussock is one plant that can do that. Cattle prefer grass and normal pickings like clover, but we get very hard winters here with severe frosts and often a lot of snow. When there is 6 inches (150 mm) lying on the ground, the only thing showing will be the silver and the red tussock, which actually breaks the snow so that an animal can find something to eat. When there is nothing else he will turn it into a shaving brush and if you are not careful that tussock is dead. The other way to kill it, of course, is with fire. The timing of fire is very critical for retaining sward cover. When we used to fire this sort of country, we would put a match to it in the spring when it had the full summer ahead of it to regrow from the roots which lie dormant over the winter. If you were to put a fire through it now, in the autumn, there would be no time for the top to regenerate and it would be utter disaster. Remember, a tussock grows as slowly as a tree and can be destroyed as quickly.

After nine hours in our new saddles all we wanted to do was collapse into a hot bath which, as we arrived at the Pinneys' comfortable house, we were thankfully able to do.

# CHAPTER THREE

# Lakes and Landscapes

The next day, while Jacky titivated the horses and prepared them for the serious business ahead, and Clyde and Carol flew back to Gisborne, we went round Dunrobin with Bernard. He gave us a fascinating introduction to the joys and problems of being a Southland farmer, energetically pursuing one train of thought after another so that we were hard pressed to keep up.

The history of farming in New Zealand has been a series of bonanzas and slumps; often something quite unexpected has come along to save the day or, more likely, when desperate and faced with ruin the resourceful farmers have pulled something new out of the hat. One such story Bernard told us as he tore up handfuls of different grasses, giving a running commentary on each.

'Look', he said, 'Yorkshire fog!' (*Holcus lanatus*). 'Not considered a good grass in most places, but up here any grass is good and actually it is quite a bulky food producer. And this is extremely interesting – Chewings fescue (*Festuca rubra*) came out from somewhere in England in the last century and found its perfect habitat for seed production here. It is a very hard-wearing grass and for the first quarter of this century Wimbledon, Lords and a large number of the first airfields were sown down with a seed which could only be produced in bulk in one place on this globe – the land you are looking at. It's not a good food producer at all but it is particularly suited for lawns and so on. At the peak of one of the slumps, when New Zealand farming was on its knees, there were several farmers in this district who were getting fat cheques from this seed. Then someone discovered a small location in Oregon, in America, which had an identical climate – a mountain valley 1,000 feet up near the coast with heavy frosts in winter and high winds in summer – and the monopoly was broken. Ironically the fertility in this district has now been improved to such an extent that you can't grow Chewings fescue in any quantity any more. The rye grass, clovers and cocksfoot just swamp it. Now this is blue wheat grass, one of the half-dozen indigenous New Zealand grasses. You'll only find that where the grazing has been very light.'

Bernard also took us into some beautiful patches of native bush, high on a ridge. There he pointed out how one could tell there were deer about by the way the Broadleaf trees had been grazed as high as the animals could reach. He showed us olerias and hebes just like the ones in our garden at home and waxed ardent about the kowhai's glorious yellow flowers and the value of its very hard wood.

'It was particularly good for posts or timber rails in the old days,' he told us. 'It never breaks. We used to burn it on the fire in winter; it was just like coal. It's also an excellent nectar producer and attracts the bellbirds, waxeyes, tuis and bush pigeons. They just love it.'

At that moment a bellbird (*Anthornis melanuea*) appeared above our heads and perched on a branch to peer inquisitively down at us. Immediately Bernard began to imitate its call, whistling and warbling, but although he was able to approach it quite closely it only put its head on one side and looked at him, refusing to reciprocate. Later we were often to hear the characteristic liquid notes coming from the bush but the birds were seldom as easy to see, being an insignificant olive green.

We learned a lot from Bernard, not least an appreciation of the complexity of the problems facing those who cared, as he did, about both the production and protection of the land in New Zealand. So much has been changed and most of the mistakes are now irreversible. Nearly all the introductions of plants and animals have proved disastrous to the ecosystem, although a few have formed the basis of New Zealand's economy. Sheep are still the main farm animal and although many farmers are diversifying into deer, goats and other sources of income, this is not going to change overnight just because the price for lambs is currently very low. In New Zealand 3 million people share a land the size of Britain with 70 million sheep. We were about to set off into the part least populated by people and most by sheep, where the national average of twenty-three sheep per person was probably exceeded a thousand fold. We would find a landscape empty of man, but much influenced by him.

All around us on the ridge was the sound of sheep bleating and they had been moving in line across the hill ever since we had arrived.

'You see, even here they are disturbed by our presence,' Bernard pointed out. 'Up in the back country they never see anyone and that is one of the reasons people may be reluctant to let you cross their properties. You must be careful never to make the sheep panic.'

Landscape conservation has long been Bernard Pinney's special interest. In the afternoon he took me to see his new forestry plantations, where he has insisted that every effort is made to blend them into the countryside. The edges have been scalloped to get away from the intrusive straight lines which regrettably are a common feature of conifer plantations – and not just in New Zealand. In every corner and odd angle, willow, alder and birch have been planted to soften the contours and every piece of waste ground has been fenced off and planted up, often with a pond in the middle.

'The staff here think I'm mad,' said Bernard. 'They call these little amenity plots "poncy bits of trees", but they are beginning to get the idea at the same time. There are a lot more duck here for shooting, thanks to the ponds, and the stock like the shelter.'

Farm tracks had been carefully sited so as not to be visible from a distance and, as Bernard pointed out forcefully, this is no more difficult to do than to create the grossly visible scars of roads and fence lines which deface so much of the country. In several places along the edges of the plantations were growing one of the largest and most attractive of the many native hebes of New Zealand. Called *Koromiko* it has long white flowers and grows nearly as big as a tree itself. I also saw the first example of a plant with which we were to become all too familiar, the bush lawyer. There are many varieties of this member of the rose family and they all have extremely sharp curved barbs which cling equally well to clothes or flesh. Sheep can get caught in it and die; we soon learned to recognize and avoid it. An interesting incongruity about this plant is that the very effective protection with which it is provided through its spines and prickles against being eaten by animals did not evolve for that reason since there were no creatures in the country likely to harm it. Instead, the thorns were simply there to help it climb up trees, but now that the country is liberally stocked with domestic and wild herbivores this coincidental adaptation must prove very useful for the plant.

Most of the remaining native flora, however, lack protection against the introduced species and have in any case found their habitats greatly disturbed by everything from burning to competition from all the aerially sown and fertilized grasses. This is particularly true in the higher mountains, where the flora is extraordinarily rich, consisting of about a thousand species, which range from dwarf trees to tiny alpine flowers to create the effect of miniature rock gardens. Although they seem to have little or no economic value today, their disappearance saps the country's natural resources and a day will surely come when their loss will be regretted. Plants which have adapted to a specific environment over millions of years can rapidly be supplanted by alien species, but in time their value will be recognized as binders of the soil, nourishing sources of food, symbiotic partners with useful insects and in other complex interrelationships of nature not yet properly understood. Retaining diverse habitats in the countryside is the key to the survival of the

Sheep moving across the hill. In remote places, when disturbed by strangers, they will often head for a gate, where they may crowd together dangerously.

various forms of life which occupy it. In New Zealand, where so many foreign imports upset the balance, it is a particularly difficult state of affairs to bring about.

Bernard rode again with us to Centre Hill Station, our next night's stop. We talked about rabbits and he told us how changed we would find Molesworth from the days when it was so overgrazed with sheep and overrun with rabbits that it had to be abandoned. Now only cattle were found there and the stockmen who worked those were the élite of their breed. John Morrison, with whom we were to stay that night, was one such and we would doubtless meet others on our travels.

We rode through some wild tussock swampland on the way to Centre Hill. This was mainly red tussock (*Chionochloa rubra*), the largest of all the tussocks, rising to over 6 feet (2 m) in height and usually an indication of wet land with poor drainage. The clumps were a fine sight, reddish-orange in the late afternoon sunshine and blending together as they stretched away to the rolling hills and swirling mist in the distance.

'This is a piece of primeval New Zealand,' said Bernard, 'and look what they are doing to it. There are streams meandering through that marsh which drain it slowly and prevent erosion. Now they've gone and dug straight drainage ditches which will do more harm than good, silting up as well as spoiling the landscape.'

Already we were beginning to fall under the spell of the high country. Fortunately there are a growing number of people who, like Bernard, are sensitive to the beauty and value of tussock grasslands and who are working to protect them. We wished him goodbye at Centre Hill and rode on alone.

At the Mavora Lakes New Zealand television caught up with us and we were filmed cantering along the water's edge and talking about our ride. We had little to say, being then only on the verge of setting out alone at last, but the clip was shown nationally and it was seen and remembered by a high proportion of those whom we were later to telephone asking for permission to cross their land. It helped that we had been introduced in this way.

The lakes lie at the end of a long track. There is a resident warden, but no tourist facilities other than for camping. It is a place of legendary beauty, a glacial valley surrounded by high mountains leading down to two blue lakes in whose waters are reflected dark green beech woods, while below the surface swim giant trout.

Mavora means My Darling in Gaelic; the lakes were named after the horse belonging to one of the early Scottish settlers of Southland. Roy McKenzie, the warden, told us that some dedicated fishermen had been coming to the lakes from Europe and America for decades. They used to say that it was the best fishing to be found anywhere in the world, including Alaska and Iceland, but sadly, Roy told us, things were changing. 'Youngsters from the city' were churning up the hillsides with their trail bikes. Roy had had fences broken down and locked gates smashed five times in the last month, but what really upset him was that they were grossly overfishing the lakes. Selling wild trout and salmon is illegal in New Zealand and they may not be served in restaurants. This is a very sensible way of limiting catches, since they are only for the fisherman himself and his family. Poaching is therefore mostly only for devilment and Roy had been finding sacks of abandoned fish in the woods, which he had had to bury.

'There are scuba divers who come with spear guns and torches and they don't just fish in the lakes,' he said. 'They clean out the surrounding ponds and the streams running in. They are killing our breeding stock and they are terribly hard to catch as almost everything they do, except using spear guns, is perfectly legal.'

This was all a recent development and Roy sounded desperate as he saw the paradise for which he was responsible being damaged without being able to do very much about it. A report written in 1975 said, 'Brown trout in the waters are abundant and of excellent size and fighting quality . . . The fishing is self-supporting in that adequate spawning gravels are available in the rivers and streams . . . Since access has been made easy, angling pressure has increased enormously. To date there are no indications that there is any deterioration in trout stocks due to angling pressure.'

That had been true for a dozen years and should have remained so indefinitely. New Zealand's great lakes are extraordinarily resilient to heavy fishing and seem able to replenish themselves to an astonishing degree during the close season, even after, as in Lake Taupo, literally tons of fish have been taken on good days.

Another danger to fishing comes from aerial topdressing of fertilizer on the land around the lakes. Phosphates and nitrogen enrich the water, causing a bloom of algae and upsetting the delicate balance which produces such fine fish. Once it begins this process is very hard to reverse.

We camped beside the lake in a sheltered dell where we were able to park Kowhai out of sight behind some bushes. The horses grazed in a convenient small paddock nearby. There was plenty of grass but no water and so we fetched buckets for them from the lake.

Even dry, dead sticks of *Nothofagus* burn badly so it took us a very long time to boil the billy and make tea. Surrounded by such breathtaking beauty and being at last properly on our way, we could not be other than happy in spite of the showers of rain which drove us to shelter in the back of the truck. With the ramp down and a couple of straw bales to lie on we could stretch out in the dry and read, glad that, unlike the other campers we could see along the shore, we did not have to wrestle with a damp tent.

A very tame New Zealand robin (*Petroica australis*) came for crumbs. It hopped on to the toe of my boot and answered back when I whistled. With white underparts and a pale yellowish breast it was not as colourful as our redbreast, but it was just as inquisitive and cheeky. This was one bird that looked as though it would have survived competition from the unrelated but very similar English robin. But it never had to for the surprising reason that all the imported robins were males, since the drab females would not have sold so well to the settlers who wished to introduce them.

In the early evening, when the sky cleared, Jacky sent me off to catch a trout for dinner, saying she would see to the horses and sort out our camp. I had a collapsible rod, some dry flies and high hopes. Louella and I walked through the beech woods to look for a suitable spot to fish. Under the trees it was open with no undergrowth and very pretty, but we were struck by the silence. There were almost no birds to be seen or heard.

It was not always so; once these woods teemed with native birds like woods anywhere else until the introduced weasels, stoats, ferrets and feral cats arrived to prey on them. Weasels and cats in particular, being good climbers, were able to seek out their nests and play havoc with their populations. Being better adapted to survive these predators, the British birds have replaced them in most habitats, but pure stands of native forest appear not to be very attractive to the new arrivals yet. Hence the silence.

There was no one else around on the lake shore and no sign of fish rising, but I cast away hopefully for an hour or so without raising a glimmer of response from the depths. In places the trees overhung the water and were reflected in its still surface. It was a strongly evocative scene for me as I grew up by a wooded lake in Ireland, where the English beech trees created exactly the same effect. There giant pike and bony red perch were plentiful and I fished a lot. Here I returned empty-handed but happy to the hot soup and bread Louella and Jacky had prepared, having little faith in my piscatorial abilities, a view which was to be confirmed time and again as I consistently failed to land any of New Zealand's legendary monsters, which the tourist brochures tell you will practically jump into the landing net.

That night we slept in Kowhai and the weather threw one of its celebrated dramatic changes at us. In New Zealand 20 January is the equivalent of 20 July in the northern hemisphere and we were at the equivalent latitude of Venice, yet during the evening a heavy hail shower fell. The mountains around, still snow capped on the distant peaks were, by nightfall, dusted white for some distance down their sides, and the temperature plummeted. At nine o'clock, the wind dropped and the lake became glassily smooth again. I walked down to the shore to look across its surface to where the last rays of the sun

North Mavora Lake, famous for its brown trout. Now, as access is being improved, these are threatened by poachers, who are even using diving gear to pursue them.

were catching the snow on top of Mount Mavora far to the north.

Jacky slung her hammock in the body of the truck, while Louella and I stretched out on the shelf above the cab. Icy condensation dripped on us from the tin roof a few inches above our heads, our sleeping bags on the hard surface failed to keep out the cold and we passed a miserably restless, freezing night. In the morning we found that the water in the billy had frozen over and everything was foggy and covered in hoar frost. This was not the hot New Zealand summer we had been promised.

Soon, however, the sun came out, the fog cleared, our fingers and toes thawed and, after making some porridge for breakfast, we could saddle up and ride off. Jacky came with us for the first couple of hours as we followed the lake shore through more glorious beech woods before emerging on to marvellous open country which resembled the highlands of Scotland. We stopped to talk to a family who were fishing on the shore. They, too, had had no success but the parents said they had once walked the route we were following and gave us some helpful directions about the later stages, where they said it was easy to get lost.

We followed the meandering Mararoa River, past gravel beaches, bogs, tussocks and limpid brooks – a captivating empty landscape with no other people or animals, just the three of us alone. Manaaki and Wahine were for the first time laden with full saddlebags, which they took to well, appearing not to be bothered by them although it was certainly the first time they had had to carry anything other than a saddle. We stopped frequently to check that they were not starting to rub.

Beyond the boundary between the Mavora Lakes park and Elfin Bay property was a wide beach in a curve of the river and there we stopped, unsaddled the horses and had a picnic at the water's edge. We had been warned that there was no holding paddock for the horses at the Taipo Hut, one of the basic government cabins for walkers, where we planned to spend the night, and so we would have to find some way of tethering them. We had brought with us two 'corkscrew' pickets with swivel tops which we had hoped to train the horses to use on such occasions. This seemed a good moment to try them out since Jacky was there to help us catch them again if the system failed. We tied bowlines around the horses' necks and at first they grazed contentedly. However, when they reached the end and felt themselves anchored, each in turn panicked. Manaaki dragged his picket out, while Wahine managed to get a leg tangled and stood shivering with tension until we were able to untie her. We would have to try something else if we wanted to find them still there in the morning.

Jacky now left us to ride back to Kowhai and then drive round to Mount Nicholas station, which we hoped to reach the next day. On her way through the woods beside the lake she met the father of the family with whom we had spoken. This time he was alone and stark naked. He walked with her for some time, chatting amiably about this and that, then said, 'By the way, I hope you don't mind, but I'm not wearing any clothes.' 'Oh really,' replied Jacky, 'I hadn't noticed.' Her suspicions that the South Islanders were a strange lot compared with her people in the North, were considerably reinforced. She assured us when we next met, that such things did not happen in Gisborne.

We forded the river and headed on up the valley. Ominous bogs, which we skirted, and deep gullies made progress slow and it did not look as though anyone had been that way on a horse for a long time. All went well, however, until we reached another fence about which we had not been warned and which appeared to have no gate in it. Feeling sure there must be one we wasted some time riding along it, first in one direction then the other, to find it. All of a sudden it dawned on me that the fence was of a design which allowed it to be lowered by 'walking' the wires down a couple of posts until they were flat on the ground and almost slack. When we had done this there was still some tension in the wires but with my foot on them Louella was able to lead Manaaki across safely. Wahine did not like the look of the wire, put a forefoot tentatively on it and, before I could stop her pulled back, neatly catching her shoe and rearing up. The tension in the wire increased dramatically and I was thrown sideways into the fence post with Wahine's full weight against me for a moment until her shoe flew off and she shot backwards, as the strain was released.

The shoe, when I picked it up, was twisted into an 'S' shape and I could only find four bent nails. This presented us with a problem as we had a long way to go. I was not sure that I had the wherewithal to replace the bent shoe and there would be no one who could help us until we reached Elfin Bay Station the next day. If Wahine went lame we might be in difficulties, yet we were now over halfway to our night's stop and it seemed pointless to turn back, as Jacky would have left long before we could get there. We carried on and fortunately the going was soft so Wahine did not seem to notice the absence of the shoe. We managed to get hopelessly lost avoiding the deeper bogs and only found the Taipo Hut late in the afternoon. It was neat and modern, set in an exposed position on a ridge above the river, next to a suspension footbridge.

I now set about trying to straighten and replace Wahine's shoe. The only tools I had were my old Swiss army knife and a pair of fencing pliers, which I had thought it wise to carry in case desperate measures were called for, such as one of the horses becoming entangled in wire. Luckily there was a large rock outside the hut with a knob at one end which I was able to use as an anvil. Trimming the hoof with the knife took a while but Wahine was well-behaved and stood quite still so that at last I had a fair fit. I have always preferred not to shoe my own horses, since we have an excellent local blacksmith in Cornwall and I am afraid of doing more harm than good. However, the four surviving nails went in true and I was quite pleased with the result.

While Louella gave the horses a good graze on some lush grass near the hut, I went off along the Mararoa to try my luck again at fishing. The swirls and pools at the many bends in the river looked promising, and several times I caught sight of good-sized trout; but none liked the look of my flies and again I returned empty handed.

Inside the hut were four double bunks with mattresses as well as running water so that we were able to brew up some instant packet soup and look forward to a good night's sleep. We carried only the most basic rations in our saddlebags, mainly biscuits and dried fruit.

We tied the horses to a strong rail, watched them for a time to see that they settled down and went to bed. At midnight the wind rose and the horses became restless. Out we went to find it was raining and they were trying to pull free. We calmed them down but had to revisit them every hour and at the two o'clock inspection we found that Manaaki had broken free. Luckily he was standing some way off, not wanting to leave on his own. If Wahine had been the one to escape, we suspected she would have gone. Since he did not like the torch and galloped off if we shone it we had to catch him in the dark, tripping over tussocks and trying to keep the worry and frustration out of our voices as we walked up to him. Eventually we caught him but through listening out for further trouble we hardly slept and were up at first light ready to set off soon after since there was little point in waiting around.

The horses seemed fine after their tethered night, though they had not accepted the idea of a straight neck rope as we had hoped they would. Our Camargue horses were always tied this way and never tried to fight the rope. We later discovered that our New Zealand ones preferred to be tied up by their bridles, something guaranteed with most horses to result in broken reins. Clyde had bought us some excellent woven nylon snaffle bridles from Gisborne which were virtually unbreakable and on which the reins were easily parted. Just leaving the reins trailing was, to our surprise, quite safe as they knew not to tread on them and would not wander far off with them like that. Although it meant they had to graze with their bits still in, we never had any more trouble with them.

The horses were still not fully used to carrying saddle bags and so we started the morning walking beside them so as to ease them gently into what promised to be a hard day. Rain threatened, too, and it was cold and cloudy. Nothing, however, could spoil the pristine beauty of the wild country we climbed up to, following at first a small stream called the Pond Burn, then making our way across country up towards a low saddle at about 2,500 feet (762 m). The ground was very wet, alternating between deep muddy cattle tracks and rocky moraines left behind by the glaciers which formed the valley. This was hard going for the horses and I kept worrying about Wahine's shoe, but it held well.

Great stands of indigenous scrub came right down to the valley on either side and for much of the time we found the easiest going on the very edge of it, where we could dodge in and out of the trees on firmer ground. There was a lark singing, not up in the air above our heads, but perched on a branch. This confused me at the time and I wondered if I were mixing it up with the New Zealand pipit (*Anthus novaeseelandiae*) which looks very like it, but its song is quite different from that of a lark. I later learnt that this is indeed a strange change which seems to have come over our skylarks when they were introduced into New Zealand. At home in England they sing beautifully and without a pause as they fly up into the sky, and they continue to do so on the way down, but apparently they never sing when perching.

Once over the saddle the trees closed in and we found ourselves following a delightful tumbling stream which we had to ford several times. This was the Pass Burn, which we now stayed close to as the ground became steeper and we had to lead the horses down a precipitous track which dropped 1,000 feet (300 m) to the Greenstone River. Louella, whose boots had slippery soles, fell and was trodden on by Manaaki twice but was luckily not badly hurt.

One of the Maori names for the South Island is Te Wahu Pounamu, 'the place of greenstone', since this very valuable and beautiful stone was only found there and that only in a few remote and inaccessible places on the west coast. Pieces of the finest quality nephrite (jade) could be translucent when polished. They were made into ear and neck pendants and treasured for their beauty and permanence, but it was its hardness as a cutting tool that gave greenstone its greatest value; having no metal, the Maori used it for weapons, adzes and chisels. It was to fashion greenstone that the fine intricate carving for which the Maori are world famous evolved. Prior to the arrival of the Europeans, greenstone was being traded through both islands, with trails leading over the southern Alps in several places along which raw stone and finished items were carried. The Greenstone River seems to have been so named because one of these tracks ran along it, rather than because the stone was found in its bed.

It is a wild, turbulent river, which falls through a deep thickly wooded gorge down to Lake Wakatipu. We had been told we would have trouble crossing it if the water was high and that we should take great care not to be swept down into the gorge. Also Roy MacKenzie had said he thought the Metherells, owners of the Elfin Bay property, sometimes drove cattle through the woods on the southern side of the river which, if true, would mean that we would not have to cross over at all.

We started down the right bank and were soon in dense woodland. There was a narrow path across which lay many fallen tree trunks, but we were able to squeeze the horses past without rubbing off their saddle bags on the trees. Then it suddenly petered out and we were confronted by dense bush. I pushed a way through for 100 yards (91 m) or so to come out high above the gorge, across which was stretched an aluminium suspension footbridge. Far below, in a completely inaccessible pool between two waterfalls, lay three colossal trout. Although we knew there were maintained walking trails through this country we had seen no one since leaving Lake Mavora and this smart new bridge was quite a surprise. It was also quite useless for horses, but from the end a clear trail led on downstream and so with quite a lot of difficulty we dragged the horses through the undergrowth and on to the track. This led us to the Sly Burn and another modern hut, but the path continued back up the hill the way we had come and after a long search we established that there was no way on towards the lake. This meant we had to retrace our steps upstream to where we had first joined the river. It had been raining heavily for some hours and our spirits had dampened. However, at the junction of the Pass Burn, we found a good ford, crossed safely and were soon on the Greenstone Trail, where there were markers and the welcome security of knowing where we were again. The disadvantage was that it was a trail designed for walkers and not for horses; it was often steep and narrow so that we, too, walked more than we rode. The rain stopped and the sunlight broke through the fresh green beech leaves in occasional glades to dapple ferns and foxgloves. Just like home, we thought.

For a while we had seen fresh footprints where there was mud on the path. There was one set only and they were going our way. Round a corner, where the sound of the river drowned the horses' steps, we came on a figure sitting by the water's edge, staring into its flow. He was very dark, Maori I thought, with moustache and beard, a rucksack and fishing gear. We greeted him and asked if he had caught any fish.

'Two today, two yesterday,' he replied expressionlessly and, since he seemed disinclined to chat, we left him and rode on. The Taipo Hut had had a total of sixty visitors for the year which, since most were families or groups, meant that on only one or two days a month on average would you be likely to meet someone walking here.

Soon afterwards the trail crossed the river again, but this time the suspension bridge was just wide enough to lead the horses across. To our surprise they made no fuss, which was just as well as there seemed to be no alternative. We now left the river and soon reached Lake Rere, an idyllic, dark, circular mere surrounded by woods and hills. There were some horses grazing on the edge and these, after throwing up their heads in alarm as we rode into view, came over to accost our mounts. Through a gate, which removed us from their attentions, the path widened to become a farm track as it passed through a dark and open beech wood. Soon afterwards we reached the shore of Lake Wakatipu. The third biggest lake in New Zealand, it is an amazing sight being 52 miles (84 km) long and yet barely reaching 3 miles (5 km) wide throughout its length. It is shaped like a giant lying on his side with his knees drawn up. High mountains drop sheer to the water on all sides and their slopes continue to create a

Meeting stock horses grazing at the edge of Lake Rere. Encounters with other horses were often alarming when they tried to make friends with our mounts.

depth well below sea level. The lake is very cold, the temperature barely alternating between winter and summer, and it pulsates. One of the Maori legends about Wakatipu, which is said to mean 'Trough of the Monster', is that a girl who was stolen by the giant set fire to him on a bed of ferns; he melted to form the lake, but his heart still beats. Every few minutes the level of the water rises and falls due to a peculiar phenomenon which scientists call a seiche. The word comes from the local name for a similar oscillation which occurs on the surface of Lake Geneva. Such oscillations are quite common, although their causes are obscure. They seem to be similar to mini tides and may be brought about by changes in wind direction, barometric pressure or even earthquakes.

A good canter along the lakeside brought us to the homestead of the Metherells, whose forebears came from a village of the same name 13 miles (21 km) from our home in Cornwall. They asked us in for tea and excellent homemade scones, while Greg, the son, kindly removed Wahine's shoe and put it back with eight new nails. Theirs is a hard and lonely life, as although the modern tourist mecca of Queenstown is an hour away across the lake by speedboat, they prefer to drive for three hours to Mossburn because shopping is cheaper there. They receive mail just twice a week from the steamer *Earnslaw*, which plies up and down the lake. As do many outstation families in New Zealand, Mary Metherell educated all four of her children through the nationwide correspondence course, and they have lived at Elfin Bay for twenty-eight years without once taking a holiday. Knowing that the Queenstown area is famous for its skiing Louella asked Bill Metherell if he himself had ever skied. 'I don't have to play in the stuff, I work in it,' he answered gruffly.

They have 15,000 acres (6,700 hectares) of hard country to look after and in the winter it must be incredibly bleak, with the wind howling across the lake to build up breakers on the shore and no easy route up to their high land.

Jacky arrived on Star just as we were about to leave, having taken two-and-a-half hours to ride over from Mount Nicholas Station. We all rode back there together and by the time we arrived we had been travelling for ten-and-a-half hours, which was a long day for both horses and riders, none of whom had had much sleep the previous night.

The 8 mile (13 km) bulldozed track along the lakeside had recently been made by the Metherells as the only all-weather access to Elfin Bay. Alongside it grew a tumble of weeds and flowers which were almost all European in origin. Blackberries and sweetbrier, of course, but the fine stands of foxgloves pushing through the bracken looked too familiar to be believable, while below them grew dandelions, daisies and both red and white clover. There were, it is true, big bushes of purple hebes, but they are such a familiar sight in English gardens that I found myself thinking of them as garden escapees rather than one of the few examples of indigenous vegetation. The only truly exotic elements in the landscape were the cabbage trees (*Cordyline australis*). They are the largest lilies in the world but look more like tall cactuses, dotting the Europeanized landscape like incongruous intruders. They have survived through being almost completely immune to fire, thriving on the ashy soil and lack of competition when the grass and scrub were burned off.

Our first sight of Mount Nicholas Station as we rounded a headland in the evening sunlight was impressive. In the otherwise barren lakeside landscape was a bay where magnificent old conifers surrounded a homestead. Immaculate lawns stretched down to post and rail fences surrounding horse paddocks with palomino mares and foals. A smart range of farm workers' quarters, where we were to lodge, stood next to the lakeshore from which a solid jetty projected. The house, hidden by the trees, was the by now familiar modern

Cabbage trees, the largest lilies in the world, give an exotic feel to an otherwise largely European landscape.

bungalow, comfortable and labour saving but relatively undistinguished, in which most New Zealanders live. The ambiance, however, was that of an English country house. This was an effect after which the early settlers strove consciously, attempting to recreate the grandeur of their homeland. The trees they had brought with them grew fast and tall so that within a hundred years it was easy to give the semblance of a noble park. They were sensible not to try to emulate the cold baronial buildings which would have completed the scene, since they would have been quite impracticable for a working family, but their absence always seemed to lend an air of unfulfilled expectancy to the scene. With nothing in between one property and the next in the high country, with no hamlets, pubs, ruins or smallholdings – the sort of man-made intrusions in the landscape which are virtually inescapable for any length of time in Europe or indeed in most of mainland Asia – one comes to expect more of each settlement than the relatively simple homesteads which are all even the grandest names among high country stations really consist of.

Mount Nicholas is huge, nearly four times the size of Mount Linton, yet with little over a quarter the number of sheep. It is wild and difficult country back from the lake, where the mountains rise sheer and steep. The original homestead was far inland up a deep valley and there was no access via the lake, since there were no boats. The owner told me that two Indian army officers lived there at one time with their sisters, one of whom committed suicide, driven crazy by the loneliness. Mustering the sheep would keep the men away for weeks at a time and life must have been very arduous. Today one of the sources of income is the tourists who come across the lake from time to time from Queenstown to see a 'real working sheep station'.

We rode through Walter Peak Station, another huge property with an exhibition of old machinery and even a café, next morning just as a tourist boat was discharging its chattering cargo ashore. They completely ignored us, assuming we were part of the natural scenery, which we took as a compliment. It set us up for the day ahead, which was just as well as it turned out to be a hard one.

Jacky cooling Manaaki's feet in the icy water of Lake Wakatipu.

# CHAPTER FOUR

# Miners and Musterers

Bruce Douglas, the manager of Cecil Peak Station, had told me on the telephone that we should make it to his homestead around the big headland opposite Queenstown. Once there had been an old track that way, but no one had been through on a horse for some years and we might have 'a spot of bother'.

At first all went well and we were able to canter for a mile or two along a good lane through head-high bracken. Louella was riding Star as Manaaki had quite a nasty cut on the shin where Wahine had kicked him and also a small sore starting on his back, where one of the saddle bags was rubbing.

When the lane ended we had to follow narrow cattle and sheep tracks along the hillside, which became progressively steeper and more overgrown. For three hours we led the horses along unpromising ledges high above the lake, seeking ways through. At one point we were following a sandy track under an overhanging bluff with a virtually sheer drop on our left. I left Louella holding the horses and went ahead to see if it were possible to continue round the next corner, since it would be very difficult to turn them round if it was not. Some animals had slithered down a 60-foot (20 m) slide but there was a rock in the middle which no horse could pass without serious injury as it had a sharp edge and left a gap next to the cliff only a few inches wide. I sat down and pondered gloomily, since further progress at any level on the mountainside seemed impossible and Jacky would by then have driven halfway to Queenstown round the lake, which made going back pointless. Then I noticed a really narrow track around the outside edge of the bluff. It looked barely passable for a man, let alone a horse, and a slip for either could be fatal, but there was no alternative. We took off the saddles, since they would have scraped against the cliff, and I led Wahine round with my eyes shut as I am not good at heights. She followed easily and I tied her to a bush before going back to get Star. But before I could do so he broke away from Louella and tried to join his sister. In his panic he took the wrong route and appeared at the top of the lethal slide. It was a bad moment. Louella could not come up behind him as she might chase him over. As I scrambled up the loose sand I knew that if he did try to come down that way he would not only kill himself but quite probably me too. He stayed, and was in turn led safely round. It was very hot and we were all sweating hard by then.

Later there was another scare when the path petered out completely on the edge of a deep gorge and we had to make a big detour through dense scrub. This consisted largely of matagouri or wild Irishman (*Discaria toumatou*), the almost universal New Zealand thorn bush. It tends to grow in thickets, sometimes creeping along the ground, sometimes as a small tree up to 20 feet (7 m) tall, but always covered with long thorns. These are always described in the literature as 'fearsome' and 'exceptionally hard' – so much so that the Maori used them as tattooing needles. We found them surprisingly soft compared to blackthorn, for instance, which is also poisonous, but they were nonetheless painful and best avoided. There were also stands of manuka (*Leptospernum scoparium*), also called the 'tea tree', since the early settlers made tea from its green leaves. It is sinewy and impossible to break, so that making a path through it is very difficult. Interestingly we noticed that the pronunciation differed in the two islands, the accent being on the first syllable in the north (to rhyme with tarn) and on the second in the south. There was gorse, too, and occasional creepers of bush lawyer.

Lots of animal tracks led through these thickets, but they tended to be tunnels only a foot or two high and well meshed above. Crawling on all fours, we took it in turns to reconnoitre a route. Dragging the horses through was hard on them and the saddles, but easier than it looked because Wahine was very brave and never baulked, except when we encountered bush lawyer, while Star would follow her anywhere.

Several times we had to drop right down to the lake shore and then climb high up, so that we were fairly exhausted by the time the going improved and we were able to make better speed on to Cecil Peak station. There we found Bruce with his wife and children tailing and dipping 1,800 lambs. He had kindly agreed to take us across the lake in the station's barge, but asked if we were in a hurry as he wanted to finish the job first, if possible. We helped and were rewarded with tea before the crossing. The horses were good as gold about going on board, but halfway over a sudden wind sprang up and it became quite rough, rolling the barge from side to side. They did not like that at all and became quite worried until Louella took their minds off it with handfuls of hay.

We landed at the Remarkables Station, belonging to the Jardine family, which lies under the mountains that dominate the district and

Last of a breed: one of the old school of drovers.

Dipping lambs at Cecil Peak Station. Farmers' wives are very much part of the workforce everywhere.

the property that bears their name. They were named in 1857 by the surveyor who first saw them from far off and spotted their unusual character. There is a stirring description of them by the father of the present owners of the station in his book about his life there, *Shadows on the Hill.*

There are many larger and higher ranges, but few more unusual or strikingly beautiful. The morning sun of summer sends searching rays into the blue mists that veil the plunging bluffs, spotlighting a jagged peak here or a rugged bluff crowned with golden tussock there, until the full warm sun of afternoon reveals every spur.

In winter, the bluffs, too steep to hold the snow, range like black guardsmen up the snowfilled chutes. The peaks stand sharp against a brittle sky and the slightest wind sends snow banners flying somewhere along the face.

Spring spawns the avalanches that thunder down the chutes until only scattered drifts remain, to bejewel the black of bluff and gold of tussock beneath the summer sun.

The barge on which we crossed Lake Wakatipu from Cecil Peak Station (opposite) to the Remarkables Station.

Moon-backed at night they stand, a wild black silhouette of primeval mystery, untold ages apart from the hurrying lights and traffic on the roads below.

We stayed in the shearers' quarters next to the old woolshed by the lake shore, a magically undisturbed and tranquil group of venerable buildings. Silent and deserted as they were, we could almost hear the echoes of the few hectic days in the year when tens of thousands of sheep pass through them to be shorn or crutched. Dark and shadowy inside, the old shed was originally begun in 1863 just after the first sheep were driven into the district. It felt like being below decks in an old sailing vessel, black beams and posts in a confusing pattern, coated in lanolin, shiny and smooth from use.

Outside in the sunshine were families of quails, cheeky and unafraid. The native quail was wiped out quite early on by the settlers, since it was easy to shoot and was unable to cope with the fires, nesting in a shallow depression in the open and often being roasted alive. Early illustrations show them as charming, plump little birds, but by 1870 they were already extinct. The Californian quail (*Lophortyx californica*) was introduced to replace them and is now common. They, too, are delightful, especially the males, which have a floppy black crest that makes them look like Elizabethan courtiers. They paraded past us, bossily shepherding dozens of young ranging from the half-grown product of early broods to bumble bee-sized chicks which must have just hatched.

We spent a couple of days sampling the sights and delights of Queenstown. After all, we thought, the horses needed a rest and we were greatly enjoying the company of Dick and Jilly Jardine, who generously lent us a car so we did not need to go everywhere in Kowhai and who arranged picnics and visits for us. We even had a chance to fly with a friend of theirs in a helicopter to see how the land lay ahead. We planned to follow a long abandoned miners' track over a high saddle and there was a good chance we would get lost.

The original settlers of the land around Lake Wakatipu in 1860 were tough men who forced their way through appallingly hard country. 'Speargrass, often more than three feet high, and masses of matagouri constantly impeded us, especially in the gullies. Our trousers from the thighs downwards were filled with blood and it was with the greatest difficulty that our poor horses and pack mule could be urged to move forward,' wrote one of them, W. G. Rees, a cousin of W. G. Grace, the immortal cricketer. The other was a Russian, Paul Nicholai Balthasar Tunzelmann von Alderflug, reputedly a godson of the Czar, and usually known simply as von Tunzelmann. These two were the only survivors of a party of five which had set out together and they took possession of one side of the lake each. Within a year they had lodged their claims to the land and returned with several thousand sheep. A year later gold was discovered on Rees's land and the biggest gold rush ever seen in New Zealand began. He was given minimal compensation by the government for his land, was done down by his partners and left the district a few years later to become a stock inspector. Von Tunzelmann was eventually ruined by the rabbits.

Some of the thousands of miners who hurried in made large fortunes quickly. Others fought and gambled as wild men arrived from America, Italy, Ireland and Australia to try their luck. Many were veterans of the earlier gold rushes in California and Australia but there seems to have been rather less crime than in other countries.

Soon there were eighty goldfields being worked by over 11,000 miners, including a few thousand Chinese, who were the targets of much suspicion and racial prejudice. Special taxes were levied on them on arrival 'in order to safeguard the race purity of the people of New Zealand'. In fact most were sent out by merchants in China with the specific aim of earning enough to return with the necessary capital to start a business of their own. Moreover, when their population reached its nineteenth-century maximum of 5,004, only nine were women, so that they were hardly likely to have had a population explosion even if they had stayed. By 1935 there were less than a hundred Chinese families in the whole country.

The Chinese miners tended to rework the ground abandoned by the Europeans but still bearing enough gold to reward diligence. A nice word for this practice, which I had not realized had an antipodean mining origin, is 'fossicking'.

They also dug incredibly long water channels around the sides of the mountains above the gold-bearing Arrow and Shotover Rivers in order to flush gold from the inaccessible gullies running into them. Often the traces of these channels are the only remaining signs of the intense activity which took place in those wild and now deserted valleys. Arrowtown, once a rowdy mining settlement, is today known as the prettiest small town in New Zealand. The saloons and stores have become boutiques and curio shops, while the original stone Bank of New Zealand is now an excellent museum. There are even gold pans for hire by the day.

We rode up the Arrow River, following a four wheel drive track which crossed and recrossed the stream in a series of fords. We passed some families happily shovelling sand into pans and sluicing it around before peering eagerly in, hoping for a nugget. Higher up there were also one or two more serious prospectors with generators and portable dredging machines sucking sand up from the river bed. As far as Macetown it was pleasant, easy riding, through groves of willows and past occasional overgrown ruins. There we found an attractive ghost town where only the stone foundations of most of the buildings remained, set among tall conifers.

Here we left the tourist trail to continue up the Arrow River. This was the route of a miners' pack track to Lake Wanaka a hundred years ago, but it had not been used for decades and now was only followed occasionally by a musterer on foot. Once again, when we had asked if we would get through on horses, we had been told that we should make it but might have a little difficulty. We were beginning to discover a trait in the New Zealand character which made even the kindest of men unable to resist the temptation to test strangers, especially poms, so as to see if they were any good. Time and again we found that the information or directions given us were the minimum required and were unsupported by warnings of difficulties or advice on how to overcome them. The result of this was that we were always on our mettle not to fail, but also never quite sure what lay ahead.

This time we had the advantage of having reconnoitred the route

A prospector with wet suit and portable dredging machine looking for gold in the Arrow River.

by helicopter while staying with the Jardines. From the air our route had looked just possible, although there was no track on either side of the river and we would have to follow its bed up a couple of narrow gorges. The critical information we had gleaned was which ridge to follow in order to reach Roses Saddle, where we would be able to cross over the mountain range.

That day I was riding Star and Louella was back on Manaaki, whose cut had healed thanks to Jacky standing with him for hours in the icy water of the lake. That morning, for the first time, all three horses had refused to allow themselves to be caught, racing round their paddock and kicking their heels in the air for an hour. Three days on good grass without any exercise had given them ideas. Once cornered, Wahine was found to be lame on the same foot on which I had had to replace the shoe at the Taipo Hut. There was some heat in the hoof and I removed the shoe so as to relieve any pressure.

Manaaki enjoyed splashing through rivers and kicked up the water in a spray, which kept us both wet, but it was a warm day and we were in good spirits. For a while all went well and we were able to make good time through the scrub and occasional open stretches on one bank or the other. Then we came to the hard part. Sometimes it was possible to follow the stream bed, but there were deep pools and boulders which were difficult to negotiate. We could not dismount and lead the horses through the water as they would be unable to avoid trampling on us, while the sides of the valley rose straight up from the river, very steep and overgrown with matagouri thorn and wild Spaniard, or speargrass (*Aciphylla*). This last was the plant that had given W. G. Rees such a lot of trouble and we now had our initiation to its 'fearsome sword-like leaves'. The points were, we found, needle sharp and drew blood instantly, while the blades had jagged knife edges which could not be brushed past without damage. Growing upwards in an impenetrable cluster, they could impale anyone unwary enough to fall on them and stock clearly left them well alone. As with bush lawyer, this lethal defence is probably also accidental rather than protective, being an adaptation to dry conditions. The Maori used to extract a much-prized aromatic oil from the moisture contained in the stiff, spiny leaves.

It was too much to ask the horses to push through the speargrass clumps and I tried pulling the plants up to clear a path where there was no way round. Once or twice I succeeded in dragging them out by the roots, but it was a painful business. Matters were not made easier by the side streams which made the slopes a boggy swamp in which we and the horses floundered. We tried climbing higher, only to reach impassable bluffs where we teetered on ledges above dangerous drops to the river below. It was exhausting work and several times it looked as though we were beaten. Once, back in the river bed, I was leading Star through a waist-deep pool around a small cliff while Louella tried to see if she could ride Manaaki over it. Suddenly the ground beneath them gave way and they somersaulted sideways, falling a good 15 feet (4.5 m) on to their backs in the river. I watched helplessly, terrified they might be killed on impact. Miraculously, apart from a mouthful of mud and gravel for Louella and a small cut on one of Manaaki's feet, they were both uninjured, but Louella became much less talkative for the next few hours and was clearly shaken.

At last I persuaded myself that we had reached the ridge up which the track should lead. It looked quite an easy climb from below and so we left the river and started up. For the first few hundred yards all went well, but then it became steeper and steeper until the gallant horses were straining up an almost vertical tussocky slope while we struggled and slipped beside them. One of our problems was that the

The first stretch of the Arrow River beyond the ghost town of Macetown.

soles of Louella's boots were smooth, so that her feet were constantly going from under her when she would take off down the mountain on her backside abandoning Manaaki, who, feeling insecure, would then try to push Star and me off the narrow sheep track on which we were precariously perched. At the same time my good old Moroccan boots, which I had had made in Fez and which had served me well during our ride through China, fell apart, the whole sole parting from the upper. I managed to tie them together with string, but was hobbling from then on.

About 600 feet (200 m) above the river we came to a small level patch where we were able to unsaddle the horses, give them a rest and stretch out for half an hour ourselves. By now it was 3.00 p.m. and I was beginning to suspect we were on the wrong ridge. Map and compass were tricky to align in the extremely broken mountainscape where each valley looked much like another, but I was not certain until we came to an abrupt precipice between us and the next ridge to the north, which had to be the right one. From where we were I could even make out a faint track leading towards the saddle.

My fury with myself at having made such a stupid mistake was forgotten in the terror of the descent back to the river. Luckily the horses and Louella were much braver than I am about heights and scrambled down like cats. A tricky stretch of the most difficult river passage yet took us around a corner and to the feet of another steep bluff, up which we dragged the horses.

'This must be the right one,' I said, trying to sound optimistic, but Louella remained understandably dubious until we had climbed a good 1,000 feet (300 m) and could see the path ahead. This path, little more than a sheep track, followed the crest of a ridge; only when it zigzagged up a steep section could we see that it had been man-made.

At Roses Saddle, which is 4,200 feet (1,280 m), we were rewarded with a superb 360 degree view of snow-capped peaks of over 6,000 feet (1,829 m) under an aquamarine sky with barely a puff of cloud and with only a pleasant breeze coming up from Lake Wanaka. The first part of the descent on the other side was the steepest yet and I, suffering from vertigo, had to find a way round, although the horses seemed ready to follow us faithfully down anything. Soon we were on an easy track and then it was not far to the Roses Hut. Our first musterers' hut was a gem of its kind. Nestling beside a small beech wood on the edge of a ravine, a clear brook running past the door, it was built of corrugated iron lined with hardboard. Inside the single room were six bunks, on which were smelly old mattresses with the stuffing coming out, and an excellent old range. We boiled our billy on this and made tea while grazing the tired horses on the good fresh grass around the hut. Sadly there was again no paddock nor anywhere to tie them once they had eaten their fill, except the foundations of the hut itself. There was a good view, a great sense of security about the scene and a huge feeling of relief at having arrived. Washing in the icy stream, eating supper by the hot range, reading by candlelight for an hour or two, then curling up in a warm sleeping bag exhausted made a delightful end to the day. Even though the horses stamped restlessly all night, never allowing us a straight hour of sleep, nothing could dampen our spirits.

There was a glorious stillness as we rode down the valley early in the morning through crisp, very clear air. We were extremely conscious of a tremendous sense of space; a sensation such as I have felt in Europe only when ski-ing in the high Alps. The silence was broken first by the *peet peet* of a pipit, followed by a song thrush greeting the day with clear musical notes from a blackberry patch down in the gorge. The sheep, catching sight of us, began to bleat on the far hill and move nervously in file. Finally, as we neared the stream and could hear the sound of rushing water, the peace was

Roses Hut on Motatapu Station, basic but very welcome.

The spartan interior of Roses Hut, generally used by musterers.

destroyed by a pair of paradise ducks (*Tadorna variegata*). Desperate in their efforts to draw our attention away from their young they circled our heads, crying in unison. The female is more colourful than the male, so that at first we assumed that their sexes were the other way around. She has a white head, bright chestnut body and white wings, while he is apparently black all over, including the head, on which the blue-green sheen cannot be seen at a distance. Lady Barker called them 'the most beautiful plumaged birds I ever saw belonging to the duck tribe'. The duck gives a strident, high-pitched, intrusive call, which the drake answers with a deep, off-key grunt. This mobbing is to no avail as all it does is to draw attention to the existence of helpless young ('very good eating, quite as delicate as the famous canvas-back' – Lady Barker again), to which they constantly return to reassure themselves that they are safe before flying back to scream at the intruders.

At Motatapu Station, Jacky was walking Wahine round and round in a good green paddock. Star and Manaaki were soon making up for lost time and grazing busily. We drove into Wanaka to buy ourselves boots and were lucky to find in a sale some excellent ones, as worn by musterers. That evening I broke my pair in by fishing the Motatapu River. Once again I caught nothing, but while disentangling my line from a tree I was joined by the first two fantails (*Rhipidura fuliginosa*) I had seen in New Zealand. Restless and charming, they fluttered long tails like Victorian ladies flirting their fans and were un-mistakably interested in what I was doing. One even perched for a moment on the end of my rod. Unlike other birds, fantails look straight at one and I was captivated by these two, who quite made up for my failing even to see a fish.

Apart from pigeons in places like the Piazza San Marco and Trafalgar Square, I cannot remember any occasions in my life when wild birds have perched on me or something I was holding. Yet here in New Zealand it had already happened twice. What a delight it must have been to travel through this country when the very great numbers of melodious small birds were still there and all as unafraid of man.

The hot weather showed no sign of breaking, Wahine was still quite lame, the other two horses were tired and nothing but a hard slog over the Lindis Pass lay ahead of us for the next day or two of riding. Since it would be nearly all along roads we decided to skip it and drive in the truck to Lake Tekapo, where once again we would be in good wild country.

# CHAPTER FIVE

# Sheep, Snow and Erewhon

G odley Peaks Station, where we started riding again, was
another property which impressed us hugely with its efficient and innovative approach to farming. Most high
country is leased from the Crown, the runholders usually owning
only a relatively small amount of land around the homestead. Bruce
Scott and his young partner Andrew Morris have about 250 acres
(100 hectares) on the flat land by the lake shore, which they irrigate
with ingenious modern machines. Water piped from unfailing
springs in the hills develops sufficient pressure both to drive the
machines at a snail's pace across the wide flat paddocks and to squirt
itself out through rotating jets above, which pulsate like slowly
revolving helicopter blades. The contrast of the rich green pasture
produced by this method with the bare hillside around is dramatic
and it is an irrigation scheme people come a long way to see. The grass
meadow fescue, once thought of as a weed, in association with the
white clover which has arrived spontaneously produces a compatible
crop requiring no additional nitrogen.

They also have the most modern woolshed imaginable for their
fine merino fleeces to receive the best possible treatment. I thought I
was in a dairy when I first went in. With spotlessly clean steel and
white-painted surfaces, without a trace of evidence that animals had
ever passed through, it could not have been more different from the
fine old shed at the Remarkables Station. Eight shearers could work
at the clinically clean shearing stands. They use hand clippers, which
are only half as fast as electric ones, but more wool can be left on to
help the sheep survive the severe winters and they now find that the
wool grows faster that way.

The rolling tables for the fleeces are slatted so that the loose wool
and rubbish falls through and all the wool is graded and sorted on
site. Below there is a room like an engineering workshop with wheels
and grindstone for sharpening the blades.

Merinos are the sheep which produce the finest wool and they live

Merino sheep are the lifeblood of the high country. They can produce some of the finest wool in the world and this has remained a profitable enterprise.

in the highest country. They were the first sheep in New Zealand, Captain Cook having landed two in 1773, although those failed to survive. Later importations from Australia did better, especially up in the mountains where it is cold. It is also free of weeds, which is important as seeds cannot be carded out of the wool and so spoil the price.

Across the lake at Mount Gerald Station Joe Frazer has had the world record price for wool (NZ$200 = £75 per kilo) for the last five years. This is an artificial record as the wool is bought as a publicity exercise by a Japanese company who weave it into fabulously expensive men's suits, but it indicates the fineness. This goes down as low as $17\frac{1}{2}$ to 18 microns, as low or even lower than can be achieved with the mohair from angora goats.

The sheep farmers who produce this fine merino wool are among the few in New Zealand who have done reasonably well in the last few years, when most others have been feeling the pinch badly. The demand for, and hence the price of, their fine produce has held up. With the hard work, dedication and sheer pride they put into its production, they deserve that it should be so.

There is, however, pressure on them from new and unexpected quarters. Legislation has long existed to protect the high country, to restrict overstocking, burning and other forms of misuse of the landscape. Under the Land Act of 1948, the Land Settlement Board was made responsible for the Crown lands leased to runholders. The policy laid down that it was required to 'recognize the unique and sensitive nature of the high country and give special attention to all matters affecting high country landscapes'. In 1977 legislation was passed making provision for the Crown to enter into covenants with landholders to protect land for its natural, scientific, scenic or cultural interests.

At the same time the whole complex question of the 'fair annual rents' which the Crown is obliged by law to charge for pastoral leases has been under review. Rents used to be set at a rate per thousand stock units of improved carrying capacity – in other words, a fixed sum was paid calculated on how many animals could be carried on the high land. Quite recently this was changed so that rent became a percentage of the value of the land exclusive of improvements, but defining exactly what that means has proved difficult. Whether justified or not, the rents are still extremely low, well under NZ$1.00 per 10 hectares, and the sum they bring in is less than the cost of administration to the Crown. The Crown is contractually obliged to renew leases in perpetuity and to give exclusive use of them. The suggestion has recently been made that the Maori have a claim to much of the Crown land and that the pastoral leases should be handed over to them to control and collect the revenue. The possibility that this might come about appalled most runholders.

'Those people are only interested in getting something for nothing. They will push our rents up to uneconomic levels, push us off the land and then it will become scrub again. My grandfather cleared this land from useless bush and we have made it what it is. The Maori have never lived here. What right have they to interfere?' was the general opinion.

The problem for these farmers is that change is coming at them fast from several directions at once. As a result attitudes are tending to polarize between extremists on both sides. There have been a series of proposals for 'retiring' land or otherwise protecting it for conservation purposes. The government's policy is more and more one of conservation of natural resources with an emphasis on promoting tourism and access to the countryside. This process has been greatly speeded up by the rapid growth in environmental awareness and activism, especially in the cities, and the public demand for change makes the farmers feel under threat and so become defensive. Since the sinking of Greenpeace's ship *Rainbow Warrior* by French undercover agents in July 1985, the environmental movement in New Zealand has found a new confidence and a lot of legislation has been passed to protect the country's fragile ecology. However, the farmers in particular resent the idea that anyone else may know better how to care for their land. The suggestion that some farmers overgrazed the land was guaranteed to produce a strong reaction.

'Those damned greenies, environmentalists and government people don't know what they are talking about,' was a fairly typical response. 'None of the landslips and screes around here are caused by man. This is a new land and that is just nature's way of settling it down. Don't you think we understand and love this land better than anyone else? I am not having a bunch of greenies coming here and telling me what to do.'

'The erosion you saw today would have happened anyway. It's nothing to do with the sheep. They don't damage the hill and anyway merinos don't like company, so you'll never see more than a few in any one place.'

To be fair, recent scientific studies have shown that much of the visible erosion is, in fact, much more ancient than previously supposed, in some cases over 1,000 years old, while some of the screes may be much older. Earthquakes and storms can also be responsible for sudden damage.

However the basic premise that the high country is fragile and requires sensitive management was accepted by most of those I spoke to in the next few weeks, although usually with strong reservations about the need for change.

'It is true that there are always a few rotten apples in every barrel who go too far, but this land needs stocking and should not be abandoned,' was the commonly held view among the farmers.

Staying on the shores of Lake Tekapo, we could understand anyone feeling passionately about the land. The evening light on the hills across the lake was breathtakingly beautiful. At sunset Louella and I looked over at the scenery we would be riding through for the next few days, the ranges of empty, inviting mountains, and I felt my heart leap with anticipation.

We slept in a hut at the very head of the lake, where the solitude and peace were absolute. Backed by a cosy old fir wood, it was a comfortable green and white cottage with a small verandah, which looked out across the astonishing flats filling the valley floor. Through these meandered channels of snow melt carrying the silt which over the millenia will eventually fill the entire lake. So far they have silted up only about half the narrowing valley leading up to the snow-covered peaks at its head and so there are several million years to go yet before the lake will be gone. Pale blue and calm, it gave no indication of the fierce storms which can whip up suddenly to capsize unwary dinghies caught out in the middle.

The moon was gibbous, nearly full and already well up by the time the sun disappeared. We had to strain our ears to hear any sound; the faint lowing of a Hereford cow for her calf hidden in the reeds below us; Canada geese calling in flight somewhere far away; a very gentle susurration of the pine trees; peace.

The Rangitata River with its many streams and dangerous quicksands is notorious for drowning people.

We had been warned that there were quicksands in the flats and we should ride as far up the valley as possible before attempting to cross. The horses, who had spent a contented night in some secure sheep yards, were keen and the valley was still in shadow and cool as we rode into the dawn. For an hour we headed upstream then turned and began to ford the succession of rivers. They were deep enough to wet the horses' girths and as they were opaque it was hard to tell where was shallow and where there were holes. However, we hit no soft spots and came through safely each time. Between the streams were endless wastes of stony ground, across which the horses picked their way reluctantly. It took another hour to reach the far shore and Lilybank Station, named after the Mount Cook lilies, which used to

grow there in profusion. The correct name for these outstanding plants is mountain buttercup (*Ranunculus lyalli*) and in many places they do still grow abundantly, although they are exceedingly difficult to cultivate in gardens. They stand 2–4 feet high and have pure white flowers up to 5 inches across with golden stamens.

We were invited in to tea by two well-mannered and friendly children. Their father, Gary Joll, is a big game hunter with a large collection of mounted heads from all over the world. Going into his living room felt like entering a baronial hall where the grandfather had been in the Indian army or had served in Africa and brought back kudu, buffalo, and every imaginable sort of antelope.

Today Americans and Germans go to hunt at Lilybank. Gary guarantees a kill or they get their money back – and so far no one has had a free week. Several hundred red deer, as well as fallow deer, thar and chamois are kept in a 10,000 acre (4,000 hectares) enclosure from which they cannot escape and so his confidence is well founded, although his guests do stalk in the mountains behind as well. They fly in to this otherwise rather inaccessible station from Mount Cook, landing on the grass strip, and the Jolls have equipped four luxury apartments for them. Most of the hunting is done on foot, though horses are sometimes used to take people up the hill.

Chamois were introduced in 1907 with the specific intention of widening the variety of game animals available, so as to 'induce the world traveller to include New Zealand in his itinerary.' The original stock were donated by the Emperor of Austria, who arranged for about 300 chamois to be driven out of the mountains – an almost incredible undertaking, which I do not believe has been repeated since. Thirty died in the process, but six does and two bucks were selected and all arrived safely. They appear to be the ancestors of all the chamois in New Zealand today.

Himalayan thar are true goats, except that the females have four teats. The Duke of Bedford imported some thar from India to England in 1897 and in 1905 he presented six of their offspring to the New Zealand government. One jumped overboard on the journey out but the rest did well and were eventually liberated, like the chamois, in the Mount Cook area.

Julie Joll, the fourteen-year-old daughter, rode with us some of the way to Mount Gerald Station, out next port of call. She was just about to go back to boarding school, a common choice for the children of remote runholders in preference to the correspondence course. She was endearingly horse mad, talking non-stop about her big black horse Monug, how only she could catch him, how she had broken him herself and how no one else could get him to cross water. 'He uses his great strength not to harm you but to your best advantage. And he pines for me when I go back to school . . .'

It was too hot to do anything but lie and gasp that afternoon at the comfortable Mount Gerald shearers' quarters. The exceptional heat wave was continuing, the ground was too hot to walk on barefoot and the sun was unbearable for more than a few minutes. Everyone said it was most unusual and would not last.

In the relative cool of the evening I went down to the lake shore to try my luck again. We had seen some nice fish as we rode round the lake but I had still caught nothing big enough to eat. A pretty river ran through the property; a deep pool overhung by a willow looked tempting for a swim but contained no fish. The shore was muddy and shallow. I had to wade out up to my waist in order to cast into deeper water. Not that anything responded when I did.

Then, once again, almost as though the birds took pity on my constant failure as a fisherman, I had another beautiful ornithological experience. The day before, Andrew Morris of Godley Peaks Station had taken us to a small nature reserve around a marshy pool on their land, where we had seen a variety of ducks and waders, in particular a flock of pied stilts (*Himantopus himantopus*). These elegant birds, pacing about in the water on their long legs, are quite common throughout the Far East. They even turn up in England very occasionally and are recorded as having bred here once. What we had been hoping to see were the extremely rare black stilts (*Himantopus novaezealandiae*), one of the world's rarest birds, only found in New Zealand and with barely forty pairs left. There were none to be seen in the pool, although Andrew said some had bred there.

Now on the empty lakeside I was disturbed by what sounded like a puppy yapping. I looked round and saw two black birds flying towards me. They circled my head quite closely, continuing to scream high-pitched abuse, their long red legs trailing out a body's length behind them. Why they should have made such a point of mobbing me I cannot imagine, unless I had strayed near their nest. But it was the last day of January, late in the season for them to be breeding, and I like to think they were just being curious, so giving me a rare treat.

I moved back to the river mouth, where I saw two good-sized fish. One of them followed my fly a couple of times, then struck. I began to play it, already looking forward to returning in triumph with a delicious meal, but suddenly the line went slack and that was that. Corned beef and rice was what we ate that evening, and very good it was too.

I slept badly, kept awake by the sheepdogs' barking and by worrying about what we were asking the horses to do the next day. Ahead of us lay the Two Thumb range, named after twin peaks like giant thumbs over 8,000 feet (2,500 m) high, and the northern boundary of the Mackenzie country, which we would now be leaving. James McKenzie, after whom the country (with a slight change of spelling) was named, fell foul of the law in 1855, when he was caught with 1,000 stolen sheep. Arrested and gaoled for five years, he – and his dog Friday, to whom he gave commands in Gaelic – soon became a legend. What is less well known is that the whole affair may have been a mistake, with McKenzie an innocent victim. He was pardoned after serving nine months of his sentence and never heard of again.

The Mackenzie country stirs a strong emotional chord in New Zealanders, typifying perhaps their independence and pioneering spirit. Peter Newton, in one of his few lyrical passages in *High Country Journey* says:

The Mackenzie Country – somehow there is a fascination in the very name. It is a land of legend, a land of vast spaces, unattractive, yet with a vast appeal; a land of contrasts – endless flats and famous mountains; cloudless skies, heat and snow and bitter cold; a land almost of drought yet noted for its rivers and wonderful lakes. And it is a land of fine homes and fine people, a people who have made it a land worthy of the pioneers who founded it.

Leaving at 7.00 a.m., we climbed straight up the track behind Mount Gerald, riding through hay fields due east into the rising sun. It was still below the ridge above us, so that we were in shadow and cool, but behind us it lit up the far side of the lake. Andrew Morris had told us proudly that Godley Peaks seen from Mount Gerald was even more beautiful than the reverse view which we had seen on our first evening at Lake Tekapo – and we had not believed him, since it seemed impossible. Now we saw that he was right. Lake Tekapo in the dawn must rate as one of the most beautiful places on earth. Shadows lay across the tall screes which were reflected in the turquoise waters of the lake. Far to the right, up the valley, sparkled great glaciers and sugar icing peaks. Down to the left lay the isolated woodland of Motuariki Island, a splash of tender green in the uncompromising hardness around. The matagouri bushes around us were wet with dew, glistening with cobwebs and dotted with little white tufts which we assumed to be spiders' nests. They looked as though they had been decked with flags.

It took us one-and-a-half hours to climb the 2,000 feet (600 m) up from the lake level to the first ridge. There we left the track through a 'Taranaki' gate in the fence. These are gates made of barbed wire and sheep netting stretched tight between end posts, very familiar to us already through the New Zealand influence on our own farm. Joe Frazer had kindly marked the turn-off point the day before with a rag tied to a tussock.

From here on it was hard, steep going, mostly on foot. After a while we found outselves filing along a faint sheep track on the top of a

Walking up the big ridge high above Lake Tekapo gave me twinges of vertigo. The great sweeps of country dropped away very steeply on both sides.

narrow ridge. I had twinges of vertigo as well as something close to agoraphobia at the sight of the great sweeping expanses of space on all sides. Although I recovered as the day wore on, I could not bring myself to mount and so increase my height above the all too slender ridge beneath my feet. As a result I walked even when the ridge levelled out and the going was quite easy for the horses. Louella was fearless and leapt on and off her mount with aplomb.

The late Ngaio Marsh, whose marvellous autobiography *Black Beech and Honeydew* should be essential background reading for anyone visiting New Zealand, shared my fear. 'I am badly affected with height vertigo,' she writes. 'Edges are anathema to me and I find it difficult to believe those psychiatrists who tell us that people who think: "If I should leap!" never do so. I am firmly persuaded that for tuppence, I would. It is no good telling us poor-spirited acrophobes, if that is the word for us, that there's no earthly reason why we should jump off sky-scrapers or over cliffs; we know there jolly well is: we might do so for the sheer horror of it.'

Leaving the ridge to cut across to the Stag Saddle at another 2,000 feet (600 m) higher was not easy. From a distance the scree looked like fine gravel, pleasant to walk through. All too often, when we came to cross it, we found that it was in fact composed of big jagged stones jumbled loosely together, which made it very hard going for the horses. In places the rocks were too big for them to face without real danger of breaking a leg and we would have to try to find a way around, but sometimes this was impossible and we had to lead them carefully through.

Just below the saddle was an enchanting small tarn of crystal clear water, with a delicate fringe of green weed around its margin, but no fish. The backcloth of our last view of Lake Tekapo with Mount Cook, at 12,346 feet (3,763 m) the highest mountain in New Zealand, Mount Tasman and the whole showy spread of the Southern Alps was an unforgettable sight as we stood the horses in the water for five minutes to cool down their poor feet.

From here on, over the saddle and down the other side, it was walking all the way for all of us. There seemed to be no best route and we had quite an uncomfortable time negotiating steep tussock slopes interspersed with painful screes and dangerous boggy patches. We were looking forward to reaching the Royal Hut, so named because Prince Charles visited it by helicopter in 1973. It was marked on the map as lying not far below us, but it was early afternoon before we reached it. The royal association of the hut had given us the idea that it would be rather special and we had been looking forward to arriving somewhere comfortable where we could rest ourselves and the horses overnight. Instead, it was a prime example of the genre of musterers' hut which Louella was later to describe as 'vandalized bus shelter'.

There was no shade and the sun was beating down mercilessly. Nowhere to tie the horses, a pile of empty beer bottles by the door, a rotting fleece or two, flies and an unappetizing dark interior of bunks and tattered mattresses was the prospect that faced us. There was a fenced paddock nearby and even an astonishingly short and bumpy airstrip, which I paced at barely 250 yards (228 m), next to the stream bed. There was nothing to tempt us to stay and so we decided to give the horses a good two hours' rest before carrying on in the cool of the evening. We lay and sweltered in the heat, and we read.

I was finishing Samuel Butler's classic, *Erewhon*, which I had been saving up to read in the very country where it was written. Butler emigrated to New Zealand in 1860 when he was twenty-five years old, having quarrelled with his clergyman father when he refused to go into the church himself. Although he only stayed four years, he was to

Giving the horses a drink at a tarn at 6,000 ft just below the Stag Saddle.

become the most famous and one of the most rapidly successful runholders of the high country in that time. With £4,000 capital he staked his claim to the remote piece of territory we were now entering, proved that it was good sheep country, bought up surrounding leases and doubled his money when he pulled out.

A brilliant and cultivated man, he filled half his tiny hut with a piano on which he composed music in the style of Handel and played Bach fugues. He also wrote articles for the local paper and these subsequently formed the basis of *Erewhon*. It is an entertaining book in the tradition of *Gulliver's Travels*, being a satire on contemporary life set in an imaginary country. Butler read Darwin's *Origin of the Species* soon after his arrival in New Zealand and it took him by storm, giving him a bone to chew for the rest of his life, during which he antagonized almost everyone by his rejection of both conventional religion and the new evolutionary theories. Unfortunately, perhaps, his highly critical enthusiasm for Darwin was based on philosophical arguments concerning men and machines. He has the inhabitants of Erewhon abolishing machines as dangerous competitors in the struggle for existence. They also punish disease as a crime and so produce a healthy and beautiful race. His New Zealand observations might have been more rewarding to posterity if he had taken more interest in what was happening to the natural world about him at that pivotal time and place in the country's history.

At the beginning of *Erewhon* he faithfully describes the landscape around his first property, Mesopotamia, 'The land between Two Rivers', and he captures very well the breathtaking beauty combined with, and to some extent enhanced by, the hardness of the life demanded of those living in it. He also appreciated the particular pleasures of riding through such country: 'There came upon me a delicious sense of peace, a fullness of contentment which I do not believe can be felt by any but those who have spent days consecutively on horse back, or at any rate in the open air.' His description of a woolshed fitted perfectly the old one we had seen at the Remarkables: 'A roomy place, built somewhat on the same plan as a cathedral, with aisles on either side full of pens for the sheep, a great nave, at the upper end of which the shearers work, and a further space for wool sorters and packers.'

The heat was still oppressive when we saddled up again at about four o'clock, but there was something in the air which felt like change and we had been warned of the dangers of being caught out in bad weather high up. Another pass lay ahead and we thought it best to cross it while the weather held.

For the first hour we were still heading blind across country between scree slopes of such steepness that it seemed impossible that the stones were not constantly falling. We came to a small, muddy tarn where thirty black-backed gulls as well as a noisy flock of paradise ducks were breeding, and at last we caught sight of a clear track leading up to the pass. It looked a long, hot climb and we gave the horses a last drink before tackling it. The reward at the top was another view, this time out over Mesopotamia to the wide Rangitata river, which Samuel Butler must have known well.

Right at the crest there was a bowed piece of iron, part of a draught bullock's yoke, stuck in the ground, which gave the name Bullock Bow Saddle to the place. Incredible though it seems, bullock carts are supposed to have been dragged this way at one time. Peter Newton, who took this route, writes, 'By all accounts those old bullockies would take their wagons anywhere, but it looked an impossible track to me.'

Close by was the skeleton of a horse, which we later learned had had a heart attack on reaching the ridge. Its whitened bones lay nearly as they had fallen. In Europe they would have been scattered

The Felt Hut on Mesopotamia Station. A perfect end to a long day.

by foxes or other animals, but none of the introduced carnivores had yet reached that altitude.

We could see far below us the clump of beech wood where the map indicated there was a hut, but it was another hard downhill slog, leading the horses, before we arrived. I think all twelve of our feet were pretty sore by then, although luckily our new boots were a good fit and their gripping soles had made the day's walking a lot easier. Since leaving Lake Tekapo (2,342 feet /714 m) we had climbed 4,000 feet (1,200 m) to the Stag Saddle, dropped 2,000 feet (600 m) to the Royal Hut, climbed another 1,250 feet (381 m) to the Bullock Bow Saddle and finally dropped 2,200 feet (670 m) to our destination, the Felt Hut, at 3,350 feet (1,021 m). There, to our great relief, we found plenty of thick grass on a beautiful river bank below the trees, where small waterfalls in the stream splashed a bank of wild flowers. We had not expected a sylvan glade and it was all the more enjoyable to be able to brew up some supper and relax in such charming surroundings.

There was even a line in *Erewhon* which fitted our mood exactly and I read it out to Louella: 'Exploring is delightful to look forward to and back upon, but it is not comfortable at the time, unless it be of such an easy nature as not to deserve the name.'

# CHAPTER SIX

# *Mesopotamia: The Land Between Two Rivers*

The search for strong contrasts has always been one of my reasons for travelling. I enjoy a comfortable bed more after sleeping rough and good food is much more satisfying if I have been hungry recently. New Zealand is a great place for contrasts. The landscape is a constant surprise, never more so than in the South Island high country, where the cosy intimacy of a tiny musterers' hut sheltering in a copse of old gnarled trees is set against the wide open space of the mountains. The inside of the Felt Hut was like a witch's den, where blackened pots hung over the ashes of an open fire, mutton fat glistened on the rough table and a few bent spoons hung from nails between the cobwebs. We hardly saw a homestead or private house in the country which was not immaculate and redolent of the woman's touch; most husbands seemed helpful and domesticated. Yet the huts, and even many of the shearers' quarters, where men were on their own, seemed almost aggressively filthy. It was as though being away from female influence made it incumbent on real Kiwis to reject any risk of being thought to need frippery. The same character trait shows in the way strangers are treated. A more generous, open-hearted people it would be hard to find, and yet they seemed to have an innate need to be gruff to the point of rudeness on first acquaintance. Often they would apologize for this later, as though it had been a mannerism they could not control.

From a temperature of 30°C (86°F) when we were crossing the passes, it dropped to 12°C (53°F) the next day. We awoke snug enough in the Felt Hut, having slept on our woollen saddle cloths and kept the fire going all night. Outside the air was bracing but it was such a pretty spot that we were extremely cheerful as we washed and brushed our teeth in the stream at the same time as watering the horses. They had had a good night, too, with plenty of grazing. Two belligerent little tomtits (*Petroica macrocephala*) hopped and fluttered around us, indicating clearly that this was their territory. They

A more generous open-hearted people it would be hard to find.

looked quite like our English tits but are in fact flycatchers, closely related to the New Zealand robins.

We boiled water for some tea and had a cup of muesli before saddling up with an apple each in our pockets for lunch. Already we were beginning to feel fit and healthy, full of confidence and optimism in spite of the weather. It was just as well we had decided not to stay up at the Royal Hut. An icy wind had brought low cloud down to just above our heads and we were soon groping our way through a wet fog. Luckily there was a good track to follow now, but higher up between the passes it would have been quite unpleasant.

After climbing quite high up again to cross the romantically named Moonlight Gully and another ridge, we suddenly burst out into sunshine and the wonderful prospect of the wide Rangitata River across Butler Downs with the trees of the Mesopotamia homestead way below. We could see why Samuel Butler fought so hard to win this country. It looked rich and inviting as the sun broke through in shafts to light it up like the promised land. When Butler and his neighbour fell out after establishing that it was good sheep country, they raced to Christchurch to register their claims and both appear to have bent the rules in the struggle which Butler eventually won. In the book which chronicles his time there, *A First Year in Canterbury Settlement*, he also gives a good description of the national character:

New Zealand seems far better adapted to develop and maintain in health the physical than the intellectual nature. The fact is, people here are busy making money; that is the inducement that led them to come in the first instance, and they show their sense in devoting their energies to the work. Yet, after all, it may be questioned whether the intellect is not as well schooled here as at home, though in a very different manner. Men are as shrewd and sensible, as alive to the humorous, and as hard-headed. Moreover, there is much nonsense in the old country from which people here are free. There is little conventionalism, little formality, and much liberality of sentiment; very little sectarianism, and, as a general rule, a healthy, sensible tone in conversation, which I like much. But it does not do to speak of John Sebastian Bach's Fugues or Pre-Raphaelite pictures.

Anthony Trollope, who went there a couple of decades later, reported something else for which the New Zealand male remains famous: 'He is very fond of getting drunk.' On this subject Butler commented that it was necessary for the newly arrived colonials to be kept constantly occupied if they were not to turn into drunkards. We never saw any signs of drink being a problem, although it is constantly raised as a serious issue in New Zealand politics. Of more note to me was the celebrated touchiness of New Zealanders to any sort of criticism. In his book, *New Zealand*, William J. Cameron states 'One has to be brave to write a book on the subject of New Zealand if it contains unpalatable truth' and it is true that ever since we decided to go there we were warned by well-meaning Kiwi friends to be careful what we said about the country afterwards.

As we rode down to Mesopotamia, a pair of keas flew swearing over our heads. More than any other birds these native alpine parrots (*Nestor notabilis*), only found in the South Island, symbolize the conflicting views of nature in New Zealand. Quite large green birds with bright crimson patches under the wings, they have mischievous, comical natures which make them rather endearing, although their sharp, curved bills are best avoided. They have a magpie's acquisitiveness for any shiny or unfamiliar objects and there are innumerable stories of the trouble they have caused. Sir Julius von Haast, the pioneer explorer who named Mount Tasman, lost his entire collection of native plants when a kea pushed them into the river. They are omnivorous, and although their diet is normally confined to fruit, insects and carrion some have developed an obnoxious habit of pecking the backs of live sheep, causing damage and, at times, death. Arguments range about how widespread this

The alpine parrot of the South Island, the Kea, has a bad reputation with farmers as a sheep killer.

deviant behaviour is, with extreme views held on both sides. We met no high country farmer who did not swear that 'killer keas' did indeed attack sheep, some describing flocks being driven mad by the predation so that they stampeded to their death over cliffs. Other people said it was only the occasional rogue who developed a taste for sheep's kidney fat, which it had discovered through playing with the wool on the back and then probing deeper. If that murderer could be eliminated then the rest would give no trouble.

The problem was more severe before vaccines, which prevent fatal infection developing from minor pecks. A bounty was put on keas and during one eight-year period it was paid on almost 30,000 birds without apparently having any effect on their numbers. It is still permissible to shoot them on land where they cause damage, but elsewhere they are fully protected. The issue causes much bad blood between farmers and conservationists, causing an unhealthy polarization of views.

We often heard the birds' wild, penetrating calls in the early morning when we were staying at stations. They sounded like

peacocks, which seemed perfectly in keeping with the grand atmosphere of the woods which usually surrounded the homesteads. Jacky,
coming from the North Island, and never having heard the cry of
keas before, had also thought they must be peacocks. We all felt a bit
foolish when we learnt the truth, although later we did stay at several
properties where peacocks were kept and did well because of the
absence of foxes.

Mesopotamia is one of the legendary high country stations. Owned
by the Prouting family since 1946, it runs to some 100,000 acres
(40,000 hectares) and has had many ups and downs during its
history. The land which was so good for sheep also suited rabbits
ideally and twice the owners were nearly ruined by them. The
techniques of using baited carrots to poison them were initiated
there, with 150,000 rabbits being taken in one year.

Laurie Prouting, the present owner, had been one of the pioneers
of catching wild red deer by helicopter, a sporting way of earning a
living which must rate among the most dangerous ever invented,
since in the early days it often involved leaping off the skid on to a
stag's back in order to 'bulldog' it to the ground, usually in deep
snow. Now Mesopotamia carries a very large herd of deer, some of
which we saw when we rode along the deer fence beside Scour
Stream on our way to the house. Unusually, this was of two storeys,
painted blue and white with a neat garden and swimming pool. It all
looked very welcoming but there was no one at home. We rode on
down to a tiny school, one of the smallest in New Zealand, where the
seven pupils, mostly called Prouting, came out to see us. We told
them about our ride through China as an impromptu geography
lesson while they admired our horses. The remains of Butler's sod
cottage were next to the school.

We returned to the homestead and waited by the old stable
building, which was made almost entirely out of forty-gallon oil
drums beaten flat. There was a grassy meadow with buttercups and a
little stream running through it for the horses. We discovered that
they had an insatiable appetite for the windfall apples from a tree in
the orchard and this made them much easier to catch from then on as
we always made a point of having some spare ones with us.

When Laurie Prouting and his brother Ray eventually appeared
we learnt that Laurie had climbed Mount Cook a couple of days
before. Two mountaineers had been killed while he was there, the
latest of the great many lives that Mount Cook has claimed since it
was first climbed by three New Zealanders in 1894.

Samuel Butler first saw Mount Cook in 1860 from the Two
Thumb Range, which we had just crossed, perhaps from the exact
spot where we stopped and looked back at it for the last time. 'I was
struck almost breathless by the wonderful mountain that burst upon

Our last view of the Southern Alps and Mount Cook from the top of the Two Thumb Range. This was probably the same spot from which Samuel Butler first saw the mountains.

my sight,' he wrote. 'There is a glorious field for the members of the Alpine Club here. Mount Cook awaits them and he who first scales it will be crowned with undying laurels: for my part, though it is hazardous to say this of any mountain, I do not think that any human being will ever reach its top.'

The Maori name for the mountain is Aorangi, usually translated as Cloud Piercer, but in reality there are several different stories concerning the legendary heroes who first saw it, or who were themselves turned into mountains, which give varying origins for the name.

Laurie gave us directions for crossing the Rangitata, warning us that there were bad quicksands which could be as much as 30 feet (9 m) across with only a crust of shingle on top and deep water below into which a horse could disappear. With the by now familiar glee at putting the wind up poms he told us some gory stories about previous riders who had lost their horses in the river, and some who had just managed to save them when only their heads had remained above the surface. The most famous death at this crossing was that of Dr Andrew Sinclair, one time Colonial Secretary and a distinguished scientist, who had been travelling with Julius von Haast when he was swept away and drowned while attempting to cross on foot. We rode past his grave in a small cemetery on the river flats as we headed out towards the river itself. We were lucky; the water level was low and although there were over a dozen stream beds to cross, some of them quite substantial rivers, and it took us one and a half hours to reach the far bank, we barely felt a soft spot. Peter Newton also crossed the Rangitata a bit upstream from our route and he wrote that 'it was the one river of the whole trip that he was anxious to get behind him.' He did ride into a soft patch and 'the whole surface trembled for half a chain around', his horse being down over its knees, but he too came safely through.

We rode on across easy, open country, stopping to unsaddle and graze the horses for an hour on the shore of Lake Camp near a collection of deserted summer shacks, known in the bottom of South Island as 'cribs' and in the North Island as baches. It was a peaceful and pretty spot. Lying in the sun, eating an apple, I realized that there was nothing I could see which told me we were not in Cornwall. The patch of meadow was strewn with familiar wild flowers. Daisies, dandelions, buttercups and red clover grew among the common grasses, cocksfoot and fescue, of home. Willows and alders fringed the lake edge, while a clump of introduced pines grew up the hill on the far side. Only the hill itself was covered with native tussock, but from a distance it might as well have been heathland.

Of course, lots of plants which were brought to New Zealand failed to become established, sometimes in spite of considerable effort. Primroses, bluebells, cowslips, heathers and violets are not seen, except where cultivated with care in gardens. Violets would thrive, it was thought, in association with guinea pigs, which would eat the plants that competed with them but leave the violets alone. As a result guinea pigs were introduced, but neither survived in the wild. For a time it was thought that a balance had been reached and that native species would hold their own against the intruders, but on the whole most have failed to do so and in much of the country the change to a European view such as we were looking at seems to be permanent.

At Hakatere 22,000 ewes were having their hooves treated for footrot and the sound of their bleating was audible a good mile before we arrived. The manager, Wayne Parnham, good-naturedly reshod Manaaki and Star that evening after stopping work. Apart from being a celebrated blacksmith, Wayne has a great reputation as an endurance rider. These events, which are popular in New Zealand,

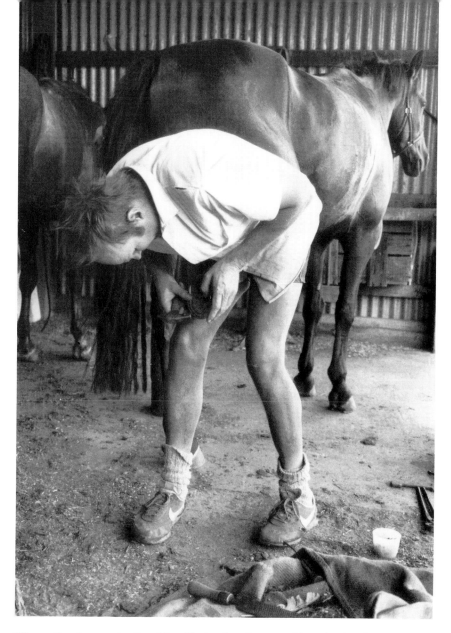

Wayne Parnham, a leading New Zealand endurance rider, shoeing Star. The condition of the horses' feet and shoes is a constant concern on very long rides.

involve rides of 50 miles (80 km) in about four hours and 100 miles (160 km) in ten, which seemed very hard on the horses as well as making the speeds we were averaging seem rather tame. They are strictly controlled, with a vet in attendance who disqualifies any horse whose heartbeat rises above sixty to sixty-five beats per minute. However, at the end of a track race the horses' heartbeats are often up to 200 beats per minute, making endurance riding less hard on the horse than racing in some respects.

The route past Lake Heron to the Rakaia River followed a bulldozed track and was mostly good going along which we could canter. It was a cold, blustery day with rain showers sweeping up from the south, which fortunately put them in our backs, and we were glad to make good time. Lake Heron is a beautiful, big lake and boasts some of the best fishing in New Zealand, having lots of trout as well as landlocked salmon which were introduced but cannot escape from the lake and so do not grow to a great size. On both the Rangitata and the Rakaia Rivers huge migratory salmon, known in their native North America as chinook, have been caught. In the twenties each river produced a monster of over 42 pounds (19 kg), but the weather did not tempt us to linger and try our luck.

The Rakaia at its junction with the Mathias proved the hardest to cross of the three big rivers we had met so far. There were great mounds of shingle which the horses did not enjoy picking their way through and some of the streams were deeper than any we had yet met. One of these gave us some trouble as we had to search for some time to find a promising crossing point where the water rippled over shallows. As we cast along the bank we hit the first proper quicksand and it was quite frightening to feel the whole area around us shaking. Taking to the water instead I set off across, shouting to Louella to stay put and see how I got on. Halfway over I experienced an acute sense of disorientation as the water rushing past made me feel that I was being swept downstream while in fact the horse was pushing up at an angle against the stream. We arrived safely and I called to Louella to wait while I took the camera out of its waterproof bag to record her crossing. As she neared the bank, Manaaki, being smaller, had to swim and it looked for a moment as though they might be swept away by the current, but then he touched bottom again and they scrambled up the bank. She was wet to the waist but safe.

We crossed the very tip of Manuka Point, one of the most isolated stations and only accessible by fording the river. On Rabbit Island, beyond the Mathias River, we stopped for Louella to wring out her clothes and then rode on across more river followed by wide grassy flats to reach Mount Algidus. Thanks to Mona Anderson, who lived there for twenty-three years, this remote station is as well known as any in the South Island. Her books, in particular *A River Rules My Life*, describe the hardships and humour of station life during and for nearly two decades after the war.

As we neared the homestead we passed a shallow lake from which a hundred Canada geese rose to fly honking overhead. These used to form an important part of the diet on Mount Algidus during the summer months, although even they were protected for a time. Mona Anderson describes how the station cook made delicious brawn from them and her own embarrassment when she had just roasted ten birds and the ranger arrived as she was carving. Although it was still illegal to kill them he had turned a blind eye and joined in the feast. They are now regarded as a serious pest, stripping pastures bare, fouling land and breeding uncontrollably.

Mount Algidus is known as some of the roughest land in the high country. Cut off from the outside world by the treacherous Wilberforce River, the most dangerous river in Canterbury and one which has taken many lives, it is a country which men are proud to have worked on.

We stopped briefly at the homestead to talk to Sally Nell, Mona Anderson's successor, and to listen carefully to her directions for crossing the Wilberforce. There was a fantastic view from there across to the rugged, scrub-covered cliff face of Mount Oakden Station opposite; upstream the river bed widened to provide a flat grey carpet leading back to the mountains of the Birdwood Range with Goat Hill rising up in the centre above dense beech and pine woods in the foreground. It was pleasant to ride through these as the combination of scorching sun and cold wind had been tiring out on the river. From there on it was easy cantering country across the flats and the Wilberforce itself was almost an anticlimax, being shallow and easily fordable. Halfway across we caught a glimpse of a small yellow and white truck in the distance at the head of Lake Coleridge. The last hour passed quickly as we hurried to rejoin Jacky and get out of the wind.

Her news was not good. Kowhai was playing up badly and she doubted if the engine would last much longer. Even with only one horse on board it had been a struggle grinding up steep hills and there was clearly something seriously wrong. We limped as far as Lake Coleridge Station where we tracked down Jim Murchison, the owner, who amiably allowed us to leave the horses in a good overgrown paddock for as long as we liked. Deciding to take the weekend off and sort out our mechanical problems, we chugged and backfired at a steady 25 mph (40 kph) for nearly three hours to Christchurch Airport. There we abandoned Kowhai in the car park, where her emblazoned sides proclaimed to all emerging from Arrivals that 'Robin and Louella Hanbury-Tenison Riding Through New Zealand Support Riding for the Disabled'. We then hired a small car and drove out to Banks Peninsula and down a long farm track to the property at Hickory Bay of Kit and Robyn Grigg, who had helped plan our journey. Although it was 11 p.m. when we arrived, we found a great welcome at their attractive old house overlooking the sea.

(*Overleaf*) Louella and Manaaki nearly being washed away crossing one of the Rakaia River streams.

'There's just one problem about tomorrow,' said Robyn, as she showed us our comfortable quarters. 'As a local councillor there is something I simply must attend. You are welcome to come too if you would like to but you may find it boring. It's Waitangi Day, which commemorates the signing of the treaty between the Maori and the Crown in 1840, and the Governor General is coming to Okains Bay just round the corner from here. It's the first time ever that this has happened in the South Island and quite a lot of people are expected.'

'Try and keep me away,' I replied as we said goodnight.

Watering the horses in the high country.

Robin and Louella on Wahine and Manaaki with Mt Cook behind.

Louella with Godley River and Southern Alps (including Mt Cook) behind.

Scree erosion above the Wilberforce River.

Maori warriors challenging the visitors on the *marae* at Okains Bay.

The irrigation scheme at Godley Peaks Station.

Rainbow at sunset from Deep Creek Hut.

In Jon Hamilton's jet boat on the Waimakariri.

Looking back over Mt White Station.

Louella and Robin with Bill Chisholm and his saddle.

The Awatere River meandering down from the high country.

Clyde Langford on his land after Cyclone Bola.

# CHAPTER SEVEN

# Waitangi Day

The Treaty of Waitangi was signed on 6 February 1840 by Captain Hobson, the first Lieutenant-Governor, and forty-five Maori chiefs. Later another 500 chiefs throughout New Zealand were persuaded by missionaries and other British representatives to sign. Long regarded as the Maori Magna Carta, it is a short but highly controversial document, the full implications of which certainly escaped the original Maori signatories. Part of the problem lay in the definition of sovereignty, which in the English text was ceded to Queen Victoria. In the hastily translated Maori version, which was the one read and signed by the vast majority of the chiefs, their sovereign rights appeared to them to be confirmed and only the right to govern was relinquished. They therefore believed they were not giving much away in order to achieve a peaceful relationship with the newly arrived settlers.

It was also touch and go whether they would sign at all, many chiefs arguing against doing so. Even some of the European missionaries present objected that the Maori had not understood the treaty, although the majority urged the chiefs to accept on the basis that it would protect them. They did not have to sign. They had not been conquered in war and were still vastly superior in numbers and military strength to the British. Five years before they had signed a Declaration of Independence in front of the British Resident. The then monarch, William IV, had acknowledged this and given his assurance that he would protect them. This was mainly designed to thwart the French and Americans, who were both showing interest in making treaties of their own.

There had also been opposition to the Treaty in Britain where Lord Glenelg, the Secretary of State for the Colonies, had himself been opposed to setting in motion the creation of a new colony in New Zealand. A House of Commons select committee had pointed out in 1838 that European contact with indigenous peoples had generally been calamitous and such was already proving to be the case with the Maori. Ironically, one of the reasons for the decision to establish British sovereignty over the whole country was the rate at which the Maori population was declining due to the impact of introduced diseases which had decimated them in some areas during the previous decade. It was even forecast that they would soon die out altogether. At precisely the same time they were being assessed, even according to the ethnocentric European yardsticks of the period, as being more 'civilized' than almost any other native race.

Once the Treaty was signed the Maori could be forced to sell land to the government which was then sold on to settlers at a substantial profit, thus angering everyone. Nor were Maori given the vote, on the grounds that they owned no individual title to land; yet in the words of the English text of the Treaty itself, 'Her Majesty the Queen of England guarantees to the Chiefs and Tribes of New Zealand and to the respective families and individuals thereof the full exclusive and undisturbed possession of their Lands and Estates Forests Fisheries and other properties which they may collectively or individually possess so long as it is their wish and desire to retain the same in their possession.' They were also given 'all the Rights and Privileges of British Subjects'.

The main difficulty lay in the two races' differing attitudes towards land ownership. In common with many other people, the Maori found the concept of individual ownership of land alien; a 'sale' was only perceived as permission to cultivate the soil. Ultimate responsibility for and identification with the earth's surface lay with those who lived on it, and it was a communal duty to care for it. Only by conquest could land be alienated from its inhabitants; even then the conquerors had to live there and establish a relationship with it before it became theirs. Meanwhile the ancestral gods (*atua*) of the vanquished people would always be ready to return.

After the signing of the Treaty trouble soon developed between the Maori and the *pakehas* (Europeans). Disagreement over interpretation caused endless disputes and, in time, the Maori Wars. These in turn resulted in massive confiscations of land and deep resentment. Today, less than 5 per cent of the land remains in communal, as opposed to private, Maori ownership.

Waitangi, which means 'weeping waters', is the site of the British Resident's house which was built in 1833. In 1932 the house, with 1,200 acres (500 hectares) of land, was presented to the nation by the Governor General and after restoration it became the base for annual celebrations of the signing of the Treaty. At first these concentrated on the notion of forging one people, but in recent years the occasion has developed into one on which Maori dissatisfaction and protest have been aired. Waitangi Day became the focus of the struggle to have the Treaty ratified, which had never been done, and made enforceable in law. Repeated requests were made for the day to receive legal recognition and in 1973 it became a public holiday. Soon after, in 1975, the Waitangi Tribunal was set up to make recommendations to the government on claims relating to the practical application of the principles of the treaty. Restricted in its scope and powers at first, the Tribunal was brought increasingly into the public spotlight as it considered such matters as customary fishing rights and the Crown leases in the South Island as well as grievances over land which had allegedly been stolen or confiscated in the early days. In some cases the purchaser had acted in good faith, only to find that the vendor had not obtained the consent of all co-owners to the sale.

Okains Bay normally has a population of eighty-one. Today a couple of thousand were expected and, as some of them would certainly be protestors, there might be trouble. The Banks Peninsula consists of the remains of two massive volcanic craters, now filled by the sea, the deeply eroded sides forming hills and steep valleys in a hollow circle. It is the only noticeably volcanic area in the South Island and in the superbly sheltered harbour in its centre nestles the only attempt at a French colony (1838–49) in the country, at Akaroa.

The landscape was just as precipitous as that in the high country we had just left, but geologically and geographically quite different. Superb beaches lay in bays at the ends of the valleys. The dense forest which once covered the fertile soil has now almost all gone, replaced by scrub, tussock grassland and improved pasture.

Driving over the series of ridges between Hickory Bay and Okains Bay, we had tantalizing glimpses out to the sea and up to the romantic rock outcrops high on the hills above. The winding road down the valley was crowded with cars and people heading for the village. We passed a group of Maori sitting on the grass beside an old jalopy, which looked unlikely to move again though one man had his head buried in the engine. A feature of New Zealand life, and one in which there is a good deal of justifiable pride, is the ability to repair and maintain anything long after much of the rest of the world would have abandoned it. As a result one is constantly delighted and surprised to see ancient pieces of machinery still working on farms to provide power or perform some obscure agricultural function. Most attractive and noticeable are the old cars on the roads dating from the forties and fifties and even earlier. The high cost of shipping cars halfway round the world, taxes and other restrictions have meant that, even in times of prosperity, the European and American notion of changing cars regularly for new models has never been general in New Zealand. The Maori, usually at the bottom of the economic scale, consequently tend to drive the most amazing old rattletraps. Early American models with big fins and grinning radiator grilles seem to be especially favoured.

A fifth-generation local *pakeha* called Murray Thacker has created a museum of Maori and Colonial history at Okains Bay. There is a fine carved meeting house with, in front of it, the *marae*, the grassy courtyard where the ceremony was to take place.

The Governor General, Sir Paul Reeves, and the Deputy Prime Minister, Geoffrey Palmer, arrived by military helicopter, dropping down into a small paddock next to the church. They were greeted with a song of welcome and led to the *marae* by Maori ladies dressed in black with white feathers in their hair. These are the symbols of peaceful resistance worn by the followers of the late nineteenth-century Maori prophet Te Whiti, who protested non-violently for forty years against the invasion of his peoples' land around Mount Egmont in the North Island.

The group of dignitaries walked along the road with the imposing, white-haired figure of Sir Paul, the first Maori Governor General, in the centre. They were flanked by Maori wardens, sinister at first sight in uniform and dark glasses. The protestors in the background confined themselves to mute dissent by wearing sweatshirts with 'Aotearoa 1990, 150 years of oppression' written on the back; a reference to the approaching hundred and fiftieth anniversary of the Treaty of Waitangi. Later, during the speeches, they stood facing away from the speakers so that the message could not but be read.

More numerous than the protestors, Maori or *pakeha*, were local farmers and their families, who had come in from all around to join in the festivities, as had a number of tourists. We all poured on to the *marae*. It was the first time Louella and I had set foot on one and an extraordinary occasion on which to be doing so. The *marae* is the spiritual centre of Maori life, more important than the carved meeting house facing on to it. It is home for the *tangata whenua*, the people of the land, those who live there or belong there, and it is where they have a right to make themselves heard. It is also where visitors, *manuhiri*, are welcomed and this involves certain essential prescribed ceremonies, which vary according to the occasion. Receiving the Governor General on Waitangi Day could hardly be exceeded for importance and everything had to be done right. Although I knew a little of what to expect from my reading, I found it extremely difficult to understand the significance of all that was happening around us.

The official party included the Russian and Spanish Ambassadors and their wives as well as some senior military and naval officers. At the entrance to the *marae* they all stopped to receive the challenge *te wero*, from two men wearing *piupiu*, the flax skirts traditionally worn by both men and women. The *wero* is a ceremony only performed before high-ranking visitors and its purpose is to find out if they come in peace or not.

Sir Paul Reeves (left), the Governor General, arriving at Okains Bay on Waitangi Day. With him was Geoffrey Palmer, the Deputy Prime Minister.

A Maori Warden keeping an eye on potential protestors.

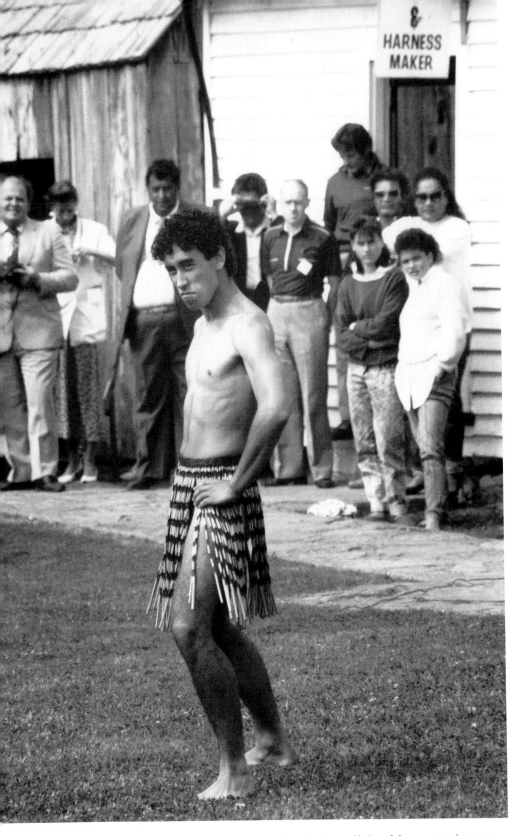

*Te wero*, the challenge. The purpose is to find out if the visitors come in peace or not.

*Te karanga*, the call of welcome. The fern frond symbolizes life and death.

Swinging his spear above his head threateningly, the younger challenger put on a most impressive display; leaping, grunting, putting out his tongue, he advanced and retired for some time before placing the *taki*, challenge dart, a small carved twig, on the ground before the *manuhiri*. When this was picked up by the Governor General the challenger turned his back on the party and led them on to the *marae*.

We then heard our first *karanga*, the call of welcome, delivered by a most elegant lady dressed all in black with a feather in her hair and a frond of fern in her hand. The last, being dark on one side and light on the other, symbolized life and death and was shaken continuously. The *karanga* is always made in a high-pitched voice by a woman and although there are basic calls and responses there is no set pattern, since it represents deep emotions and strongly held feelings. Each one is therefore appropriate to the occasion on which it is delivered.

As the guests took their places on two rows of seats placed at an angle across the *marae* a chorus of a couple of dozen attractive Maori girls, also all wearing *piupiu* skirts, started to sing, sway and move their hands in charming unison. This was *te powhiri*, the welcome, which wards off evil spirits and ensures the visitors' safe arrival on the *marae* itself. After the song everyone stood with eyes lowered to remember the spirits of the dead, an essential element whenever people enter a *marae*; and then the speeches began. Always begun and ended in Maori, sometimes delivered with great passion, they continued for the next two hours.

First the *tangata whenua* greeted and addressed their guests, using every opportunity to air grievances and to use the occasion to score points. The day before, some 430 rural sub post offices had been closed throughout New Zealand, causing much anger. Part of a government economy drive, the move was deeply unpopular with everyone in the rural districts we had been through and was widely seen as an attack on already hard-pressed farming communities and country people by urban politicians. The loss of income to the country stores housing most of the post offices would lead to the closure of many and the further isolation of people, especially those living in the under-populated South Island. This verbal attack was clearly aimed at the Deputy Prime Minister.

There was much talk, addressed directly to the Governor General, of the role of the Crown in Maori affairs. 'The Crown has been with us from the start. It is the one brake on our society which will stop attrition by one side on the other. We want that to continue so that we may be protected under its mantle,' was the view put forward.

At the same time the steps taken by the present government to change the status of the Treaty of Waitangi were recognized. 'The greatest act of government since the Treaty itself,' declaimed Tipene O'Regan, the Chairman of the Ngati Tahu Maori Trust Board and the leading speaker of the *tangata whenua*. He emphasized however that the cases at present before the courts concerning the South Island were vital to the future of Maori-*pakeha* relations, saying, 'The North Island is your time bomb. We are just the fuse.' And time, they all agreed, was running out. Progress, they implied, must be made before 1990, the hundred and fiftieth anniversary of the Treaty, or there would be trouble. 'You may have created a tiger, but we all have to ride it,' was a telling point he made.

One after the other they rose to speak, wonderful orators declaiming in the sonorous Maori language, of which to my regret I understood barely a word, but the sound of which was already highly satisfactory in my ears. The resonance and surety of the vowels, the confidence and explosive quality of the consonants gave great force to what was being said.

The chorus of Maori girls taking a rest while listening to a speech. After each speech they sang a song.

*Nau mai* and *haere mai*, both meaning 'welcome', I could recognize and also the names of some of the famous tribal groups such as *Ngati Porou*, *Ngati Tahu*, the local Maori, and *Ngati Whatua*, pronounced 'Narty Fattua' with great emphasis. At the end the booming, embracing greeting was thrice repeated, *Tena koutou, tena koutou, tena koutou.*'

In reply the Deputy Prime Minister concentrated on pointing out how much his government had done and was doing for the Maori. He saluted Murray Thacker for creating such a fine museum and went on to point out the many contributions *pakehas* had been making to the Maori cause. 'Some of us are sixth generation New Zealanders and this is our country too, remember. We have no other place to go.'

The Governor General spoke with great force and assurance, following the correct procedure of answering the challenges and referring to all the different tribes present. Speaking as a Maori he was able to echo much of what had been said, agreeing that 'time is not on our side', but warning of a white backlash if matters were

Sir Paul Reeves, the first Maori Governor General, on the *marae*. Behind him sit the other visitors.

pushed too hard. Reconciliation was his very proper theme. He spoke of the 'special partnership and social contract which is so distinctly ours' and he developed the idea of what constitutes a New Zealander. Standing alone on the *marae*, as had all the other speakers, he seemed to epitomize all that was best about the country – the energy and opportunity and the happy mix of Europe and Polynesia, which have made such a surprisingly robust small nation far out in the Pacific. If only the dialogue about the problems it faces could always be held freely on the *marae*, where opposing views are respected and debated, rather than in the press and parliament where all too often they are trivialized or polarized.

It was a very moving moment and one which affected almost everyone present. I saw Jacky in the crowd with tears running down her face. Although she had grown up on the East Cape surrounded by Maori (to whom she had an amiably paternalistic attitude I sometimes found shocking) and, like many New Zealanders, knew a lot of Maori words, she had never visited a *marae* before. She told me afterwards that the experience had opened her eyes. Most of the *pakeha* present had also never witnessed Maori oratory and indeed many *pakeha* New Zealanders hardly ever get to know a Maori. Sadly the close relationship which mixed the blood of the two races has parted in recent years and there is a growing suspicion on both sides. This can only be an unhealthy trend and one which is in the interests of neither side. The growing Maori self-awareness and independence of spirit is not going to disappear conveniently for the dominant *pakeha*. Instead it should be welcomed as a dynamic contribution to the culture and character of the country.

There were moments of light relief among the serious and passionate speeches. The Spanish Ambassador made a witty speech about his country's early designs on the islands. He had several of the staff of his Embassy there as well as the officers from a visiting sail training ship. These he made come forward and sing Asturias, the Spanish National Anthem, which they did very well, though looking acutely embarrassed.

Also present was a bearded figure in black robes with a black conical hat, the famous Wizard of Christchurch. The best known of the eccentric speakers who daily harangue the crowds in the city's Cathedral Square, his favourite subjects are the Queen, the Church and the dangers of female emancipation. With him was a group of men in the uniforms of British colonial redcoats who sang *Amazing Grace* rather beautifully. The Maori girls' chorus were, of course, regular contributors to the theatrical sense of occasion which seems to develop so spontaneously and well on a *marae*.

Near the end there was a demonstration. The silent protestors had assembled near the front of the crowd; the Maori wardens had gathered around them. Suddenly a young Maori man stepped forward and began to speak on the *marae*. This is something everyone has a right to do and no-one stopped him, although the Maori wardens moved in closer. He had a leaf wreath around his head which he took off and threw on the grass, apparently challenging the Governor General to pick it up. The elders of the *tangata whenua* shouted in outrage and there was a moment of tense confrontation as both sides squared up to each other while the police and TV cameras came closer. Then Tipene O'Regan stepped forward in his fine flax and feather cloak to speak commandingly and start singing a Maori hymn, in which everyone joined, thus leaving the protestors out-manoeuvred.

As soon as the song finished the visitors were invited to cross the *marae* where they all shook hands and performed the *hongi* (pressed noses) with their hosts. The tension immediately relaxed with everyone laughing and chatting. Even the protestors stopped looking

Jacky with the famous wizard of Christchurch. He is usually to be found in the cathedral square in Christchurch, where he daily harangues the crowds.

grim and mingled amiably with the crowd. It is hard to do otherwise on a *marae*.

We spoke briefly to Sir Paul and Lady Reeves, who were interested in how our ride was going. When, after being introduced to the Deputy Prime Minister, I told him in response to the usual question as to how I found New Zealand that the environmental problems interested me, he deftly passed me to the man standing next to him, saying 'Ah, then you should talk to Ken Piddington here, who is the head of the Department of Conservation.' Sadly there was no time to talk then as they were just off to an official reception and soon afterwards Mr Piddington, who had suggested I should call on him in Wellington, was made head of the Environment Division at the World Bank.

After 1984, when the Labour Government decided to discontinue most farm subsidies, there was a dramatic drop in farm incomes. However, the Prime Minister resisted the temptation, to which all his

Tipene O'Regan wearing a flax cloak and speaking vehemently in Maori.

predecessors would have succumbed, to step in and help the farmers out. Instead he illustrated his view of the new role of farming by stating in 1986, 'No longer could it be said that a collapse of the farm industry would bring about a collapse of the New Zealand economy.' What he meant was that although the process would undoubtedly be painful and traumatic the time had come to stop supporting unsustainable businesses; farmers would have to stand on their own feet. This policy, coming at the same time as a burgeoning awareness of and concern for the environment by the huge urban majority of the population, seemed to me to offer opportunities for interesting new approaches. I would have welcomed a chance to pursue these questions with government policy-makers, but it was not to be.

Throughout the proceedings one of the most striking figures had been that of the local Anglican vicar, Martin Warren. A tall, grey-haired man in pale green shirt and trousers, he looked vaguely familiar. 'Hanbury-Tenison,' he said when we were introduced. 'Weren't we at Magdalen together a very long time ago?' We were. Next morning we went to morning service at his church in Akaroa, where we listened to a powerful sermon on sin and personal responsibility. Margaret Thatcher would have approved. He also referred to the Waitangi Tribunal and made a nice analogy between marriage with all its difficulties and Maori-*pakeha* relations.

Akaroa was almost painfully beautiful. The harbour, formed from the flooded crater of one of the Banks Peninsula volcanoes, looked more like a lovely lake than an arm of the sea. We saw our first pohutukawa trees (*Metrosideros excelsa*) growing along the shore. Here, at the very southern limit of their range, they were covered in glorious red bottlebrush flowers which were reflected in the calm blue water, though in the subtropical north they flower at Christmas and are therefore known as New Zealand's Christmas tree. A French colony was on the point of being established at Akaroa in 1840, Captain Jean Langlois having thought that he had bought the whole of Banks Peninsula from the Ngai Tahu tribe. However, when he stopped at Waitangi on his return with the first sixty-three emigrants, he found that the Treaty had just been signed and New Zealand was now a British colony. The French settlers stayed in spite of this and as a result Akaroa has a delightfully Gallic feel to it. Many of the old stone and clapboard houses have been preserved and there are excellent seafood restaurants, one of which we visited with our hosts Robyn and Kit Grigg.

Their farm, over the hill at Hickory Bay, is down a private road and has an inaccessible and therefore undisturbed beach beyond the farmhouse. There we gathered large, succulent mussels by the bucketful and watched a completely unafraid yellow-eyed penguin (*Megadyptes antipodes*) which simply stood on a rock looking self-

I found myself looking straight into a large whiskery face with melancholy eyes . . .

conscious and stared at us. As it is one of the rarest penguins in the world, there being only a few hundred left, I went back alone later to try to get some photographs. Creeping quietly between some large rocks, I made my way to a boulder in the centre, behind which I hid. Peering slowly over the top I found myself looking straight into a large whiskery face with melancholy eyes gazing myopically into mine. It was quite frightening, as for a moment I had no idea what it was. Then, slowly turning my head and looking round, I realized that I had crept into the middle of a colony of fur seals (*Arctocephalus forsteri*). There were at least a dozen all round me and I must have walked within inches of one on my way in. When my nearest neighbour yawned, giving a satisfied grunt at the end, he revealed big teeth and I wondered if seals ever bit people. That was silly, I told myself. I had only to stand up and they would all flop back into the sea in a panic. I stood up. A couple of heads I had not noticed were lifted to glance incuriously at me and then lowered, but none of the seals showed the least alarm. It must have been horribly easy for the whalers and sealers to kill them when the shores teemed with seals which had never seen man before. I decided to enjoy the moment and stop worrying. It was wonderful. As my eyes became accustomed to picking out a glimpse of brown fur among the rocks and seaweed, I would see a hind flipper raised casually here and there as a stout, contented animal lay on its back in the shallows, or scratched itself with the small residual claw on its forelimb. There was a strong, acrid smell emanating from them. No-one had warned me that I might meet seals on the beach and it had not crossed my mind that I would do so. It occurred to me that all the books which say that there were only two mammals (bats) in New Zealand before man arrived were wrong.

In the Galapagos Islands I once swam underwater with a group of female sea lions. They flirted around me as I dived through a tunnel under the reef and came almost nose to nose to look into my face mask. That, too, had been an experience of pure magic until the huge shape of the male had risen like a submarine from the depths and chased me ignominiously back to the boat. Now I began to wonder if I were trespassing again and should perhaps leave while all was still peaceful. I tiptoed away, receiving barely a glance as I passed. Only those lucky enough to have had similar experiences will understand the elation I felt as I ran back to tell everyone about it.

# CHAPTER EIGHT

# Academics and Art

Lincoln College, near Christchurch, is one of the world's oldest schools of agriculture. Only the Royal Agricultural College at Cirencester, at which I once studied, and the Ontario Agricultural College at Guelph in Canada were established earlier. I had several introductions to members of the staff at Lincoln, whose brains I hoped to pick. I spent a valuable morning listening to them, while Louella and Jacky went shopping in Christchurch.

We ranged over a whole lot of subjects which had been bothering me in the high country. It is easy to adopt a high moral tone about conservation issues, but things look very different if you are hungry or have to make a living for your family from poor land. I wanted to know what the experts felt should be done with remote and fragile regions. I expected purely commercial answers and was pleasantly surprised to find enlightened concern for the whole biosphere and a very real understanding of both the mistakes of the past and the problems to be solved in the future.

For a start, the significance of the role agriculture has played in New Zealand's history was explained to me. It has always constituted a large proportion of the national economy and today it still generates about one fifth of the country's wealth. Most of the country, particularly in the North Island, was originally forested and a huge effort was made by the early settlers to clear it. Now it is deeply depressing for farmers to see the land on which they, their fathers and their grandfathers struggled and sweated over the years become uneconomic.

'Should it perhaps never have been farmed in the first place,' I asked, 'or would the settlers have been better concentrating on forestry production instead of agriculture?'

The trouble with that argument, I was told, was that for years in the nineteenth and early twentieth centuries the world was flooded with forest products from all parts of the globe. If it would have been viable then it would probably have been done. As it was, it was sheep and dairy cows that made the country grow.

'But what if things had been done differently?' I pressed my point. 'With the benefit of hindsight, how could the environment have been managed better?'

It was important for me to understand, the experts said, the difference between high country and hill country. Much of the erosion we had seen in the high country was actually caused by the land settling down geologically and not by man or rabbits. That was not to say the introduced plants and animals had not made matters worse and had this been understood at the outset a lot of the higher land would never have been alienated for private use. In other words, it would have been made into a series of national parks and conservation areas. The same would have applied to much of the original forest in the North Island.

Much more critical was the steep but not alpine hill country, especially that on the east coast of the North Island where we were heading. That land was basically unstable and should never have been cleared for agriculture by the removal of the original trees and scrub. Replacing them with forestry might have been a better option, but even that would not have been the answer. With hindsight it is now clear it should have been left alone. One particular event, I was told, had exacerbated the soil erosion problem critically. This was the Easter flood of 1938, when so much soil had been shifted and so many fences buried that a great many farmers were ruined. It was this natural disaster which precipitated the advent of the Soil Conservation Council and the associated Acts of Parliament dedicated to soil conservation. In answer to my question as to whether the disaster was in fact natural or man-made, all were agreed that the rain was natural enough as the cause but the effect would not have occurred had it not been for the removal of the scrub. Such exceptional rainfalls were probably cyclical anyway, occurring perhaps every fifty years or so. In the light of events that were to follow, this was a prophetic discussion.

We went on to discuss the whole fascinating question of the extensively disturbed balance of nature in New Zealand. This is a problem which the country probably has to a greater extent than anywhere else. I ventured my opinion that 'while all conservation involves some management, to attempt it here seems hopeless. Almost everywhere in the world conservation is largely a matter of leaving nature alone, with the exception of possibly eliminating a few pests.' In Britain we have more or less disposed of the coypu and it might be a good thing if we wiped out the mink; of course we have to reduce pollution drastically, but most of our habitats will renew spontaneously if given a chance, as I was finding with my own wildflower meadows. However, in New Zealand the rabbits aren't going to go away, nor are the moas going to come back. The whole evolutionary system has been so broken down by man's arrival and all the pests he brought with him that it seemed to me impossible to sort things out.

I was assured that while New Zealand's history from the first day of settlement had indeed been a chapter of errors, efforts were now being made to correct the mistakes of the past. I was quite right that it was not an easy task. Red deer were still causing grave damage to the beech forests, stoats were doing dreadful things to the bird life and now opossums were becoming a plague, with the added complication that they were TB carriers as well as highly destructive.

Opossums were one of the very few exotic introductions intended for profit rather than sentiment or sport. They were expected to form the basis of a fur industry and indeed still do so, many thousands of skins being sold for about $5 (£2) each. Wrongly named, like much of New Zealand's flora and fauna, they should properly be called phalangers, as the true opossum only comes from the Americas and these were introduced from Australia. First released in 1858, official enthusiasm for their liberation continued well into the twentieth century with the Auckland Acclimatisation Society gushing in 1917 that 'we shall be doing a great service to the country in stocking these large areas with this valuable and harmless animal.' Although farmers and fruit growers were protesting at the damage being done to their crops, it was not until 1956 that the opossum was declared a noxious animal.

Where the native forests are concerned, the problem has now been identified as arising from a combination of deer and opossum. The deer remove the undergrowth which lets the opossums in; they in turn destroy the canopies of the trees, creating open glades which encourage the deer.

The Government did seem to be committed to passing legislation which would help protect the environment. They had recently signed the World Heritage covenant, created new national parks and allocated considerable funds to conservation. The trouble was that most farmers still did not regard conservation as a legitimate land use. But that, too, was changing. Many recognized the value of covenanting important features on their land such as remnant native forests or wetlands to the Queen Elizabeth II National Trust, thus protecting them in perpetuity.

I sympathized with the difficulties the farmers faced in coming to terms with such a change of outlook, since I had lived through a similar experience myself. For most of the twenty-eight years that I have farmed sheep and cattle in Cornwall the emphasis of professional agricultural advice was on intensification, with grants for the removal of hedges and the draining of marshes, and encouragement for increased use of fertilizers and pesticides. Gradually that

Opossums are killed as vermin and the skins sold for fur. They were introduced from Australia and released in great numbers in the 19th century.

emphasis has changed and in recent years, for all sorts of economic and social reasons, British farmers are being urged to concentrate more on conservation.

Such a radical change of perspective never comes easily and most of us have had to reassess our position and take into consideration the value of all sorts of odd things like butterflies, wildflowers, frogs, hardwoods, bracken, hawks, owls, bats and badgers. Traditionally these were all economically insignificant or minor pests we could ignore or destroy as it pleased us. For me the crunch came with badgers, always plentiful but inoffensive neighbours in my woods.

There is a tenuous and much debated link between badgers and tuberculosis in cattle, which led our Ministry of Agriculture to declare a quiet war on them.

When I discovered that all land for 4 miles to the north of my home had been cleared of badgers and a notice arrived informing me that bait marking was about to begin, to assess whether those on my land should be exterminated too, I decided that I had to fight. I tore the notice up and forbade the Ministry entry. They told me that they had the right. The World Wildlife Fund made my farm a test case, undertaking to pay my legal fees should I be taken to court on this issue. The Ministry backed off and my badgers are still there.

I learnt a lot, and did much heart-searching while the battle was on as it is much easier to avoid conflict at such times and let others bear the brunt. The war is not over and never will be. Now that we have many red deer on the farm I live under the constant threat of TB occurring here, being attributed to the badgers and presenting me with impossible choices. Fortunately, research continues and an oral vaccine for badgers may become practicable. The alternative is the ultimate extinction of another of our indigenous mammals, because that is the stark choice. We either learn to live with them, inconvenient though it may at times be, or we wipe them out and live in a barren land.

In New Zealand the picture is a very different one and the problem even greater. Nature can never be beaten into submission with impunity. We simply do not know enough about the long-term effects of our actions to risk it. Sooner or later, unless great care is taken, quite unforeseen disaster will strike. Beneficial plants and animals become pests. Improved land fails or slips. In New Zealand, where everything, the land, the animals and man are all so new, it is especially hard to forecast the future. Perhaps the research into finding an oral vaccine against TB in badgers in England may lead to a similar solution being found to the opossum problem 12,000 miles (20,000 km) away.

There is a tendency in New Zealand to see everything new and unwelcome as a foreign plot; a by-product of the well-documented xenophobia and chauvinism, I suppose. Many times we were told that all the human rights activism and Maori protest was actually being orchestrated by Libyans wanting to undermine the country. Interference is deeply resented in all areas, but nowhere more than by farmers. As always, the press bears a responsibility for highlighting extreme examples and feeding fears. When unashamedly partisan this just encourages prejudice and polarization between perfectly reconcilable views. After all, everyone must really want to see racial harmony prevail between Maori and *pakeha*, though recent extremist claims by Maori activists sound alarmingly militant. But activists do not want war, they want to be listened to and they want their rights.

It can be against no citizen's long-term interests for New Zealand to continue to be a clean and healthy land where farming makes a real contribution to the economy. Yet to hear extreme conservationists talk, all farmers, and notably the big high country runholders, are greedy rapists of the soil, who only want to squeeze every penny they can out of land which should all be abandoned to nature. This is patently nonsense. We had seen for ourselves something of the hard work and dedication which goes into farming that most inhospitable of regions. We had seen the superb stock which can be reared on such land and discovered how passionately those who lived there cared for it all. However, we had also glimpsed how fragile it was and how much sensitivity needs to be exercised in looking after it.

The farming press, especially that financed by the commercial interests of fertilizer and pesticide manufacturers, tends to portray all 'greenies' as fanatics dedicated to bringing all stock farming to an end. I read alarmist articles which first dismissed conservationists and thinking consumers alike as neurotic, then 'revealed' that the purpose behind the animal welfare movement was to turn everyone into a vegetarian or a vegan.

A week after I was at Lincoln College a Press Release was issued to promote a new magazine *Farm Progress*, produced by the Agricultural Chemical and Animal Remedies Manufacturers Association. In it environmental, consumer and animal rights groups are classified together as 'extremists'. Their long-term aims are spelled out as: 'The banning of all pesticides . . . An end to the commercial use of animals on farms . . . The abolition of the use of all "artificial products" in the production of farmed animals.'

In a country where agriculture has always underpinned the economy and still does, such talk raises blood pressure to dangerous levels. The environmentalists are not going to go away but neither are the farmers and both would be better off if they could learn to work together towards solutions instead of slanging each other. A song from the old musical *Oklahoma* kept going through my head as we rode through the countryside: 'Oh the farmer and the greenie (cowboy in the original) should be friends . . .'

At Lincoln College, and later when I had time to read through the piles of scientific papers and conference reports they kindly gave me, I realized how much good work was being done on these issues, which must give hope that the resourceful New Zealanders will work things out in time. Far better to have a press which behaves irresponsibly at both extremes but is free than one which is muzzled as in Malaysia, where criticism of human rights or deforestation can result in closure and prison.

Sheep being unloaded at Addington saleyards, Christchurch. Agriculture is central to New Zealand's economy and there are 70 million sheep to 3 million people in the country.

Discussions and meetings are an obsession in New Zealand; with all the problems they face at the moment perhaps that is not such a bad thing but they do carry it to extremes. One report I read broke down local government into over 1,000 statutory bodies: 231 Territorial Authorities, 135 Community Councils, 22 United or Regional Councils, 209 Special Purpose Authorities, and 407 Statutory National Boards. All that in a land of 3 million people! Since the same people sit on several different committees one cannot help feeling that they would do better simply to get on with the job.

Several scientific writers saw the era of traditional high country farming coming to an end, to be replaced by a mix of use involving grazing the better lower land while abandoning the high steepland to walkers and wildlife. 'It has not been easy for many land occupiers . . . to accept that major errors in land management were made and that rehabilitation is likely to be slow, costly and may require fundamental changes in land use,' wrote Chris Kerr, one of the scientists I met, in the opening paper of the 1987 Hill and High Country Seminar.

Others illustrated how fragile the mountains are and how susceptible to damage by all sorts of wildlife, native as well as introduced. 'Some such alpine systems have such low productivity that they cannot stand grazing even by grasshoppers.' 'It was surprise enough to observe the recovery of alpine grasses and buttercups when deer were reduced in the wetter mountains. It is even more surprising to discover how deer had been imposing hunger on takahe and kea and affecting their habitats in turn. Hungry takahe quietly become extinct. Hungry kea first make others pay.' (Both these are quotes from a paper in the same seminar by Professor Kevin O'Connor.) The takahe (*Notornis mantelli*) is a large, plump, blue flightless rail thought to be extinct until its rediscovery in 1948 a hundred years after the first one to be recorded by Europeans was caught (and subsequent killed, cooked and eaten) by a party of sealers. Only four specimens were collected during the next fifty years, then a small and dwindling population was found in a remote valley in the Southern Alps. It lives on tussock shoots and insects. Lack of competition or predators led to its stout and defenceless condition. When deer arrived to eat its food, it was unable to cope.

The 'killer keas' seem less wicked if the cause of their occasional attacks on sheep is understood to be hunger brought about by the very same sheep eating their natural food, although I do not expect that argument to carry much weight with farmers suffering their depredations.

The scientists also suggested, although quite subtly, that both opposing camps might sometimes be as interested in control and effective ownership of the areas concerned as in what was for the best from environmental or economic standpoints.

The garage examining Kowhai had identified serious trouble.

'The engine's completely shot. There's a valve gone and the pistons are slapping around,' said the foreman, showing me some tortured pieces of metal.

'What will it cost to put right?' I asked nervously.

'Four thousand dollars for an overhaul, $2,000 for a short block, or I could get you a second-hand engine for about $850. That's what I would recommend.'

It was going to take a couple of days but matters could have been worse and at least we had an excuse to see the garden city of Christchurch, the most English place in New Zealand. With fine stone buildings, a neo-Gothic cathedral, excellent museums and a willow-lined river called the Avon meandering through the centre, it was the perfect place to break down.

For some years I have collected Newlyn School pictures, particularly the work of an artist called Thomas Cooper Gotch (1854–1931), one of the last of the Pre-Raphaelites. On a wild impulse, and remembering Samuel Butler's remark that it did not do to speak of such things in New Zealand, I asked at the McDougall Art Gallery if they had any paintings of his. The curator told me he had three minutes before another meeting, but it was over an hour before we parted. Charming and extremely knowledgeable, he took me down to the basement store where I was allowed to glimpse an amazing collection of pictures, many privately owned and just passing through for exhibition or restoration. Notable for me were some *plein-air* landscapes by Frank Bramley (1857–1915) and a superb portrait of Bramley by William Wainwright (1855–1931), who also painted the best-known portrait of Gotch. Both were leading members of the Newlyn School. They did have a Gotch, but in such bad repair that I was only allowed to see a photograph of it. Called *Consent*, it will, when restored, be a lovely Victorian picture of a daughter asking her father's permission to marry.

By this stage I must have proved my credentials as the curator paused and said 'It's funny you should be asking about Gotch. I had a lady in here last week with four portraits by him. If you like, I'll ring her and ask if she minds you calling round.' And so it was that I found myself taking tea with Mrs Moss, who, with her sister and two brothers, had been painted by my favourite artist some sixty-five years ago in England and remembered the occasion well.

'Such a nice man,' she told me. 'he had a ginger beard and a real way with children.'

The delicate watercolours, among the most delightful child portraits I have ever seen, hung in the room where we sat. Outside Sunset Cottage was a totally English townscape and I was overcome by a sense of unreality. Gotch never went to New Zealand, though he did paint in Australia, and the last thing I had expected on waking that morning had been to see any of his work. The portraits will stay in the family where they belong and if I ever return to Christchurch I will ask if I may call for tea again.

Another extraordinary experience awaited us in Christchurch. Exactly ten years previously I had been in the Borneo rain forest leading a large Royal Geographical Society expedition of scientists. One of the best pieces of equipment we had with us, which helped most with the logistics and made life particularly enjoyable, was the jet boat provided by Hamilton Marine of Christchurch. Jon Hamilton and his son Mike had brought us the boat themselves and shown us how to get the best out of it through the fourteen rapids and 90 miles (145 km) between our Base Camp and Marudi, the nearest small town. Jon had written with useful advice on our route through

The Waimakariri River runs through a melodramatic gorge. We went several miles up it in Jon Hamilton's jet boat.

New Zealand and now he offered to take us by jet boat up the Waimakariri River to reconnoitre the next stage of our journey. The Waimak, as it is called by locals, runs through a dramatic gorge with perpendicular bare rock walls. For a time a single-track railway line built in the last century teeters alongside, then it becomes true wilderness.

Jon Hamilton and his father Sir William invented and perfected jet boats in order to be able to travel up the wild, shallow rivers of the South Island to their sheep station at Irishman's Creek on the Tekapo River. They did much of the original testing in the fifties on the Waimak, which they were the first to ascend thanks to this novel means of transport. Instead of using a propellor, which strikes rocks or gravel beds, water is sucked through a turbine and expelled at the stern so that the boat almost flies and can, if necessary, even scrape across banks with impunity. Speeding up through the powerful rapids under the wild, untouched, romantic cliffs was an exhilarating experience. Jon is probably the most experienced jet boat driver in the world and he knows and loves this stretch of water like no other. It has been his escape from the cares of running a large engineering company, somewhere he can go, often alone, and taunt the elements. The Waimak is a worthy opponent, being subject to rapid and lethal floods, its bed strewn with jagged rocks, which, if struck, spell instant sinking for a small fibreglass boat and probable death by drowning for its occupants. Lady Barker wrote in February 1868:

We have been nearly washed away, by all the creeks and rivers in the country overflowing their banks. Christchurch particularly was in great danger from the chance of the Waimakariri returning to its old channel, in which case it would sweep away the town. For several hours half the streets were under water, the people going about in boats, and the Avon was spread out like a lake over its banks for miles. The weather had been unusually sultry for some weeks, and during the last five days the heat had been far greater, even in the hills, than anyone could remember.

Jon was an enthusiastic guide, pointing out fish in clear pools and telling stories about the camps his family had made in inaccessible bays, where they could safely leave equipment since so few others had ever attempted the river in those days. Once, when going up alone in a big flood, he had come upon four men in a rubber dinghy who had been trapped for some hours in a whirlpool out of which they had not sufficient strength to paddle themselves. He had thrown them a rope and towed them out.

At the head of the gorge was a place between two gravel beds where wool used to be carried across the river from Mount White Station to Craigieburn, until one day an entire year's shearing had been lost in flood water. This was the spot where we, too, had planned to cross once we resumed our ride and it was the excuse for our boat trip.

We pulled into a backwater to see a school of gigantic chinook salmon below the boat. Their departure as we landed seemed almost leisurely, as though they knew they had nothing to fear from us. Though hardly up to the New Zealand record of 64 pounds (29 kg), they were the biggest salmon I have ever seen.

We climbed a small bluff and sat looking up river. A storm cloud was gathering over Mount Binser and a rainbow arced across the valley. The water flowed quite fast and we doubted if the horses would make it safely across, especially as rain was coming. To avoid the ford would mean riding several miles round by road, and so we decided to skip that stretch and start again at Mount White Station itself.

# CHAPTER NINE

# Riding in the Rain

There is a special pleasure about travel that comes from living within limited horizons. The problems of each day are immediately resolvable, rather than long term ones such as business affairs and overdrafts. Life is very satisfactory when everything can be planned out within a manageable framework. This is, of course, the escapist side of travel but that should not prevent one relishing it.

We left Christchurch in pouring rain but euphoric at having sorted everything out so that we could remount our horses and resume our journey. On the way back to Lake Coleridge Station, where we had left the horses in the care of Jim Murchison, we stopped at a small place called Darfield to try to buy feed for them. The farm suppliers (called in New Zealand a stock and station agency) Wrightson, Dalgety had none, but the boss offered to try to find some while we had a bite to eat at the café. He rang some farmers and then drove in his own car for half an hour to fetch us a sack of chaff and a bale of good lucerne hay. For these he charged us only the small amount he had had to pay the farmers themselves; another example of the spontaneous generosity and help to be found throughout the country, but much slower to reveal itself in the South Island. In *Out of Africa*, Karen Blixen has the following to say about hospitality. 'In pioneer countries hospitality is a necessity of life, not to the travellers alone, but to the settlers. A visitor is a friend. He brings news, good or bad, which is bread to the hungry minds in lonely places.'

This African approach softens the sting of accepting help from strangers in a foreign land. Sadly we found, especially in the South Island, that while the instinct to provide for the traveller was there, the thirst for news and conversation was often lacking. One of the hardest things to take about the New Zealand character is the contrast between their natural generosity and the lack of charm or interest with which it is so often given.

It took us all a good hour to catch the horses, who had made up their minds that they liked Lake Coleridge Station and would be happy to stay there, but at last they were loaded.

From Christchurch back to our new starting point at Mount White was over a hundred miles, but the road led through some beautiful country along the edge of the large Craigieburn Forest Park. Once all the lower slopes of the Craigieburn Range were forested, with alpine scrub and grassland above. Only the highest ridges and alpine tops above 6,000 feet (1,800 m) were bare rock and screes. Samuel Butler was there in 1860 and described 'impenetrable thickets of matagouri scrub'. He lit the first recorded fire, although there probably were earlier ones started by moa hunters or by lightning. The land was quickly cleared for sheep and by the early part of this century erosion was accelerating and causing problems. The first areas of surviving woodland had been declared state forest in 1898 and later much more pastoral land was retired from farming to increase the acreage of forest. Most of the slopes visible from the road are still bare, however, and it is necessary to walk into the park to reach the best vegetation.

There is an extensive limestone outcrop around Castle Hill Station, which makes the grazing sweet there. The most dramatic evidence of this is the great natural white battlement on a hilltop which gives the station its name. The homestead below used to be a staging post on the coach road, which was built in one year (1865) by 1,000 men under appalling conditions, providing Christchurch with access to the west coast port of Greymouth. The high slopes above have been developed as ski fields and are much used in winter, although it is a dangerous area for avalanches. In 1918 the then owner of the station lost almost his entire flock in exceptionally heavy snow. It is country where even in the summer the weather can suddenly turn foul and we were glad to be through it quickly and safely.

Mount White is another of the great stations about which several books have been written. Peter Newton not only rode through it by the same route we planned to take but he was later the manager and wrote *The Boss's Story* about his time there. He describes it as 'one of the best-balanced runs in the back country', consisting as it does of a huge and varied acreage; as remote as anywhere in the South Island and subject to 'more than its share of snow', it is a fine station with land ranging from remote hinterland down to flat terraces next to the Waimakariri River. It is the sort of country which stirs the hearts of a musterers and makes all who work there fiercely proud and defensive of the hard lives they lead. For all the hardship they do seem to thrive. In *The Boss's Story* there is a photograph taken in the early fifties of the present manager, Ray Marshall, sitting on a rail in the homestead yards with a gang of other young musterers. The man we met some thirty-five years later still wore shorts, had all his hair and looked barely a day older.

Keen to be back in the saddle, we were up at 5.30 a.m. the next morning. Ray gave us careful advice on the route ahead.

'Look at those high clouds,' he said. 'They're a sure sign of a nor'easter on the way and that will bring high winds and rain. You don't want to be caught on the top in that. It's a long way, but I should try and get over the Saddle today if you can; you'll have to shift as it usually takes two days.'

It had rained hard in the night, but the day was clear and the horses were fresh. There was a delay at the start when we found that Louella's hat had been left behind. She would probably need it against both sun and rain before we were through and so we went back for it. It was eight o'clock by the time we rode up from the station to look back over the sweep of the Mount White paddocks and then ahead from the first ridge to the wild and glorious country beyond. There was a surprising amount of manuka and it was in flower, small white blossoms giving off a faint, pleasant aroma. Left alone this hardy plant can form the nurse crop of a new beech forest by providing shelter for the young trees without swamping them, but here it was still being grazed by sheep and cattle; some of it had even been burnt recently, though whether this was accidental or not we could not tell.

Five hours' good easy ambling, with lots of soft cantering, brought us to Anderson's Hut at the foot of the ridge leading up to Esk Head and the saddle in the Dampier Range. We had now come 20 miles (32 km) from Mount White and musterers would normally camp here before bringing the sheep down from one of the isolated high blocks ahead the next day. We decided to rest the horses, who were sweating but still keen, for an hour or so and then, if the cloud had not come down to make the crossing too dangerous, to carry on before the weather broke. On either side of the ridge were deep valleys which looked rich and green from above. In Anderson's Stream to our left there were little meadows and patches of virgin beech forest. In the hot afternoon sunshine it looked an idyllic place to live, about as cut off from the outside world as could be imagined. With trout in the stream and red deer on the hill life should be easy. Good tall tussock grass grew right up to the ridge and there were few signs of erosion, yet Peter Newton describes this as 'one of the worst corners for snow in the whole length of the province.'

What struck us most as we led the horses on foot up the steeper stretches of the ridge was the utter peace. Almost no one ever goes up there. A walker or a hunter every month or so, perhaps; the musterers once or twice a year, but for the rest of the time it is left alone. Although it clearly is grazed, there were no sheep to be seen, no cattle and not even any of the red deer, which used to be especially common until, in the 1960s, it became worthwhile to catch them.

(*Above*) Anderson's Hut on Mount White Station is tucked under a beech wood below Esk Head. (*Below*) Wild empty country, it looks benign but can be cruel when the weather changes.

As we emerged from a clump of beech and manuka scrub the increasingly splendid view behind us began to build. At the top of the ridge we had to make quite a tricky traverse to the right across some screes in order to get above the saddle, as its face was guarded by sheer slopes. Halfway round we reached a small, deep tarn, into which a tiny ice-cold stream trickled, from which we and the horses drank thankfully after the climb. The tarn was no bigger than a swimming pool, its water dark and clear of weed. As we walked away from it I glanced back over my shoulder and saw a large fish move on the surface. It seemed impossible that anyone would have bothered to stock such an extremely isolated place with trout and yet no fish could have made its way up the steep damp slope into which our little stream disappeared on leaving the tarn. Perhaps it was an eel, as they are plentiful in New Zealand and grow to a huge size. We heard of specimens 6 feet (1.5 m) long and almost as thick as a man's thigh in the big lakes far below, but would one have wriggled up so high?

From the saddle itself we had views in all directions to rival any we were to see in that famously beautiful country. Rain showers to the north over a succession of high ranges added to the dramatic effect. Thunder echoed off the hills around. The temperature plummeted and the rain came, but not before we had seen enough to feel a great sense of achievement.

It was a long haul down to Deep Creek Hut and we did not find our way across the ravine after which it is named until six o'clock. Then the joy of a mug of tea followed by some chicken soup from a package and a couple of buns we had brought with us from Mount White, while we stretched out on the hard bunks and listened to the rain outside. There was a tattered copy of *Everyman's Book of Heroic and Patriotic Verse* in the hut, with pencilled notes in the margin and underlinings for emphasis. As our wet clothes steamed in front of the fire I read favourite poems by Kipling and Henry Newbolt aloud in the candlelight to Louella.

In the night we heard the eerie, high-pitched cry of the morepork (*Ninox novaeseelandiae*), New Zealand's native owl, which does sound just as though it is pleading for food. A hundred years earlier there was an even stranger call to be heard, especially on wet nights. The large laughing owl (*Sceloglaux albifacies*) was described by one of those who heard it as uttering 'a series of dismal shrieks frequently repeated'. Sadly it fell prey early on to the introduced predators. Early ornithologists reported that it flew weakly on short, feeble wings, preferring to walk quickly away from trouble with long strides of its short, powerful legs. One can imagine how quickly wild cats must have taken advantage of that behaviour; it was soon extinct.

We rode east along the south branch of the Hurunui River for 5–6 miles (8–9 km) to call on Chris and Sally Bridgeman, who bought Esk

Head Station six years ago. For 120 years before that it was owned by the same family, managed for nearly sixty years by one man and since then by his grandson. Chris's expensive new broom, which included major investment in fencing and roads, had been followed by the slump in farm prices and rapidly escalating interest rates rising to 27 per cent on the money he had borrowed to upgrade the place. It was a sadly familiar story but the Bridgemans were cheerful and seemed confident everything would come right in time, although their ambitious plans to start deer farming had had to be postponed.

They had a message for us from Jacky, saying that Kowhai was giving trouble again and she had returned to Christchurch to have a new head gasket fitted. They were generous with advice and offers of hospitality but we felt we should push on. Sally made us a pile of sandwiches and Chris gave me a key to a gate on our route ahead.

'The last person who rode through left all the gates open and all the sheep escaped,' he said. 'It's incredible how stupid people can be, so I've had to put a lock on it. Send the key back when you reach a post office.'

We kept hearing stories of idiot behaviour by previous travellers which made the kindness we received all the more surprising, although it must have strengthened these isolated farmers' natural suspicion of outsiders. An American girl with no provisions and dressed in a skirt had attempted to ride over to Mount White the previous year. She had been lost on the mountain for three days and had eventually returned half starved. We also heard many stories of a Swiss couple who had been riding unshod horses and attempting to navigate with a Shell road map. We were flattered at being treated as professionals by contrast, although it did often mean our initial telephone calls were greeted with suspicion. Three days ahead of us lay St James, a station famous for the horses bred there. I had been warned that the owner, Jim Stevenson, might be reluctant to let us through and so I had been even more apologetic than usual when I rang him.

'I am an Englishman riding through New Zealand with my wife,' I said, which always sounded foolish enough without the pommy accent; that tends to be an irritant to back-country Kiwis. 'Would it be all right for us to cross your land, please?'

A gruff voice answered, 'What if my stallions start chasing you?'

'It's okay, we'll be riding geldings,' I replied.

'That makes it worse!' he roared. I had given the wrong answer, as apparently the stallions find mares less of a threat. 'The last bloody fools who tried coming through on horses lost one with a broken leg in the Boyle River.'

'We've got pretty good horses,' I said. 'Will we get through from Glenhope to St James in a day if you do give us permission?'

'I don't know, do I? I don't know how good you are. You'll have to go some.'

At that point I knew he was going to let us through and sure enough his next words confirmed it.

'When did you say this would be?'

Having much the same problem with people wanting to use my land in Cornwall for various purposes I understood his resistance, but I also knew how to get round it.

Meanwhile, we had some 60 miles (100 km) to cover. Retracing our steps along the South Branch of the Hurunui, a most attractive river running through a deep gorge, we could see big trout lying in pools far below us. Chris Bridgeman had told me that they averaged 8–9 pounds (3–4 kg) but were almost impossible to catch as they lived in deep holes under the cliffs and seldom surfaced to feed.

As we neared Lake Mason we had to negotiate some boggy ground and then push our way through matagouri bushes. There was gorse, too, the bushes nibbled by sheep into strange shapes as though a topiarist had been at work. Hearing a tinkle, Louella looked down just in time to see Manaaki's near hind shoe drop off. Once again I had to set to work with pliers, Swiss army knife and stones, but this time we had new nails with us and I was rather pleased with the result; the shoe stayed on tight for the next day and a half until we could have a new set fitted.

By Lake Mason we came on somewhere that seemed to us the most perfect setting imaginable for a house. Tall, ancient beeches sheltered an area of open parkland which ran down to the lake shore. Across the lake was a grand wooded hillside and all around were vast panoramas of mountains. Black swans, flocks of ducks and crested grebes crowded the surface of the lake and trout made rings on the still water. We led the horses through the woods along the lakeside, guiding them around fallen logs and squeezing them between trees against which the saddle bags rubbed.

A gentle climb up from the lake brought us to a ridge from which we could see out over Lake Sumner, reputedly the most beautiful lake in the entire Canterbury district at the heart of a large forest park. A whole new sort of country lay before us. The slopes far across the valley were thickly wooded from the water's edge to near the summits of the mountains. In front, at the head of the lake, were wide river flats and a welcoming basin of gentle land which contrasted dramatically with the harsh country behind us. Above us to our left was a peak called Terrible Knob (4,774 feet / 1,455 m), below us the main Hurunui River flowed into the lake, and opposite were Mac's Knob (4,688 feet / 1,429 m) and Mount Longfellow (5,785 feet / 1,898 m), the highest peak in the district. Behind the bare ridges of the Nelson tops lay the main divide, the South Island watershed.

Although still quite a difficult area to reach, it is such a beautiful place that walking trails have been opened up for what are called 'trampers' in New Zealand, suspension footbridges cross some of the more dangerous rivers and there are many huts. Most of these belong to the New Zealand Forest Service, which manages the park, although others are musterers' huts belonging to the stations whose stock graze the open areas.

It was a long, stony 1,000 feet (300 m) down to the plain and then a pleasant ride in the evening light to Lake Sumner Hut, wonderfully ramshackle but locked, although it had a useful paddock around it for the horses. A couple of miles further upstream was No. 2 Hut, a modern forestry hut with eighteen bunks. Our only problem was that it was surrounded by a smart new fence with a locked gate and only a stile for 'trampers'. Horses were clearly not expected, although the grass inside looked tempting. Frustrated at the prospect of having to leave the horses tethered outside, which would have been dangerous, and tired after quite a long day which looked like ending in torrential rain as had the one before, we rode rather desperately around the large paddock in the centre of which was the hut. Smoke curled from

Lake Sumner Hut was locked. Even the most ramshackle musterers' huts were welcome after a long day in the saddle.

the chimney, which indicated that for the first time we would be sharing with others and this, too, seemed a pity as we enjoyed being alone. At last we found a place where the fence had been broken down by people climbing over and, using the fencing pliers to remove some more staples, I was able to lower the remaining wires to the ground. Laying our coats on the wire we led the horses across safely and I later made the fence good again – much better than it had been before our arrival.

At the hut was a somewhat elderly man, who seemed as disappointed by our arrival as we were to find him already ensconced. We all greeted each other amiably enough, but when we carried our saddles inside out of the rain he pointed out rather sharply that he had just swept the floor and usually took his boots off himself indoors. We conformed and boiled our billy on the stove. He told us he had been at the hut for three days as he had not liked the look of the weather and thought it unsafe to leave.

Louella confided to me, when he went outside for a moment, that he looked like a homicidal maniac and would probably murder us in the night. While we sat up at the table reading and writing by candlelight, he crouched on his bunk in the dark staring at us. We slept badly, worrying among other things about the rain drumming on the roof and the poor horses out in it. We had given them a good rub down on arrival and there was plenty of grass for them but we could not carry their rugs with us when away from the truck and we were afraid that on such a night they might get a chill. Several times in the night I had to go out to comfort them and move their tethers, since the paddock was too big to risk letting them loose and having problems catching them next day. Our companion never stirred; when we left in the morning he was sitting gazing at the view.

Now the famous Kiwi Pack Track lay ahead. Once this was a droving route for stock being taken from Marlborough across to the gold mines on the west coast around Hokitika; then for years it was abandoned, being followed only occasionally by deer hunters. Now it has been opened again by the Forest Service as a walking trail. Running through thick, unspoiled beech forest, in which grew some of the largest red beech that we had seen, the path was often steep and narrow so that again we walked and led the horses for much of the way. We were in a different world here from that of the high ridge. Although stoats, ferrets and wild cats are to be found, the bird life is rich and for the first time we had an inkling of the 'melodious wild music' of native birds described by Joseph Banks. After the rain everything was green and wet, little brooks ran down the hillside under the trees, and ferns, fallen trees and dappled light made it like a tropical rainforest, reminding me for a moment of Borneo.

Two of New Zealand's rarer native forest birds are relatively common in this park. The kaka (*Nestor meridionalis*) is a fat, harmless relation of the kea. The Maori used to trap them to keep as pets or to eat. We heard them whistling musically in the trees, though they were hard to spot. More visible, though with softer calls, were the yellow-crowned parakeets (*Cyanoramphus auriceps*) which flew chattering overhead in small flocks.

The tiny rifleman (*Acanthisitta chloris*), New Zealand's smallest bird, was also there in large numbers. They belong to a family unknown in the rest of the world; hardly able to fly, they can only flutter from tree to tree and are very hard to catch sight of. With only primitive vocal chords, they have no proper song but make a rapid, high-pitched 'zip' which reveals their presence. It sounds more like a cricket than a bird and adds to the illusion of tropical jungle. Much more vociferous were the noisy and common tuis (*Prosthemadera novaeseelandiae*) called parson birds because of the startling white throat feathers on their dark plumage, giving the effect of a clerical collar. They have a wide repertoire of songs, but the one which I now heard, and which instantly reminded me even more of the jungle, consisted of four liquid notes reproducing the opening bar of Beethoven's Fifth Symphony. There is a bird in Borneo which repeats the same phrase endlessly and slightly off key.

The track was well marked and just wide enough for the horses, but the little wooden bridges and occasional poles laid across muddy stretches for the convenience of walkers sometimes made it difficult for them to pick their way. From near the Kiwi Saddle, which we crossed easily, there were glimpsed views of the lake far below through the trees; then a long stretch beside an open glade, through which ran the Kiwi River. Tempting meadowland covered in yellow ragwort with bright green boggy patches looked good to ride across at first, but then we felt the ground shake and thought it better to stay next to the wood. This was just as well as we later learned that a hundred horses are supposed to have been drowned in that bog over the years. It is a lethal place for animals. John Shearer, the owner of The Poplars Station, of which this valley is part, said that he no longer put stock there, but for another reason apart from the danger of animals drowning – the hunters who tended to loose off at anything that moved. He had had thirteen young steers shot out of the last batch he had turned out there, one having twenty-six bullets in its leg. Understandably he did not think highly of tourists, but he was kind to us and quite impressed by the speed and distance we had travelled. He is a great pilot and keeps a light aircraft which he uses for mustering the very inaccessible and difficult bushbound country running up to well over 6,000 feet (2,000 m).

Peter Newton described the difficulties of mustering in the old days when a full gang was employed. Being subject to tremendous rainfall and fog, the muster could be held up for days and with no natural boundaries at which to hold the sheep each night it was almost impossible to be sure of bringing them all in:

> One practice was for each man to carry just the bare necessities, in the way of bedding and food, and camp on the hill where he finished the day. With each man only half a mile or so apart, sheep were not so liable to drift back. However, this was only practicable in.fine weather and the mustering has always been a problem on these tops. All this country is subject to heavy snow and any sheep left out after the autumn muster can be written off.

Today John simply flies over the sheep and blasts a loud klaxon which effectively drives them down from the high ground into valleys where they can be managed more easily.

Fording the Hope River, we set off again from Glenhope Station up the side of the Waiau River, following another old pack track. This was the day on which we hoped to cross St James and meet Jacky again on the road into Molesworth. If we made it we would have covered a good 40 miles (67 km) and the hardest part of our journey would be over. If we failed to arrive by evening we would be in for an uncomfortable night out as there were no huts after half way. Also the horses were showing some signs of stress. Wahine had a disturbing little lump on her back and Manaaki's fetlocks were slightly swollen.

The track ran high above the river, giving me moments of vertigo, but the views were magnificent and although the weather remained threatening we cantered along in great spirits. The nor'easter was continuing and everyone had talked about how unusually bad the weather was for the time of year. An inch of rain had fallen at The Poplars the day before and there was no sign of a change for the better. The vegetation was often a mixture of broom and manuka, which looked rather similar at a glance, the introduced and the native plants growing happily together without either becoming dominant. Gorse, sweetbrier and ragwort were all common and major pests, while along the sides of the track there were thistles which had arrived with the stock, the seeds being brought in the droppings. In the undergrowth blackbirds and chaffinches sang, lulling us into believing we were at home in Cornwall, until the strange alien shriek of a parrot, the song of a tui or the sweet notes of a bellbird would remind us where we were.

The country was becoming noticeably more eroded again, with deep gullies and washouts where water had created tracks. Sometimes, near homesteads where a bulldozer had been at work, we had to look twice to see if a scar on a hillside was made by man or nature.

Up and down over spurs and into deep creeks, we covered many more miles than a straight line on the map indicated. Reaching Tin

The track to Glenhope Station running high above the Waiau River towards St James's Station. Far upstream, we had to find our way across the valley, fording the river.

Jug Hut, we learned from the exercise book in which passersby were invited to write their names that we had covered 14 miles since leaving the river two hours before. We were therefore averaging 7 mph, which is fast going for a horse across country. We travelled on past the entrance to the Magdalen Valley, which was said to be even more beautiful than that of the Waiau, though that was hard to believe. I had hoped to see if there were still poplars in the valley, all that remains of a French settlement where cheese was made for the miners over the mountains, but was unable to catch a glimpse of them. They may have inspired the name of the Poplars Range and the station itself.

Then came the moment when we had to leave the track and cross the Waiau River. It was quite a deep ford after the recent rain and there was a high, white, eroded cliff on the far bank. We had a little trouble finding our way up through the manuka which clothed the hillside, but once on the top of the terrace we found another track and believed ourselves home and dry.

We were wrong. After resting by a stream to eat a couple of hard-boiled eggs and share an orange while the horses grazed, we remounted and started to climb over Charlie's Saddle at about 2,500 feet (750 m). At this point it began to rain really hard and did not let up for the next three hours. We plodded on, soon soaked to the skin in spite of our Barbours and now quite cold as the temperature dropped; Louella had been stung on the face by a wasp the day before and her mouth was swollen and numb. For a time we followed the Edwards River up to near its source, then we had to veer off south east to pick up a path down Peter's Valley to the old St James's homestead and the road. In poor visibility and torrential rain we needed the compass and some careful map reading not to get lost and bogged down in a big swamp.

Near the homestead, as we slithered along a recently bulldozed track, now running with water like a river, some stallions did at last appear. They looked wildly at us, their eyes rolling, then cantered off without bothering us further. The buildings were deserted, the house empty. We sheltered miserably under a tree, the rain tipping down our necks; then, to our relief, Kowhai appeared and Jacky, with a big, welcoming grin, climbed out. We rubbed the horses down, gave them a big feed, put on their New Zealand rugs and turned them loose in some good grassy stockyards for the night. Since there was nowhere obvious for us to camp and the rain showed no sign of letting up, we decided to spoil ourselves. We drove 10 miles (16 km) or so down to Hanmer Springs, an alpine health spa, where we checked into a luxurious motel. They had a washing machine and a drying room which we took over for the evening, so that by morning all our filthy clothes were clean and dry again. While the machines did their work we crossed the road to the thermal pool where we lay and soaked in boiling sulphurous water, easing our many aches. It was just what we needed at that moment and the timing could not have been better. There was even an excellent little restaurant in town run by a Dutch couple, where we spoiled ourselves further with mussels, roast lamb and good New Zealand wine.

That night we used the almost-forgotten luxury of the telephone in our room to ring home. We had sent our two-and-a-half-year-old son Merlin a postcard some weeks before in which we told him that my horse was called Wahine and had a sore foot. He had been considering this since the postcard had been read to him and his first words when he came on the line were 'Daddy, how is One Whinney's foot?' From then on that was her name.

CHAPTER TEN

# Lake Tennyson
# and Molesworth

Lake Tennyson had always been a fixed point on our itinerary. It lies between St James Station and the legendary Molesworth Station and I had said all along that that was one place where I must stop and catch a fish at last. Refreshed after our night in Hanmer Springs and clean in our scrubbed clothes, we picnicked on the shore. The first European to see Lake Tennyson, in 1855, was a squatter called F. A. Weld, one of the very earliest South Island sheep farmers, who was later to be Premier of New Zealand and later still knighted to become Sir Frederick. He gave a clear description of the lake at the head of the Clarence River: 'It lies in an ampitheatre [sic] of lofty peaks, bold in outline, dark in colour, except where brightened by sunlight and relieved by patches of snow scattered in clefts of the rock.'

The view was the same for us, including the patches of snow, but half a gale was blowing white horses across the surface of the water and a big black rain cloud loomed over the far end of the lake 2 miles (3 km) away to the north. It was impossible to cast a fly but I was determined and followed the shore round to a bay where I could almost put the wind behind me. Still no luck. In desperation I walked back to where the Clarence flowed out of the lake over a rapid interrupted by beds of weed. Almost at once I had a bite and moments later I had landed a fish just on the legal minimum of 9 inches. No matter that it was barely large enough to eat, I had done what I set out to do and my honour was satisfied.

At Lake Tennyson I saw my first wrybill (*Anarhynchus frontalis*), one of the most peculiar little birds in the world and one found only in New Zealand. It is, I believe, the sole bird with a beak which bends to the side, always to the right. No one knows why it has this strange anomaly. It used to be thought that it made life easier when chasing small insects around pebbles, but research and observation fails to confirm this. As, in common with other small plovers, it spends much of its time on lake shores and beside the sea, I like the idea of an evolutionary advantage accruing to a species which can proceed endlessly clockwise, probing under the seaward edge of stones for freshly deposited food washed in by the last wave.

Asymmetry in nature is fairly rare but not by any means unknown in other creatures, although I can think of no other irregular birds. The male narwhal's unicorn-like elongated tusk is an overgrown left tooth and it spirals to the left. Again no one appears to know why. Male fiddler crabs, the only crustaceans to court, do so by waving one greatly enlarged and brightly coloured front claw outside their burrows in the hope of attracting females. In their case it appears to be the right claw that grows. When I asked an entymologist friend for further examples, he muttered something about 'the genitalia of certain lepidoptera' and I decided to pursue that particular line of research no further.

We saddled up and rode through the Crimea Range towards Tarndale. Whoever named this area must have had an obsession with the Crimean War. Perhaps Weld himself had been receiving newspapers from home. There are Inkerman, Balaclava, Sebastopol and Cardigan Ridges, a Nightingale Stream, a Raglan Range and a Mount Turk. Probably there are more associated names which were not marked on our map or whose historical connection I failed to recognize. It looked hard country, with bare scraped hills stretching to the horizon, their bleakness accentuated by the hideous succession of vast electricity pylons marching obtrusively through the wilderness.

On the way into Tarndale we passed through a locked gate which prevented vehicles entering the Molesworth property but allowed horses through. This huge station, New Zealand's largest farm of nearly half a million acres (200,000 hectares), now belongs to the state. It consists of four pastoral runs, Tarndale, Dillons, St Helen's and Molesworth itself, after which the whole station is now named. All were at different times abandoned, largely as a result of infestation by rabbits and overgrazing by sheep. Today only cattle are kept – over 10,000 of them. They do well and cause less damage to the land, which is high and cold.

Conifers had been planted in blocks to bind the soil, which the frost lifted off in sheets where it was bare, leaving in places the effect of a crudely ploughed field. Surprisingly the plantations were not fenced off from stock but only the outer trees were grazed and stunted, the majority being left alone.

A smart range of old and new buildings greeted us at Tarndale, set attractively among trees by a stream in the shelter of a hill. It seemed a real oasis in the bush landscape. There were two musterers at home, the third being away taking a sick dog to the vet, a two-day journey. Ross Bolt, the head stockman, was breaking in an ugly and rebellious

Appaloosa mare in the pen. Cracking his stock whip, he made her stand still, then on command follow him around. As we watched, she learned to obey him and we had an immediate impression that Ross was someone who usually got his way. The atmosphere at Tarndale was efficient and confident. To be selected as a Molesworth stockman is an accolade and those who have worked there are always proud of the fact. The other stockman, younger at twenty and less experienced, also looked the part less than Ross. He was shorter and bespectacled, but clearly determined to prove himself. His name was Alistair Horn, but he insisted on being called Flint. When Louella asked him why he replied, 'My dad called me Flint when I was in my bassinette.' She thought he was sweet, but resisted telling him so.

They were a great pair to spend an evening with, talking exclusively in good Kiwi slang and without pretensions or complexes, just loving the hard life and the daily challenges. And it is about as tough there as anywhere in the South Island. They told us there was frost on 250 days in the year and snow can occur in any month; in the winter it is so thick that moving around the land is often virtually impossible. The cattle are not fed in winter. I asked why no hay or silage was made.

'No point,' was the reply. 'You could never get it out to them through the snow and anyway they would expect it again next year.'

Before the winter all the cattle are brought down to the lower ground where 'good tucker' has been built up for them by leaving paddocks ungrazed in the summer, and there they live out the bad weather. The old, long grass can provide food even when it is buried under snow and they have to dig for it. There are 3,000 breeding cows, producing about 2,500 calves, which are kept for two-and-a-half years before being sold. As a result 6,000 animals may be rounded up at once and driven into the yards, one of the great sights of the high country. Perhaps thirty are missed and left behind to spend the winter up in the hills. 'In a bad year most will die, last year was mild and they all survived,' said Ross.

Under the old regime, when sheep were kept, 40,000 died one year. Now only forty old ewes are kept on the hill behind Tarndale for meat and dog tucker. Soon after we arrived Ross sharpened his big knife and went in their direction looking tough. That night we feasted on roast mutton with turnips, peas, carrots and mashed potatoes, mostly grown in their vegetable garden, and covered in a good thick gravy, all cooked competently and without fuss by the two boys.

They are allowed two nights off every six weeks when, after being fetched in the truck from Molesworth, they can get into town; they are not allowed to keep any transport at Tarndale except for their horses. There was a good deal of talk about drink and girls, the latter being referred to as either real dags or real hard cases. Both are New Zealand descriptions of people with a sense of humour. A dag is also described in the Oxford English Dictionary as 'one of the locks of wool clotted with dirt about the hinder parts of a sheep'. When these dry they clatter as the sheep runs. A particularly inelegant expression used by dinkum Kiwis when telling a girl to hurry up is 'Rattle yer dags'.

Under the tough exterior of New Zealanders there is usually wit and even sensitivity well concealed. These high country musterers are part of the New Zealand mythology. In the books written by New Zealanders about their own country, they are constantly referred to as 'a very select body of men', their toughness, fortitude and hard humour extolled as the ideal Kiwi virtues. Yet Ross, for all his apparent rejection of life's fripperies, later showed us his album of photographs he had taken at Molesworth. They were evocative and subtle, capturing sunsets, the light on hills, and moments in the farming year in a way that made me envious.

New quarters had been supplied by the government the year before to replace the very spartan accommodation originally built in 1874. Instead of having to boil water in a copper, cook over an open fire and wash under a cold tap outside, they now had modern stainless steel everywhere, one reason being that unlike porcelain it does not crack in the severe winter frost. They kept it all immaculate and we were very impressed. We slept in comfortable beds and awoke to the smell of sausages being fried. Outside, the small lawn was freshly mown, the logs were neatly stacked, there was no rusty machinery lying about and the roofs and sides of the houses were gleaming with new red and white paint.

The day was overcast, with only occasional spots of sun glinting through chinks in the clouds. There was an icy wind and Ross said, 'Certain to be rain today, maybe snow if it stays this cold. We'd better check the stock up the Alma Valley.'

As we only had about 20 miles (30 km) to ride that day to reach Molesworth Station itself, we decided to go with them for the morning. We caught the horses and let out the dogs selected for the day's work. They raced around with unbridled energy, barely able to control themselves when summoned with a series of piercing whistles interspersed with oaths from Ross and Flint.

Nowhere is the training of dogs taken more seriously than in New Zealand. A boy starts to learn with his first sheepdog when he is about ten years old. He has to master seven or eight separate whistles, which he must be able to produce instantly, audible for several hundred yards and produced simply by contorting his mouth, teeth and tongue. Using fingers would be hopeless in freezing conditions and would take too long. 'Stop', 'Go away', 'Left', 'Right', 'Bark',

Ross Bolt, head stockman at Tarndale; one of 'a very select body of men'.

'Stop barking', 'Come here' and more instructions must each be clearly delivered and understood by the dog. By the time he is a man and has five or more dogs, he will have developed a different repertoire for each.

We mounted and prepared to set off. Suddenly Flint's horse, Tom, gave a series of bucks, throwing his rider over his head to land on all fours on the ground some distance away. Ross nearly 'bust a gut' laughing and it was some time before calm and decorum were restored. Luckily Flint was not hurt, although I suspect that would have been cause for even more hilarity.

Riding out with the boys and their dogs was glorious. There was a good sense of purpose – finding the bulls and separating them was important and tricky work as they tended to bunch together – but it was the sheer sense of enjoyment at what they were doing that impressed us most. This was the life they had chosen and clearly no other could ever match it. We left them far up the valley, promising eternal friendship and waving until we were out of sight. It was one of the happiest eighteen hours of the journey, and perhaps we savoured it more because the end of this stage was now in sight.

Molesworth has always been a hard place to visit and we were glad that, thanks to Bernard Pinney, we had been given permission to ride right across it. By chance our visit coincided with the first occasion when public access by vehicle was being allowed on a trial basis. As a

Riding out to muster up the Alma Valley. The young stockmen on Molesworth lead hard lives but seem to enjoy every minute.

result we were passed by a couple of cars once we reached the metalled road joining the headwaters of the Acheron and Awatere Rivers which is normally closed.

As we rested the horses by a stream, stretching ourselves out on the grass and holding their neck ropes while they grazed, a camper van pulled up. The couple on board had recognized us from our television interview at the start of our journey, which we had never seen, and insisted on pressing tea and chocolate cake on us. The living was becoming daily easier and soon we would be leaving the healthy hard life behind and having to resist temptation.

Later the driver of another vehicle rolled down his window and said, 'Hello Robin, I heard you were coming through. How's it going?' Don Stevens had served in the British Army and been on expeditions with colleagues of mine in England. He had read several of my books and we had many friends in common. Now he was working for the Department of Conservation, which is responsible for managing the recreational and conservational values of Molesworth.

It seemed we were back in a world where the glorious anonymity of the high country was left behind. There it is empty of people and feels even emptier than it really is. Never once had we felt that we were being watched from the surrounding hills. Never once did figures appear to look at us or chat when we stopped to rest. Yet that is what would happen in most other parts of the world. In China, however remote we thought ourselves to be, far out on the edge of the Gobi or high in the eastern mountains, privacy could only be achieved on the move. Whenever we halted there would soon be people.

Each stretch of the journey we had just made had been made before many times – first by the Maori on their travels in search of game and greenstone, then by the early settlers, followed by the miners and the pack trackers who supplied them. Today musterers and trampers use the same trail through the mountains, but the land is so large and the population so small that meetings are rare. Nevertheless, in spite of the silence and the space, we never felt that we were in a true wilderness untouched by man, and although the climate and the terrain could both be cruel there was always a sense of security about the country.

Don Reid, the manager of Molesworth, is the son-in-law of the legendary Bill Chisholm who made Molesworth both famous and successful. His wife Ann has lived there all her life. As a little girl in the 'fifties she grew up helping her father's stockmen and rabbiters, learning to care for young animals as well as becoming a skilled horsewoman. Now she is the mistress of Molesworth, with a daughter of her own. She was our hostess that night and we slept in even greater comfort than at Tarndale. Bill Chisholm himself we were to meet later in Blenheim, just a week before his seventy-fifth birthday. Tough, gruff and craggy, he did not try to conceal his pleasure at our visit, confessing that retirement bored him. When Louella said, as we looked through albums of old photographs of his years at Molesworth, 'What an interesting life you've led,' he snorted, 'Yes, but much too short,' which must be a good way to feel.

Many of the pictures showed huge herds of cattle being rounded up. When I said how impressed I was by how quiet they always seemed to be, he answered, 'If I ever saw the boys stirring the animals up for the camera, I would send them off.' His passion for tidiness was legendary and he was delighted when we told him that he would be proud of the boys at Tarndale.

We unloaded the horses from the truck outside his suburban house and walked them up and down the street, asking his advice about one or two girth galls and saddle sores that were developing. He was complimentary about their condition and very interested in our Camargue saddles. He produced his own Australian stock saddle, with its high cantle; he had had it forty years and it had seen hard work but it was in beautiful condition and he clearly still cleaned it regularly. His bridle dated from the Boer War and had a very clever bit which could be detached to leave a head collar to tether the horse or to facilitate catching it. We could have used that design.

He also produced his kangaroo hide stock whip and tried to teach me how to crack it on his small lawn.

'It's like casting a fly, you must do it overarm,' he explained, as I failed to produce a satisfactory report. 'You're trying too hard. Keep practising and she'll be right.'

Back at Molesworth, the main preoccupation of his successor, Don, was the sudden influx of visitors. While recognizing that it was a good thing to let the public have access to enjoy the scenery and understand what they were doing on the property, he was pessimistic about how they would behave.

The derogatory term for tourists in rural New Zealand is 'loopies' and certainly some of the behaviour we had been told about was criminally insane. Don was afraid of idiots on motorbikes chasing cattle and people leaving gates open, but what worried him most was the fear of a carelessly thrown cigarette causing a disastrous fire on the dry grassland. So much had been done to revegetate the once denuded land and to transform the previous bankrupt properties into a profitable state farm that it would be a sad irony if the very public which now owns it were to bring about its destruction.

Continuing down the Awatere River away from Molesworth we remained in spectacular country with breathtaking views each time we crossed a pass. Although we were nearing Blenheim and the coast this was still very much high country, with merino sheep on the bare tops and cattle in the valleys, where willows lined the river. After a while these began to give way to poplars as the soil improved and the valleys widened to make room for prosperous homesteads surrounded by pine trees. There were even some cabbage trees, the first we had seen since Lake Wanaka, we thought.

We stayed at Camden Station with Frank and Shelley Prouting. We had planned to ride on down to Blenheim the next day, but the horses were very tired and Jacky begged us to give them a rest. Also the road from then on was tarseal and no great pleasure to ride along. We decided to call a halt.

Frank, like his brother Laurie a famous bush pilot full of hair-raising stories of the great deer-catching days, suggested the next morning that we might like a flight in his plane. He simply wheeled the Cessna 180 out of its garage next to the house, started it up, taxied over to the paddock and took off. It took no longer than jumping into the car to go shopping.

We sailed up in the morning light towards the highest peak north of the Southern Alps – Mount Tapuaenuku (9,465 feet /2,885 m), set among a cluster of other peaks, including Mount Alarm, at the centre of the Kaikoura Range. Captain Cook called them 'The Lookers On'. This was Camden's high country directly above the homestead and we were there in seconds, although it would take a man on foot more

Down the Awatere we came on prosperous homesteads surrounded by trees.

than a day to climb up. Frank was looking out for stray sheep and also wanted to see if fresh snow had fallen on the tops. It had been bitterly cold in the night but only some frost glistened on the higher slopes, apart from patches of old snow in folds of the scree near the summit.

It was so easy soaring over the rocks in the clear air with sudden views of Molesworth one way, Blenheim and the sea the other. Two chamois leapt down across a scree and Frank dived to follow them, swooping into a deep corrie which seemed to have no outlet. We entered a patch of cloud, lost all visibility for a moment, came out into turbulence which threw the plane about as updraughts hit us crossing a ridge, and then we were swinging between high cliffs and out into the sunshine again. This was Frank's home patch and he knew every inch.

Far below, the pine and poplars in straight lines around the homesteads gave an Italianate feel to the scene. The savage contrast of the bare, wild mountains with the soft lushness in the deep valleys was the very essence of romantic imagery. We could see why people love that country so much.

As we lost height we saw some sheep across the valley moving along the hillside.

'Must be a muster,' said Frank, 'let's go and have a look.'

Frank Prouting's runway at Camden Station. The sheep were an added hazard and had to be driven off before we could land.

Sure enough we came on the shepherd striding across the hillside with his dogs. He did not look up as we flew low over him.

'Some people don't like us flying over their properties,' Frank told us. 'They say it scares the stock, but it doesn't.'

We came in to land at an impossible angle, side-slipping around the edge of an abrupt bluff behind which the diminutive runway was hidden. There were sheep on the paddock which scattered as we approached.

'I don't suppose you have too many runways like that in England,' said Frank. I replied that the only worse one I had seen was his brother Laurie's apology for a strip by the riverbed at the Royal Hut.

'Shelley rode most of your route through from Lake Wakatipu before we were married,' Frank said. 'I flew her in to that strip for the wedding and we were married up there on Mesopotamia. We spent the first night of our honeymoon in the Stone Hut, just along the valley, sharing with a dozen musterers.'

We were sharing our accommodation, the Camden shearers' quarters, with Laurie's seventeen-year-old son Malcolm, who worked for Frank. We looked in his refrigerator and the contents seemed to sum up the life of a young high country shepherd. It contained one skinned rabbit and a bar of chocolate.

# CHAPTER ELEVEN

# Wine and
# Windy Wellington

We had now ridden over 500 miles through the South Island. It was time to stop riding for a while and see something of the country before crossing over to the North Island. We stayed with Jo and Andy Grigg, the latter a cousin of Kit Grigg's at Meadowbank, their attractive property overlooking Blenheim. In their comfortable house, filled with books and music, we were able to relax for a couple of nights.

Barely fifteen years since the first vine was planted in the district the Wairau plain around Blenheim has become New Zealand's top wine-producing region. Although wine making was one of the first industries attempted by the early colonists it is only recently that the product has developed any quality. The technology to bring this revolution about came largely from the dairy industry, where the use of huge stainless-steel vats had been perfected. The major wineries now look more like dairies than traditional cellars. Fortunately this has coincided with a dramatic change in drinking habits in the country, so that today huge quantities of wine are drunk locally as well as being exported all over the world. Nearly half is grown in this one extremely sunny and warm valley lying at the northernmost end of the range of mountains which stretches without a break the entire length of the island. It was a good place to stop and unwind.

We visited the Marlborough Sounds, an outstandingly beautiful network of islands and inlets where Cook landed in 1770, climbed a hill and first saw the straits that were to bear his name. Nearby he raised the Union flag. After naming Queen Charlotte's Sound and formally taking possession of the adjacent lands, he appropriately 'drank Her Majesty's hilth in a bottle of wine and gave the empty bottle to the old man (who had attended us up the hill) with which he was highly pleased.' A fairly poor exchange for the old Maori, it would seem, and one which the British Government did not endorse, leaving the formal colonization of the territory until the signing of the Treaty of Waitangi fifty years later.

In Picton we visited a light show about New Zealand to see the
whole life of the nation flash rapidly before our eyes. Wonderful
photographs of the mountains made us realize again what fabulously
beautiful scenery we had just ridden through. The comments of the
typical New Zealanders on the screen confirmed my growing
impression that they are a straightforward but rather defensive
people. 'I wouldn't live anywhere else' and 'Real country is best'
were recurrent themes. So too were a deep distrust of large scale
enterprise and a respect for individual effort and physical prowess;
but this soon turns back to suspicion if there is a sign of success or of
anything that does not conform.

Modern New Zealanders still find it difficult to see their country as
a whole in the way that the Maori did before them. Hardly a
mountain or river throughout both islands was not named by the
Maori before the Europeans arrived, and their legends often sweep
from one end to the other in a single story. *Pakehas* identify with their
own regions, the high country of the South or the lush farmland of
the North, the ski slopes of Queenstown or the sailing waters of the
Bay of Islands.

There is still a great emphasis on the outdoor life, even though the
vast majority of the population now lives in cities, half in and around
Auckland. The role of physical achievement is testified to by the
continual excellence of New Zealand sportsmen and women in so
many fields, in spite of the tiny population. In rugby, sailing,
climbing, cricket, breeding and jumping horses and many other
sports New Zealanders are among the best in the world.

They have also led the way in many areas of social advance, having
one of the most developed welfare states anywhere. It was created in
the late 1930s under Prime Minister Michael Savage, when the
country was undergoing a period of economic prosperity. A comprehensive health-care plan and social security system were established, which were the envy of Britain ten years later when the
welfare state was being created after World War II. A newly arrived
ADC to the Governor at that period, now a member of the House of
Lords, tells the story of how his boss explained to him one of the
differences between New Zealand and 'home'. 'You know, my boy,
that we now say we take care of people from the cradle to the grave.
Well over here they go a lot further and have done for some time. You
could say that they look after you from erection to resurrection.' New
Zealand men were the first in the world to give their women the vote
and individual freedom is still the lynchpin of their political
philosophy. This does not, however, stop the majority retaining a
Victorian puritanism and a sometimes quite astonishing chauvinism
in their attitudes towards women as wives and companions, taking it
for granted that they will be content with a subservient role in

society. Gordon McLauchlan, a leading and cynical New Zealand journalist, suggests in his funny, cruel book *The Passionless People* that this may account for the disproportionate number of New Zealand women who have become writers 'to keep themselves relatively stable in their mentally and emotionally numbing roles in a materialistic society'. Ngaio Marsh wrote:

We are often told by English people how very English New Zealand is, their intention being complimentary. I think that this pronouncement may be true but not altogether in the intended sense. We are, I venture, more like the English of our pioneers' time than those of our own. We are doubly insular. We come from a group of islands at the top of the world and we have settled on a group comparable in size but infinitely more isolated, at the bottom of it. We are overwhelmingly of English, Scottish, Welsh and Irish

'People from a frontier society, with little artifice, and even less conceit . . .' Maurice Shadbolt.

stock and it seemed to me, when I came back after five years, that we had turned in on our origins. You might say, I thought, that if you put a selection of people from the British Isles into antipodean cool-storage for a century and a half and then opened the door: we are what would emerge. There have been internal changes but they have not followed those of our islands of origin. And I thought: it is the superficial changes, the things that matter least, which leap most readily to the notice of non-New Zealanders. Our voices and our manners have deteriorated to such an extent that many fourth-generation New Zealanders have a strong, muddled instinct that prompts them to regard any kind of a speech but the indigenous snarl as effeminate and even the most rudimentary forms of courtesy as gush. It is good honest kiwi to kick the English language into the gutter and it shows how independent you are if you sprawl in armchairs when old women come into their own drawing-rooms. I refuse to say lounges.

And then, I thought, how complacent we are and yet how uncertain of ourselves! Why do the young ones say so often and so proudly that they suppose New Zealand seems crude and then, if you agree: 'Well, in some ways, perhaps,' why do they look so furious? I had forgotten what we are like, I thought. We really are rum. Or so it seemed to me when I returned.

Another marvellous New Zealand writer, Maurice Shadbolt, describes the national character as follows:

Outside his country the Kiwi may seem shy, rather reserved; but this is easily explained. People from a frontier society, with little artifice, and even less conceit, go very naked in the world. It's not simply a question of manners; it is also a question of speech. The only words he knows may be too blunt. So he's careful.

And, outside New Zealand, it's likely that you'll only get the Kiwi talking vigorously on one subject – his own country. He may sometimes speak with contempt or distaste, but like a lover talking of an unfaithful mistress. For nostalgia will probably come welling through his speech. New Zealand sends many such into the world, and most return. The human Kiwi, like the bird itself, is not built for exile. He withers internally, grows old too soon. For his tragedy is that he can abandon his country yet not forget it; his country refuses to abandon him. It haunts him, as one poet put it, like a debt unpaid, a love betrayed. As it did Katherine Mansfield, who, after rejecting it, yearned to make her undiscovered country leap into the imagination of the old world.

Yet, on his native earth, he loses his diffidence. Here he is sure of himself; this, after all, is the land he has mastered. He defends it hotly against criticism, resists intrusion, is often suspicious of foreigners. But, underneath, it's still the same Kiwi speaking: a man uncertain of himself, an Adam unsure of his Eden.

An artist whose work I had hoped to see in Christchurch was Evelyn Page. One of New Zealand's best living painters, she was a friend and contemporary of the late Ngaio Marsh who, in addition to being a theatrical producer and detective story writer was also a good painter herself. Dame Ngaio, as she became in 1966, opened a retrospective exhibition of Evelyn Page's work in December 1970. It had been suggested to me that her style was not unlike that of some of the Newlyn School and that I would enjoy her pictures. To my disappointment there were very few at Christchurch, Neil Roberts, the curator of the Robert McDougall Art Gallery with whom I had discussed Gotch, having recently put together an exhibition of her life's work entitled Seven Decades. The exhibition was currently on tour at Wanganui in the North Island and I resolved to see it before we started riding again. The artist herself lived in an old people's home in Wellington, our next stop.

The horses stood up well to the three-hour crossing of Cook Strait and we were able to lodge them at the Riding for the Disabled centre just outside Wellington, where they had excellent grazing. We were allowed to sleep in the pavilion, which had a small kitchen and space for us to spread our sleeping bags on the floor.

Our main reason for visiting Wellington was to pay a visit to Louella's godmother, Jocelyn Vogel, whom she had not seen for twelve years. It was Jocelyn who had given Louella her previous trip to New Zealand as a nineteenth birthday present seventeen years earlier and we had been looking forward to staying with her this time. Sadly, she had had a bad fall, breaking her hip, shortly after we started our ride and was now in hospital, very ill. When we telephoned we were told that she might not survive the night. She was a remarkable lady, of whom Louella was extremely fond; through her, three great names in New Zealand's history were linked.

She was born in 1909 a Riddiford, her grandfather being Daniel Riddiford, Wellington agent of the New Zealand Company in the early days. The New Zealand Company was a profit-making enterprise formed prior to the signing of the Treaty of Waitangi with the avowed purpose of 'preserving the existing social and economic structure by transporting a cross-section of English society, excluding only its lowest level'. Riddiford acquired vast properties in the first tract of land to be opened up for sheep farming, the Wairarapa, a fertile valley in the south of the North Island. Unlike many he paid the Maori owners what was at the time regarded as a fair price, sixpence per acre. He became so rich and powerful that he was known as King Riddiford. Woburn, the huge mansion he rebuilt in Lower Hutt, near Wellington, was where Jocelyn grew up, surrounded by luxury. The estate was sold in 1960 and the house is now an old people's home.

She married Jim Vogel, grandson of the great Sir Julius Vogel who started his fortune among the west coast gold miners, founded the *Otago Daily Times* and eventually became premier of New Zealand for the first time in 1873. For the next fifteen years he dominated New

Zealand politics. A man of vision, it was he who gave New Zealand a proper railway system, brought in unprecedented numbers of immigrants and pioneered state forests. However, his financial policies, which depended on borrowing large sums of money, left the country deeply in debt.

Jocelyn's mother Zoe was the seventh of nine children born to governor Sir George Grey's niece, Anne Matthews, who married his manager and friend Seymour Thorne George. Louella's grandmother was the ninth child. She married a later governor's dashing young ADC, one John Gage Williams from Scorrier, Cornwall, where they soon returned to live. Louella's eight great aunts and uncles who remained in New Zealand had nineteen children and forty-eight grandchildren between them so that she has a great many cousins all over the country.

Sir George Grey had already been Governor of South Australia before his first governorship of New Zealand from 1845 to 1853. He then was posted to govern Cape Colony in South Africa before returning for a second governorship of New Zealand from 1861–68. Later still, in 1877, he became Premier for two years.

A highly cultured, liberal and controversial man, he learnt Maori and wrote *Mythology and Traditions of the New Zealanders*, a record of the oral myths of the Maori people, which did much to preserve them at a time when they might otherwise have disappeared. In his farewell address to the Maori chiefs after his first governorship he said: 'Hereafter a great nation will occupy these Islands, and with wonder and gladness they will look back upon the works of those men who assisted in founding their country; and when the children in those times ask their parents who were the men who founded so great a country, they will answer them, the men who did these things in the olden times were our ancestors. Yes, those things were done, not by our European ancestors alone, but partly also by our ancestors who were the original native inhabitants of these Islands, and then they will tell them many names, and amongst them those of my friends.'

On the whole Grey seems to have tried to defend the Maori but to have been devious in his dealings and to have allowed pressure from the settlers to sway his judgement. He is best remembered today for the Mansion House he built on Kawau Island, where the Thorne George children were brought up. There he carried the New Zealand obsession with introducing exotic species to unprecedented lengths, bringing in several varieties of kangaroo and deer as well as birds from Britain and Australia and a whole herbarium of trees and plants. Many of them are still there, including the parma wallaby, now probably extinct back in its native Australia.

We hurried round to the hospital in the morning, Louella feeling sick and nervous at seeing someone she loved so ill. Though desperately thin and wasted, Jo was really pleased to see us. There was a flower in her hair and, knowing we were coming, she had made the nurses dress her in a pretty pink bedjacket. Her poor wasted arms were covered in sores, bandaged and tied to the sides of the bed to stop her plucking at them and removing her various drips. She also had an oxygen mask on much of the time. But she knew who we were, kissed Louella, said how happy she was to meet me at last and then lay rambling confusedly while Louella held her hand. Twice she called me Jim. She was to die before the end of the week.

After we left the hospital we walked in the peace of the Botanical Gardens, a wild expanse of native bush and rare trees right in the centre of town.

In the afternoon we visited the National Art Gallery where they had some good Newlyn pictures, including an outstanding Laura Knight of a girl mending linen, but still no Evelyn Pages. On the spur of the moment, as we had an hour to spare, we took a taxi out to Sprott House, her old people's home. To our surprise we were shown to her room without any fuss even though we had no appointment. We found a very alert old lady sitting on her bed reading a romantic novel. She was full of life and the joy of living, interested in talking about pictures and delighted to be visited. We did not realize until later that she was eighty-nine years old. She told us she had one particularly good friend in the home who was ninety-four. With a twinkle in her eye she said that she did hope that she would not die too soon as they still had so much to talk about. Sadly she herself died four months later, in July.

She was so pleased that her exhibition was a success and was delighted by all the letters she was getting as a result.

'You know,' she said, 'they all say the same thing – how much humanity I put into my pictures. I don't known how good they are, but do look at my *Nude with Magnolias*. It's the last picture in the show and I did it two years ago. I think I got that one about right.' After her seventy years of painting professionally that seemed to us a wonderful approach to life.

She wanted to know all about what we were doing and when we left after an hour of non-stop dialogue, which seemed not to tire her a bit, she said she wished she were coming with us for the rest of our ride.

Later we were able to borrow a car and drive up to Wanganui to see her exhibition. In her time she had painted landscapes in China and in England, where she did a portrait of Ralph Vaughan Williams. There was a fine portrait of Sir William Hamilton, the jet boat pioneer, who had been a lifelong friend of hers, painted at Irishman's Creek, the family's sheep station, which we had missed riding through. Nor had I known of this friendship when we went boating with his son Jon on the Waimakariri, the very same day that I had gone to the Christchurch Museum to look at her pictures. Her zest for life and her great sense of colour and how to use paint come across best in her strong portraits and still lifes which instantly communicate with the viewer. Evelyn Page is a painter of whom New Zealand can be justly proud and it was good to see her talent had been properly recognized during her lifetime.

Beyond Wanganui was the site of what our guide books described as 'perhaps the most important Maori rock drawing in the North Island', at a place called Kohi. We drove up to the house of the farmer on whose land the site lay and received permission to visit it. He gave us directions to find it and, when I asked if it was much visited, replied that a proper League of Nations came, with tourists from Germany, America and all over. It was hard to believe, as the path to it along the bank of a small river was overgrown and hard to follow. The carving, when we eventually found it, was on the face of a cliff at the top of a rough track with occasional rotted wooden steps. It was dark under the trees and the place had a strong atmosphere, although the rock drawing was itself at first disappointing. Only about 4 feet square, the curved symbols on the rock meant nothing to us. They were said to represent lizards, the only figure normally portrayed realistically in Maori art, though we could not decipher them. The lizard symbolizes *whiro* meaning evil and is also the name of the god of death and decay. Sometimes they are depicted in sculpture to warn that an area is *tapu*, that is, sacred, forbidden, under strict religious restriction. We felt uneasy at Kohi and soon left.

We were now staying near Marton half a day's drive north of Wellington, having driven the horses there along National State Highway 1. It is a rich farming district where my share-farming partner Pancho was raised and where several Fullerton-Smith relations of his still live. His cousins Joe and Ali are great horse people and our three had been having first-class treatment. We were worried about their backs, which had all been showing signs of stress in the South Island, and 'One Whinney' had a nasty girth gall as well as wrinkly skin and bald patches, though no sores as yet. A potion, strong smelling and deadly poisonous, had been recommended as treatment by a friend of the Fullerton-Smiths on the New Zealand Olympics selection committee and we applied it religiously morning and evening from then on.

There was also more serious trouble with Kowhai, whose 'new' engine had given out, and we were having to go through all the tiresome and expensive business of finding another second-hand one and having it fitted. Sometimes horses are a lot less trouble than motor vehicles. However, we had to return the truck in at least the same condition as we had been lent it, so there was no alternative. Fortunately the Fullerton-Smiths knew an excellent mechanic in

The Maori rock carving at Kohi, near Waverley, represents lizards symbolizing evil.

Marton who did what was necessary quickly and efficiently.

Joe decided to ride with us for half of the first day. He had a gigantic skewbald horse called Rastafarian, which he had bought from Jacky's uncle near Gisborne. We started slowly, riding between fields of barley and hay, thinking this was really pretty tame after the high country. Joe's farm was called Tutaenui, as was the nearby town itself until the early settlers discovered what it meant – the polite translation of the Maori is 'a dung heap'. They then named it Marton after Captain Cook's birthplace in Yorkshire. The land is fertile and the farming is mixed, with Romney sheep, cattle and corn all doing well, but there too everyone was feeling the pinch of New Zealand's agricultural recession.

After a mile or so, just as we were settling down to being in the saddle again, we had a shock. Round a corner we came to a magnificent view of steep hills rippling all the way to the distant horizon like waves on a rough sea. It was the most dramatic contrast imaginable from what lay behind us. Strangely, from the ridge on which we stood, this wild, apparently uninhabited country seemed to lie below us. Both appearances were illusionary as the land was in fact rising in a series of ranges to the great volcanic plateau crowned by the North Island's highest peak, the perpetually snow-capped Mount Ruapehu at 9,173 feet (2,796 m). It is an active volcano with a simmering crater lake at its heart. Although we could see no trace of farmland or buildings on the wrinkled slopes ahead we were to find that there were trees, farms and even lakes tucked out of sight in the folds of the land. The endless green hills were criss-crossed with sheep tracks. Louella said, 'It looks like an elephant's hide.'

'I had to travel the world to appreciate this view,' said Joe as we paused to drink it in.

Thanks to Joe we were able to leave the dirt road on which we had started and cut across country, passing through his neighbours' land and seeing some very attractive fertile valleys. The most romantic spot we passed that day was a large, wooded and very isolated lake, to which Joe said he and his cousins used to carry a boat sometimes when they were boys. A great spot for fishing and camping, it reminded us of Lake Rere above Lake Wakatipu.

Joe explained how this country, like so much of New Zealand, lay right on a fault line, where the edges of the tectonic plates met, so that everything was moving. A mere two or three million years before, it had all been under the sea. Today, when bulldozers carve out a new road, they often come on pure sea sand with large, undamaged sea shells in it, although we were up a good 1,000 feet (300 m) above sea level.

'This land was all covered with scrub originally,' Joe told us. 'My great uncle used to take a tin box full of porridge with him into the bush and he would live on that and cut for a week or more until it was finished. He had the guts and determination to clear this land. It's hard to imagine the work those old boys put into it. They didn't have chainsaws either.'

New Zealanders whose families have farmed the land for several generations are understandably intensely proud of the work that has gone into clearing and taming it. People who come along and glibly suggest it might have been better left alone are on dangerous ground. I didn't argue with Joe. The land looked healthy and productive, there were large stands of trees, both native bush and new plantations, and there were few signs of erosion.

During the morning we crossed half a dozen properties and met some of Joe's neighbours as they mustered or checked their stock. One of them rode with us for a time as he was on his way to fetch some bullocks. He was wearing shorts, as do most New Zealand farmers for much of the time – sensible in that climate I suppose, although riding in them always strikes me as excessively masochistic. He showed us the way through a swamp on his boundary, where we floundered safely through a reed bed.

There were times, as we skirted around steep hillsides or followed streams, when we could have been back in the South Island, but the scale of the countryside was unmistakably smaller, proved by our constant arrival at boundary fences. Many of them seemed to lack gates and riding any distance through the North Island looked like being much more difficult without very careful planning.

In the early afternoon Ali met us with a horsebox at Otairi Station, the biggest property in the district at 12,000 acres (5,000 hectares). Joe and Rastafarian went home with her, leaving us, rather later than planned, to cross the station to Te Kumu ('The Buttocks'), a homestead at its eastern edge. From there we had a good day's route planned for us through to the Kawhatau River.

Now the landscape did become more like the high country. At first we were able to follow a good dirt track through a long green valley between the hills. As it had been a hot day the horses were sweating but we were running late and so we cantered them for much of the next hour. At last we reached the woolshed where we had been told there would be someone who would give us directions for the tricky last few miles. Unfortunately he carried the familiar relaxed approach to directions to new lengths, saying vaguely that we would probably get lost, he wasn't sure which ridge we should ride up and it would be dark before we arrived by that route anyway. Rashly, I asked why we could not ride by a more direct route around the mountain and he answered that two boundary fences lay in the way, but it would certainly be quicker if we were able to get through them. I assured him that I always carried fencing pliers for wired-up gates and we hurried off.

We began by climbing along a precipitous ridge in order to gain height. When we had dragged the tired horses to the top we found that the long hillside we then had to traverse was among the steepest we had met, with just the narrowest of sheep tracks across it. Our feet ached from walking on the awkward slope as we struggled on for more than an hour. The sky began to darken with black clouds threatening heavy rain. At one point Star, my mount for the day, slipped and fell down the slope. He was within an ace of starting to roll, in which case he would have continued for 100 feet (30 m) or more, but I hung on to his bridle and he scrambled to a halt.

At last we reached the boundary fence and the gateway, which was indeed tied up securely with barbed wire. I reached into my saddlebag for the fencing pliers, only to find that for the first time since leaving Invercargill I had left them behind. It was now far too late to turn back before nightfall and so I had to unwind each strand painfully with my bare hands, using the old Swiss army knife when the ends were too stiff or short to bend. Once through it took as long to fasten it all again securely and half an hour had been wasted before we were on our way again. Darkness was now falling, the rain was close and the prospect of a cold and wet night out was very real. There was no sign of our destination and the country we were in was deeply cut by gorges and criss-crossed by fences. We hurried on,

casting about along fence lines and following promising tracks which petered out, all the time trying to reconcile natural features with map and compass in the half light. It was nearly 9.00 p.m. before we found the final gate, which also had to be laboriously undone and wired up again, so that when at last we saw the lights of Te Kumu across a valley it was pitch dark and starting to rain.

We had expected a cold reception from Bruce and Kaye Chalmers, the young couple who had only recently taken on the job of managing this remote outstation. They would have been justified in resenting a couple of poms turning up in the middle of the night virtually without warning. Instead they were the soul of kindness and hospitality, heating up some food, although they had had their tea long before, and insisting we stayed in their house rather than down in the sheep sheds.

It rained all night, and in the morning it was blowing half a gale as well, which drove the rain horizontally. We struggled down to the paddock where the horses had spent the night to find them huddled

Usually we were able to avoid roads and those we followed were often no more than farm tracks.

together unhappily in the shelter of some poplars. They were tucked up and made no attempt to avoid being caught, which were bad signs. When we led them into a shed both started shivering and Manaaki would barely allow his back to be touched. If we tried to do so his back legs gave way, he staggered and almost fell. When we rubbed him down to dry the rain off we found the small beginnings of a saddle sore. It was only the size of a fingernail but sure to worsen if he was ridden. A long day lay ahead, which might well knock him up completely if we attempted it. We decided to stop riding for a few days and give the horses a proper rest to recover. Bruce and Kaye generously said that we could stay as long as we liked, but it made much more sense to return to Tutaenui by road as Jacky and One Whinney were still there waiting for Kowhai's new engine to be fitted. I rang Joe and caught him at breakfast.

'Glad to have you back,' he said at once. 'We were just saying that you went too soon and we still had a lot to talk about. I'll be there in an hour or so.'

# CHAPTER TWELVE

# Erosion, Earthquakes and Art Deco

Just over thirty years earlier I had been driving through the Middle East with an Irish friend in a battered Second World War American jeep. It was a dreadful vehicle which broke down constantly, but in it we had struggled through the Dasht-e-Lut and the Dasht-e-Kavir deserts of central Persia, followed impossible camel trails in the highlands of Afghanistan and eventually crossed Pakistan and entered India. There, in the Golden Temple at Amritsar, we met two young New Zealanders doing much the same thing as we were, but in a Morris Minor.

They were called Mike Allen and Bunny Gorringe. We became friends and drove on in convoy. The level crossing gates at Jullundur were closed and, as was usual, our jeep stalled. Our new friends peered helpfully into the engine as I performed a familiar trick, pouring petrol directly from a five-gallon jerry can into the carburettor, the quickest way to get the engine to start once the heat had caused the fuel to evaporate. Suddenly the petrol ignited and all three of us were in flames. Bunny and I managed to beat ours out, but Mike, who was wearing an aertex shirt and who had received the bulk of the can's contents over him, became a human torch. It took a blanket to put his flames out and by then the beard he had grown on the way out was gone, his fair hair was singed black and the skin was hanging in shreds off the whole of the top of his body.

We rushed him to the local hospital, where he was painted from head to foot with gentian violet and given a shot of morphine. For a week we nursed and fed him; it was only a small country hospital and these functions were normally performed by the relatives. Although in terrible pain he was extraordinarily brave and never blamed me for the accident, as he might well have done. After a time we moved him to a mission hospital where he made a full recovery and a month later we all drove down to Ceylon together.

We had not met since that time, but I had stayed in touch with Bunny and it was to his farm on the Kawhatau that we had planned to ride from Te Kumu. By a happy coincidence Mike was coming to stay with Bunny the next night as his daughter was at a nearby school. Kowhai was fixed, the horses were loaded and both parties arrived at the same time. Our wives were subjected to an evening of reminiscences as we each dredged up increasingly far-fetched memories of that most memorable time.

Apart from Mike's suffering stoically born, my most unpleasant recollection was of an incident I witnessed at Jullundur Hospital in the small hours one morning as I walked through the grounds to take my turn at his bedside. I remembered that his spectacles had been left in the operating theatre, an isolated building among some trees. I strolled over to fetch them and walked in to find the lights on and a dozen men holding down a fully conscious Sikh, who was screaming and praying while a surgeon wielded a scalpel over his nether regions. There was blood everywhere and it seemed that he was receiving the traditional punishment for rape.

Mike is today a successful dairy farmer in the rich Waikato region to the north. Bunny has largely handed over his family farm to his two sons, which leaves him more time for his real passion – his involvement in Catchment Control. He is President of the New Zealand Catchment Authority, a post involving endless meetings which he finds satisfying due to the achievements being made. At last the dangers of neglecting New Zealand's fragile environment are being recognized and huge efforts are being made to reverse the mistakes of the past. Bunny heaped reports and articles on me which showed the appalling effects of floods and erosion, usually the result of deforestation. They made depressing reading. Page after page carried pictures of degraded tussock grasslands, eroded screes and silted-up river beds. It seemed that almost nowhere in the country was safe.

I learned that much of the South Island was formed of deposits of loess, the fine windblown dust which can, over millenia, build up to considerable thickness. It is extremely prone to erosion, as we had seen on our last ride in Northern China, where huge areas are dissected by deep gullies and nothing grows on the barren soil. One of the difficulties in the South Island was the continuing question of identifying which erosion was natural, caused by glaciers, high rainfall and earth movement, and which was caused by man through burning and overgrazing. Around Christchurch and the Banks Peninsula the forest cover had been replaced by dense swards of grass, sown in time to prevent severe erosion. The danger there lies in excavations for building work which can expose the loess and cause rapid problems.

We were about to enter one of the worst regions for erosion in the country. The Heretaunga Plains behind Hastings and Napier were among the least attractive lowlands when Europeans arrived in the mid-nineteenth century. The Maori laid no claim to much of the land – cold, wet unhealthy swamp, which one of the earliest arrivals, the great missionary and naturalist William Colenso, described as having 'nothing whatever to recommend it – no water, no wood, no good harbour, no shelter from stormy winds'. It took the shrewd eye of Donald McLean, later a leading politician, to recognize its potential. Just as the Treaty of Waitangi was being signed, a whaler called Rhodes arranged to buy from the few Maori living there the whole of the Hawkes Bay coast up to 50 miles (80 km) inland for £150. His purchase was invalid, and McLean, first as a Land Commissioner for the government and then on his own account, took over virtually complete control of the bay. At the same time as being a Land Commissioner, he was also a Protector of Aborigines, charged with being an impartial guardian of Maori welfare, an anomalous position but one which made him extraordinarily powerful. For this he was later much disliked by other politicians, being referred to as 'absolute in power and irresponsible to authority'. Later, as the Native Minister described as being most sympathetic to Maori welfare, he worked hard to defend their rights but there seems little doubt that he feathered his own and the government's nest when the going was good.

The land acquired by these devious means had promise but was extremely prone to flooding. Today it is one of the most fertile and productive parts of the island, where orchards, vineyards and farms cover the land. This is the result of huge efforts to channel and control the three rivers running through it. Disasters dogged the settlers (some caused by their own mistakes) and it is a tribute to their grit that they kept on in the face of them. For example, an early attempt was made to stabilize the river banks by using imported willows. Within a couple of decades the trees had become a problem as they clogged stream beds so efforts were made to remove them.

Floods brought silt down on to cultivated land and washed away roads, bridges and railways. It was only the work of the local Catchment Board which eventually brought the situation under control and confirmed the prosperity of the region. However, constant care is needed to maintain the stopbanks and channels which take the water safely out to sea and to protect the forestry on the hills inland which prevents silt and shingle being carried down to block them.

By far the greatest threat to that district, and indeed to many other parts of New Zealand, is one over which man has no control whatsoever; earthquakes. At 10.47 p.m. on 3 February 1931 a colossal earthquake of 7.9 on the Richter scale, which was recorded the other side of the world at Kew, struck Hawkes Bay, demolishing virtually every building in Napier and doing great damage all along the coast. Two hundred and fifty-eight people were killed and tens of thousands made homeless. It was a massive disaster which would have ruined many societies. The resilient and determined residents of Napier simply cleared up the mess and formed a committee to rebuild the place, meeting in the Trocadero Tearooms, one of the few buildings to have survived.

The town was fortunate in having several enterprising and imaginative architects who recognized the opportunity presented by the disaster and cooperated to plan a uniform city, drawing on the best designs available in the world. These they found in America, where new ideas in building had been widely experimented with in the years leading up to the stock market crash and the Depression. Some wanted to copy the young city of Santa Barbara in California, which had itself been razed by an earthquake in 1925. It had been rebuilt in what came to be known as the Spanish Mission style, derived from the early Californian missions and emphasizing white stucco, curved parapets, twisted columns and red pantile roofs. It was simple to build and earthquake resistant. Others looked to the example of Frank Lloyd Wright and other architects who had pioneered modern architecture in Chicago earlier in the century. However, the overriding influence that became the dominant theme of the new town's architecture and made it the gem it is today was the modernistic style now called Art Deco.

I had only a hazy idea what Art Deco was until I saw Napier. Art Nouveau, with its romantic, flowery themes, was more familiar to me; it had its finest period at the same time as the best Newlyn School painters were at work at the end of the nineteenth century. Art Deco, by contrast, has clean geometrical lines, patterns and imagery in an unmistakably 'modern' style. Once that is understood it is instantly recognizable whatever form it takes. There are recurrent motifs such as zig-zags, sunbursts, parallel lines, squares, circles and leaping female figures which appear whatever material is being used, whether plain stone, colourful stained glass, highly polished wood or the metal most identified with Art Deco, chrome.

Napier has it all and whereas so much Art Deco has been fragmented and destroyed elsewhere, there it has survived extraordinarily intact. The streets of flat-roofed, two-storeyed buildings, looking at first glance like rows of Odeon cinemas, have barely an intrusive feature, save for advertisements and parking meters, and even they are not so out of keeping as they are when allied with earlier styles. Just being in Napier is peculiarly satisfying, partly because the effect of the blended styles is so pleasing, partly because it makes fall into shape so many things only glimpsed elsewhere in the world, where a poor relic of Art Deco is swamped by surrounding

Napier represents the most complete and significant group of Art Deco buildings in the world and is one of New Zealand's greatest treasures.

skyscrapers. The city is one of New Zealand's greatest and least recognized treasures, one of the few examples of stimulating architecture and design in the country. Yet when I checked a dozen comprehensive guides to New Zealand not one of them even mentioned Art Deco or the architectural interest of the place. Fortunately, in the nick of time, the inhabitants of Napier have themselves saved the town. Led by the example of the excellent museum, inappropriate development is being stopped, relatively few good buildings have been destroyed and those that remain are being restored and painted.

I had been told about Napier by a friend in England, otherwise we might have missed it. It is probably better known abroad than in New Zealand, where most people found it surprising that we should want to go there. A quote by Dr Neil Cossons, OBE, Director of the Science Museum in London and Past President of the British Museums Association, is printed on a leaflet we picked up in the Museum: 'Napier represents the most complete and significant group of Art Deco buildings in the world and is comparable with Bath as an example of a planned townscape in a cohesive style. Napier is without a doubt unique.'

The museum collection there had more surprises in the form of the unexpectedly familiar. As well as several pictures by Newlyn School painters and by Evelyn Page there was a representative collection of the work of Michael Cardew. One of Britain's greatest potters, he was a close neighbour of ours on Bodmin Moor until his death in 1982. It seems he had held a workshop in Napier twenty years before our visit.

We had decided by then that it would be unnecessarily hard on the horses to abuse their sore backs with an attempt to ride them across the Ruahine Range which lay between Bunny's farm and the coast. It was quite a tempting prospect, as it looked just possible and would have taken us through some extremely wild country. It was a great place for birdlife, too. If we camped up there we might even see kiwis, although they are quite rare everywhere. The huia (*Heteralocha acutirostris*), last reliably reported in 1907, is almost certainly extinct, although someone had suggested that if they still existed anywhere it could be in the Ruahine. They were large black birds with orange wattles, much valued by the Maori for their twelve long, white-tipped tail feathers. These were among the most treasured of Maori possessions, being preserved in special carved wooden boxes for trade with South Island tribes for greenstone and for passing on from one generation to the next. Until the Europeans arrived only high-ranking chiefs were allowed to wear them, an excellent way to preserve a rare and beautiful species. Just at the time when the birds' habitat was being reduced as the primeval forest was cut down, their feathers became fashionable as collectors' items and they were hunted ruthlessly to extinction.

The strangest thing about the huias was that they were the only birds in which the male and female had strikingly different beaks, so much so that originally they were described as two distinct species. The male has a comparatively short, straight bill used for excavating rotten logs rather as a woodpecker does. The female's bill was long and elegantly curved. With it she could probe delicately inside the log once her mate had made an opening for her.

Their song, a soft, fluting call, was described as unforgettable by those lucky enough to hear it and was even transcribed into musical notation, probably the only case of such a record being kept of an extinct species. In 1926 the distress call, the sound of which gave the species its name, was noted down as follows:

while the notes sung when searching for food went like this:

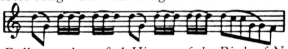

Sir Walter Buller, author of *A History of the Birds of New Zealand* (1887–8) and one of the Europeans who knew them best, wrote:

They are hopping actively from branch to branch, and at short intervals balance themselves and spread to their full extent their broad white-tipped tails, as if in sheer delight; then the sexes meet for a moment to caress each other with their beautiful ivory bills, while they utter a low, whimpering love-note; and then, without any warning, as if moved by a sudden inspiration, they bound off in company, flying and leaping in succession, to some favourite feeding-place, far away in the silent depths of the forest.

Farming friends of Bunny's, who had in the past ridden high into the mountains, had advised against our attempting it. There were, they said, steep scree slopes which were virtually unclimbable for horses and the weather high up was extremely unpredictable. The lower slopes were thickly wooded with beech and higher up shrubs and stunted trees formed an almost impenetrable barrier. Although there were some foot tracks, they could well be too narrow and too steep for horses. Moreover the whole area is a State Forest Park and we would have to apply for permission to ride through, which might well be refused for a variety of reasons. These included danger to the environment from the horses possibly introducing noxious weeds in their dung and the danger to them and to ourselves involved in taking them mountaineering. We were sure the horses could have done it but decided to be sensible. Instead we would all go in the now-healthy Kowhai, visiting friends and starting to ride again when the country seemed more suitable.

Bunny's farm lay in a region of dramatic deep white-walled gorges, through which the Kawhatau and Rangitikei Rivers ran. It was good land, less prone to slipping and well covered in trees, thanks largely to Bunny's efforts. We drove with him to a high point from which we could survey the landscape.

'Native trees don't stand alone,' he told us, 'which is why so much planting is necessary. Poplars are best for single planting as their roots help bind the soil as well as sucking up the water to stop it from becoming saturated. That's when it slips. Those trees down there are mostly lombardy with Chinese yunanenses and some hybrids.'

We looked out across countryside which could have formed the backdrop of a Renaissance painting. The poplars, craggy cliffs, clumps of native bush and fertile pastures stretched away to the mountains, where black clouds and another of New Zealand's glorious rainbows warned us of the hazards that awaited the unwary traveller up there.

The sheep on the farm were Perendale and Drysdale. Both were named after the New Zealanders who developed them, Professor Peren and Doctor Dry. The first is a dual-purpose breed, a mixture of Cheviot and Romney; the second the result of genetic experiments with the Romney which resulted in excellent carpet wool. Both are now fixed breeds and exported overseas.

The Kawhatau River runs through dramatic gorges and fertile farmland.

On the far side of the river basin we visited another Gorringe farm, run by Don White, a modest, quiet, confident man who is something of a legend for his success in dog trials. He had spent much of his life on high country runs, including several we had ridden through, so there was much to talk about as we looked over his dogs. They were Huntaways, a New Zealand breed taught to bark on command, invaluable for moving sheep on large tracks of country and for forcing flocks into yards. Don told me that their origins lay in Scottish Border Collies crossed with Scottish following dogs called 'Beardies'. Beagle blood was introduced to give them big deep voices, as well as some Labrador for size and heaven knows what else. Now they are fairly uniform black and tan, large as foxhounds.

'This is the best dog in New Zealand,' he said quietly at one point, as he fondled the ears of a rather ugly old bitch. 'She's called Sky and she has had four outings at the New Zealand championships at which she has had one third, one second, and been champion twice.' When I commented that she looked more than six years old he replied, 'They do when they are worked hard, but they enjoy life.'

They live rough, in bare kennels without straw which would get damp and attract fleas. There is shingle around the kennels to keep their pads hard and Don combs them daily to keep their coats in trim.

Sky, twice New Zealand Champion Huntaway. The dogs we saw in New Zealand were worked hard but always looked healthy.

'Dogs are like horses,' he said. 'If you like them they will respond. You have to be able to think like them.'

Having been brought up on largely canine principles by a mother who was, and still is at eighty-five, one of Ireland's leading gundog trainers, I knew what he meant, though I do not have the patience or the skill myself.

Ngaio Marsh has this to say about dogs:

In respect of dogs I am a New Zealander. I like dogs. As a rule they have pleasant dispositions and either flatter one or make one uneasily compassionate by their excessive devotion. I very much like large, sensible dogs and sporting dogs. When dogs work they are splendid. A good huntaway, streaking down a mountainside and setting a great mob of sheep in motion is a noble sight. They are dirty, however, and can be obscene and no amount of shampooing and twiddling will make anything but asses of them. In New Zealand they can give one hydatids and it would be idiotic to let them lick one's face even if one liked it. I never became reconciled to the South Kensington dogs. When they were not defecating on the doorstep they were shivering in their mistresses' embrace.

Hydatids, lethal tapeworms which kill humans and are transmitted by dogs, have now reached Britain and are spreading fast, which may in time alter our view of dogs as pets.

We drove over the mountains on a road called the Gentle Annie, which took us north of the Ruahine Range through the Kaweka State Forest Park. The Gentle Annie, which strictly refers only to the final, steepest stretch, used to be a rough old dirt droving road and it had once been our plan to ride along it. However, today much of it has been improved and riding for days along roads is no fun.

At the bottom of the pass we unloaded all three horses and rode them up to give them some exercise and to spare Kowhai, who was showing a tendency to boil. The bush on either side was thick with manuka and we decided we were wise not to have tried to force our way across country. From the top we could see right out to the coast over blankets of green conifer plantations with the rich Heretaunga plain beyond. Soon we were passing orchards and vineyards. We stayed the night at Kanui, the farm of another cousin of Louella's, Chris Wilson.

In the morning we helped Chris muster some cattle. It was a glorious, heady day with a warm gale force wind coming over the hills from the west. Flights of ducks soared past, rising off ponds which had been created by damming small creeks. Behind them trailed an ungainly pukeko (*Porphyrio porphyrio*), the New Zealand equivalent of a moorhen but much larger, its wings beating furiously, its legs stretched out behind. Jacky rode with us, bareback in shorts and full of life now she was back in her home territory of the East Coast. She admitted to feeling homesick for her children now they were so close yet, like us, she did not want our idyll together to end.

The land had been cleared by Chris's father and the calves we rounded up looked strong and healthy. Clouds of white down blew past our heads, which Chris explained were from the nodding thistles. Although the station had Californian and Scotch thistles too it was free of the variegated kind, another noxious weed like the nodding thistle.

As they rode and talked I saw a faint family likeness between Louella and Chris. It made a change to be with a relation, however distant. There is a special feeling to cousinship which takes the sting out of accepting hospitality and Chris, fair-haired and energetic, was a natural host.

Next door to Kanui was another place we wanted to visit – Gwavas, the home of Mike and Carola Hudson whose son Tom had recently come to live at Tregrehan, a beautiful house and garden near us in Cornwall. The links between Cornwall and New Zealand are so close that constant coincidences of this sort no longer surprised us and we had had to stop asking friends if there was anyone they would like us to look up on our travels.

Guavas, however, was special and as we walked around the garden with the Hudsons it felt uncannily like being at home. There were magnolias, camellias, ilex, English beech and oaks, all the trees and shrubs of a Cornish garden, which had been brought out and planted only a hundred years before. Some of the trees were massive and looked very much older. The speed at which trees grow in New Zealand always seemed unfair to me, especially as we live at a windswept 800 feet (244 m) and everything grows very slowly.

Underneath the trees a stream meandered through boggy ground with ferns, dogwood and hydrangeas on its banks. A lovely old wooden summerhouse stood in the dark shade of a huge red oak. Mike's grandmother had had it built for her to allow her some shade to rest in as she and her husband planned the garden when there were no trees, just a bare swamp.

The house was one of the largest and most attractive we had seen in New Zealand. Two-storeyed and painted green and white, it had been empty for twenty-three years and yet was in perfect condition. There seems to be little dry rot or problems with damp in New Zealand; just recurrent economic crises which make it difficult to live in such a house far out in the country. Much easier to do as the Hudsons and almost everyone else in New Zealand does, and live in a small labour-saving bungalow.

As we drove on along the coast we saw more signs of farming troubles. Pumpkins were on sale beside the road at three for $1 (about 30p), but most of the crop was being dumped in the fields for the sheep to eat. The Japanese market for them had collapsed for some reason, probably because of a glut, and there was nothing else to do with them.

We saw no point in trying to ride through this country, attractive as much of it was, since the farms tended to be small, with many paddocks and fences to be negotiated, and it would have been next to impossible to avoid roads. Instead we drove, stopping only briefly at beautiful Lake Tutira, one of the most lovely spots we saw in both islands – a place of tranquil water surrounded by old weeping willows and teeming with black swans, coots and all sorts of ducks and geese. It is a bird sanctuary and was left to the nation by the farmer and naturalist W. H. Guthrie-Smith (1861–1940) who wrote a classic book, *The Story of a New Zealand Sheep Station* (1921), about his farm, Tutira. At the same time he gave nearly all of it away to servicemen returning from the First World War, where, incidentally, proportionately more New Zealanders were killed or wounded than any other nation involved. He was a great early conservationist, who fought for legislation to protect the rapidly disappearing indigenous species and who deplored the misguided efforts of those who wished to reproduce England in the Pacific. Their 'rat-like pertinacity,' he wrote, 'has accomplished the ruin of a Fauna and Flora unique in the world.'

Later we looked out across wide lagoons alive with wildfowl to the

Looking across to the Mahia peninsula. We rode north from the tip along the far Pacific shore.

distant outline of the Mahia Peninsula. We had decided to ride from the very southern tip up to Gisborne before joining Clyde and Carol for a final week through the mountains from their farm out to East Cape.

It was dark by the time we reached the peninsula and the track was rough and tortuous, with almost impossibly steep hills for Kowhai to grind up fully loaded. The moon was full and we stopped on a high ridge to admire the nocturnal view. Sheep were silhouetted against the sky, a soft, balmy breeze made us realize we were nearing the tropics and a silver band of moonlight led across the Pacific to the distant lights of Gisborne.

# CHAPTER THIRTEEN

# Seaside and Forests

M ost Maori believe that their ancestors came by canoe from the legendary land of Hawaiki. The tribes trace their descent from the occupants of each canoe and their myths go back to Hawaiki, where the first men had their epic adventures. Maui was one of these mythical heroes, a hoaxer, who used magic tricks to catch huge quantities of fish.

One day he persuaded his jealous elder brothers to take their canoe far out of sight of land. Then, using a hook made from the jawbone of his ancestress, he caught a fish so large that it had on it trees, houses, people and even fire, the discovery of which is also attributed to Maui. Telling his brothers not to touch anything until he returned with a priest to lift the tapu, he left them alone, but they were greedy and started to cut the fish up to eat it. It writhed and twisted in agony, which generated mountains and valleys.

Thus was created the North Island, which is indeed in the shape of a fish, head downwards, its mouth at Wellington, its tail at Northland, its dorsal fin at East Cape and its pectoral at Taranaki. You have to hold the map on its side, but once you do so the image is quite clear and all the more surprising when you realize that the Polynesians who created the myth had no maps. The brothers' canoe became the South Island and the anchor stone Stewart Island.

Maui fouled-hooked New Zealand, which was perhaps only to be expected of a trickster. In the middle of the fish's back is the great curve of the hook, Hawke Bay, with the point at Cape Kidnappers where Captain Cook made his second landing. The barb was turned into Mahia Peninsula.

High on a headland at the very tip of the peninsula is a Maori farm called Onenui, which means Abundant Sand. It has some 600 owners, members of the same tribe. Brian Lloyd, the manager, was round, fat, grey-bearded and jolly. He welcomed us boisterously although it was after 9.00 p.m. His wife, Sally, insisted we had tea and cakes before going to the shearers' quarters. She and eight other

Portland Island from the sheep yards at Onenui Station.

Maori women were compiling a record of all the stories they learnt as children, stories about the sea, the rocks and the birds, and they planned to form a publishing company.

The sea is all around at Onenui, blowing in a spray on the high winds which batter from the east, where there is no land before Chile. Off the end of the peninsula, but part of the farm, lies Portland Island, where Brian had brought back 400 lambs in a barge the day before. They shear the sheep there and ship the wool back the same way, although there is a runway for light aircraft. The island is uninhabited now, though at one time there were resident keepers for the lighthouse. One of the last ones was killed by a wild bull and today the light is automatic. There have been a lot of wrecks along this coast and in daylight it was easy to see why; savage, jagged shelves of rock reach out from the shore, surfacing at some distance from the land, invisible and lethal to shipping.

The main part of the property carries 18,000 sheep and 1,500 cattle on 8,000 acres. It was very run down for years but under Brian's management had turned in a profit of NZ$100,000 last year.

We watched Brian and his gang of Maori helpers drenching lambs in the early morning, making a pretty picture with the island in the background. He showed us the way across the property and down a cleft in the cliffs to the sea shore. Before the rough overland track was cut this was the only way in and out of Onenui, vehicles having to drive along the foreshore at low tide.

It was a lovely morning and it was good to be back in the saddle. The horses were nervous of the rippling waves and rock pools, having never apparently seen the sea before, but apart from that they cantered along happily. We soon came to an abandoned farm, now part of Onenui. There was an attractive old pink and blue clapboard house, empty for six or seven years, the garden overgrown, but all in reasonable condition and crying out to be loved and lived in. We tethered the horses and explored, climbing up to the little wood above and looking out across the ocean at our feet, imagining what it would be like to live there. There was a small schoolhouse and a tiny graveyard where we read some of the inscriptions. Some were for Maori soldiers killed in the Second World War, when many Maori fought with distinction in all the armed services, but one particular infantry formation – 28 New Zealand (Maori) Battalion – is remembered with special pride. It was composed entirely of volunteers and fought with the Eighth Army from Alamein to Tunis and then through the whole of the Italian campaign. Lieutenant General Sir Bernard Freyberg VC, whom Churchill called 'the finest divisional commander in the world', said of the Maori under his command '. . . no infantry battalion had a more distinguished record, or saw more fighting, or, alas, had such heavy casualties . . .' By the end of the war they had a casualty list of 2,589, including 640 dead.

Another inscription: 'In Loving Memory of Our Dear Daughter Josephine Te Kurairirangi Hemmingsen Died 28th March, 1935, aged $1\frac{1}{2}$ years.' There were pink amaryllis around the grave. We felt we were intruding on distant private grief and so mounted up and rode away from that singularly lonely place.

Now we found ourselves riding along a most extraordinary geological structure. Narrow ridges like stone weatherboarding stretched straight as a die for several miles between the sea and the land. Covered at high tide, the rock was surprisingly soft and gave the horses few problems. They were beginning to enjoy splashing through wet sections and we felt this would be good for their feet as well as possibly getting rid of the botflies' eggs which they had been picking up on their heels for the last few days. When horses lick these off they hatch in their stomachs and become parasites.

At the end of the rocky shelf we came to a sandy beach where we could canter. That day we picnicked on two cold lobsters from Portland Island which Brian had given us. Lying on our back in the hot sun while the horses grazed the coarse sea grass on a dune we gorged ourselves, tearing the succulent white flesh out with our fingers.

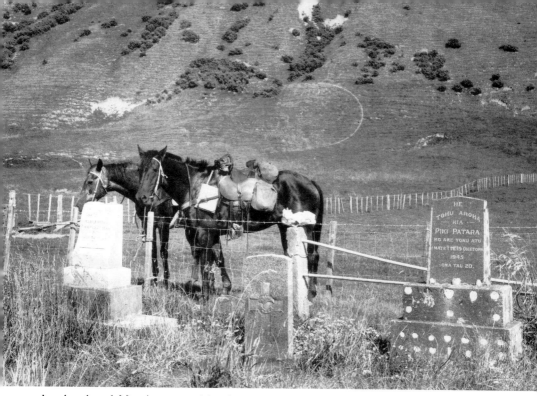

An abandoned Maori graveyard by the sea. Some of the graves remembered soldiers who had fought and died in North Africa and Italy during the Second World War.

Cantering along Pukenui Beach.

The extraordinary rock formation on the Mahia peninsula.

At the base of the peninsula we forded a tidal river and rode the 5 miles (8 km) of Pukenui Beach. Deserted, sandy and stretching from horizon to horizon in the evening haze, it seemed blissfully endless as we raced each other along it, knowing that friends of Jacky's had a comfortable beach house at Mahanga ahead and that for once there were no rabbit holes, stones or wire to look out for. Arriving hot and sweaty at the same time as Jacky and our Hungarian hosts, we decided to take all three horses out into the sea. Unsaddling and stripping off, we rode them bareback out through the waves. This was an experience I had never had before and it was incredibly exhilarating. The waves were much bigger than they looked from the shore, real surfing breakers built up across the Pacific, which threatened to throw the horses over backwards when they breasted them so that their front feet pawed at the air. They overcame their initial fear quickly and forced their way out through the waves to the deeper water beyond where, swimming properly, perhaps for the first time in their lives, they were clearly enjoying themselves as much as we were. Hanging on to their manes, we swooped over rollers and submerged beneath the water, but falling off was painless and, provided one kept away from the flailing hooves, it was not as dangerous as it seemed at first. Neither we nor the horses wanted to stop and we prolonged the fun by telling ourselves how much good it must be doing their backs. The water itself was pleasantly warm, though the evening breeze was chill and cooled the spray.

Surging back towards the beach, letting Star have his head as he followed the others home, it felt like riding a trampoline. Then his feet hit the ground with a jolt, I suddenly seemed a long way up from the ground and I flew over his head to land on the hard wet sand like a dead rabbit. Winded but very happy, I crawled up the beach for a superb dinner of goulash and champagne.

From Mahanga we rode along what we were told was 'the longest bridle path between two rivers in New Zealand'. It was the old coach road, now a grassy track climbing up into the hills parallel with the coast and giving increasingly good views back towards the Mahia Peninsula. Our informant was Ivor Riddiford, the owner of Mahanga Station. In common with many other farmers on the East Coast, he was selling his land as he was disillusioned with the economic prospects, his son was not interested in taking it on and he wanted to retire to somewhere smaller. He gave us helpful directions along the little-used track and we cantered off in high spirits.

Our friends had driven through in a four wheel drive vehicle a couple of days before and everyone assured us nothing could go wrong. It did. No-one had noticed that there was a cattle grid and double padlocked gate where the track entered a large section of forestry.

For over an hour we cast about up and down fence lines seeking a way through. It was a strong new fence with concrete posts, specifically designed not to be lowered and running at times through manuka scrub where we had to push our way, leading the horses. We were determined not to give up and return defeated. At last I found a place where two fences met and there was a narrow gap blocked with a barbed wire entanglement, which I was able to clear and then replace when we had squeezed the horses through.

Now we were on forestry tracks through dark conifer plantations, some of a good age with fine tall trees, which are always enjoyable to ride through. It was hilly country and in the valleys there were often ponds around which great tree ferns grew, the first we had seen close to. They are among the most magnificent plants to be found anywhere, rising as high as 60 feet (18 m) in some cases, with wide-spreading umbrella-like fronds. They looked incongruous to me growing in the familiar environment of a fir plantation, but seemed to co-exist well.

On the forest floor we glimpsed pheasants. Unlike the many species of small birds which were introduced out of nostalgia and a usually misguided desire to control the insect life, pheasants were brought in exclusively for sport. Paradoxically they proved the most effective pest controllers, settlers being quoted as saying that if it were not for the aid of the pheasant, they could scarcely hold their own against the depredations of crickets and other insects. They acclimatized quickly and by 1867 were so abundant in the North Island that importation was no longer necessary.

In the same year Lady Barker reported that they were arriving in the South Island too. From Waimate, in South Canterbury, she wrote:

This is one of the very few stations where pheasants have been introduced, but then, every arrangement has been made for their comfort, and a beautiful house and yard built for their reception on a flat, just beneath the high terrace on which the house stands. More than a hundred young birds were turned out last spring, and there will probably be three times that number at the end of this year. We actually had pheasant twice at dinner; the first, and probably the last time we shall taste game in New Zealand. There is a good deal of thick scrub in the clefts of the home-terrace, and this affords excellent shelter for the young. Their greatest enemies are the hawks, and every variety of trap and cunning device for the destruction of these latter are in use, but as yet without much execution among them, they are so wonderfully clever and discerning.

Originally much of the northern part of the North Island was covered in kauri forests. Kauri (*Agathis australis*) is one of the finest timbers known and it rapidly became New Zealand's chief export in the early nineteenth century. Cook had reported that the trees grew 'straight as an arrow and taper'd very little in proportion to length'. It was ideal for ships' masts and as a building material. Britain had recently lost her main source of ships' timber with the independence of her American colonies, and the rape of New Zealand began. At an incredible pace the kauri forests were cut down, logged and shipped abroad. Hundreds of millions of cubic feet of timber were removed, oxen were imported to drag the huge logs out and railways were built – as were mills and even whole towns, which died once the trees were gone and the land was laid bare.

Sadly kauri and the other main native timber trees of New Zealand such as rimu and totara grow very slowly, taking in some cases up to 700 years to reach maturity. But what trees they are when mature and what a tragedy that they could not have been exploited sustainably so that a continuing industry could have been developed which would have supplied the world with a priceless product in perpetuity, one which would have become more and more valuable as time passed and other sources disappeared. Tragically it is exactly the same story which is being acted out today in the tropical forests of Malaysia – greed and short-term need leaving behind a wasteland.

Later, before we left the country, we were able to go and visit some of the handful of remaining giants which were allowed to survive. Standing in front of the greatest of them all, Tane Mahuta, the God of the Forest, I defy anyone, however hard their heart, not to be moved close to tears. One of the largest living things on earth and among the oldest, its stupendous bulk has been growing for over 1,000 years, perhaps 2,000. Like an elephant it has an immensity and a dignity which cannot but inspire respect and awe.

By shedding their bark periodically like an old skin, kauris keep their trunks clean. The girth was massive and clear of branches for the first 30 feet. Above, the limbs sprouted to form a whole world in which ferns and orchids grew; further still the main stem soared 180 feet up into the sky to tower above the forest canopy below. In its timelessness and immutability, climatic disasters would pass it by as they had for centuries, an earthquake would hardly be noticed.

As we stood alone in the forest before Tane Mahuta we were acutely conscious of being in the presence of a tangible life force, an unmistakable animistic spirit, the Pan of the Greeks, a Buddhist tree of enlightenment, Yggdrasil the Scandinavian world tree, whose roots and branches bind heaven and earth together, the tree of Our Lord, the tree of Life.

At that moment an American tourist walked up the neat path to Tane Mahuta and, barely glancing upwards, asked us, 'Say, can you tell me if the mosquitoes here have malaria?' Wrong again about the power of nature over blind man. Or perhaps not all men; had Maori philosophy prevailed in Aotearoa the kauris would still be there.

Luckily for the New Zealand settlers they were able to replace their declining timber trade as the kauris ran out with a new introduced species, the Monterey pine (*Pinus radiata*). In the twenties and thirties hundreds of thousands of acres of poor pumice land, not that on which the kauri forests had grown, were planted largely with this single species which today accounts for over 90 per cent of New Zealand's plantation forests. There was once a problem with ichneumon wasps (which were accidentally introduced in a cargo of timber) as they bore into these trees to lay their eggs and cause a lot of damage. However, biological control through the introduction of other ichneumon wasps which are parasites of the damaging species worked effectively.

Taking only thirty years to mature, which is about two-and-a-half times as fast as in its native California, it is a model forester's tree. It is easy to transplant, resistant to disease and grows well on almost any soil. We had seen stands of *P. radiata* all the way through both islands, as well as large single trees planted in the last century and allowed to develop into fine specimens. To cap it all, it makes excellent timber which seasons quickly and can produce high quality pulp.

A hundred and fifty miles (241 km) to the west of the forest that we were riding through lay one of the largest plantations in the world, the Kaingaroa State Forest, which produces 2.6 million cubic yards (2 million m³) a year. Timber is again one of New Zealand's major exports and it brings employment and prosperity to thousands. Much of the energy for the mills comes from the geothermal power of natural steam from underground; the tree crop is regrown continuously on the same land and so far, in spite of the unusual practice of relying so heavily on a single introduced species with all the attendant dangers from viruses, pests or genetic weaknesses, *P. radiata* seems to be a continuing success story.

Even the criticism that these forests were sterile and provided no habitat for the native species is claimed to be no longer as valid as it once was, although they are certainly far less pleasing aesthetically. With constant felling and replanting a humus layer is beginning to build under the trees which allows a wide variety of understorey plants including native trees to grow and so support at least some of the indigenous birds.

The woods were pleasant enough to ride through and the forestry roads made an ideal surface for horses, but the monotony and scale of the plantations make them sterile and unattractive as a whole, whether seen from the ground or from the air. The rare glimpses we had through the trees down to the sea or up to the sky were a welcome relief. There is also today some questioning of the big business approach to forestry in New Zealand, where giant corporations control huge areas of land for such a monoculture, motivated solely by a desire for profit. It has been suggested that 'agro-forestry', where trees and farming are integrated as a single enterprise on the land, might be more satisfactory economically, socially and environmentally. At present the profitability of growing trees on the farm is too low to make it generally worthwhile to many farmers, however desirable it might be for other reasons, such as binding the soil.

For the ride into Jacky's home town of Gisborne we teamed up with her boss Ray Goldsbury, National President of New Zealand Riding for the Disabled, who took us across country through cool, bush-covered hills. We had not raised very much money for his charity but we had provided some useful publicity and he was in what we were to learn was his usual ebullient mood.

Before we left the country we were able to visit their headquarters at Ambury Park outside Auckland and meet the director Dr Jill Calvely. The work they do is quite extraordinary and we had to confess that until we saw it we had had no idea how important it was. Of course Jacky had talked cheerfully about how she jollied mentally and physically handicapped children into enjoying themselves on ponies, but we already knew that no child could resist her and simply took it for granted that it would do them good. What we had not realized was the medical significance of riding as therapy. Jill told us a series of 'miracle stories' concerning people with severe posture problems, broken necks and other disabilities, which hospitals and conventional medicine had written off as incurable but which had responded to her treatment. There is some peculiar chemistry which develops between humans and horses to induce a relaxation and mutual satisfaction which may be more therapeutic than hot baths or drugs. Even more impressive were the children themselves, some of whom had never responded at all to the efforts of their parents and nurses, but who gradually began to come alive when placed on a horse and led gently round the ring. In time some of the most hopeless cases were doing things no one would have believed possible.

Ray joined us on a nice-looking big horse called Blue which he claimed was extremely stupid, though we saw no sign of it.

'If you put an extra brain next to the one he's got he might qualify as a bloody idiot,' he said.

We stopped at Fairview Station for a cup of tea and were given some of the biggest scones we had ever seen. Our problem these last few days along the East Coast had been to resist the hospitality being thrust on us from all sides. Jacky had told us constantly that the people of the North Island would be much more welcoming than those in the South, and she beamed at being proved right.

We rode down a steep ridge to the source of Gisborne's water supply, where in a delightful valley a clear river tinkled over rounded pebbles under the shade of poplars and pollarded willows. Alongside us ran the big black pipe taking most of the water to the town. No scene could have appeared more tranquil and no one could have guessed how much it would change in the next few days.

There were flocks of Chinese and white geese dabbling in the river as well as turkeys running about in the bush beside us. We had often seen such flocks in the countryside in both islands and we asked Ray how people managed them. Were they, for instance, put in at night as in Europe, where there is a danger from foxes?

'Good heavens, no,' exclaimed Ray. 'They are wild and belong to no-one. Occasionally a hunter might shoot one, but mostly they're left alone.'

New Zealand may be having a bad time economically, I thought, but they are not exactly on the bread line yet. Where else in the world would you find almost tame poultry there for the taking but left largely alone?

In mid-afternoon we rode up to the school where Jacky's son Nick was a pupil. We had telephoned ahead to warn the schoolmaster and all fifteen pupils were outside in a flash to greet us. There was no mistaking Nick, a perfect small clone of his mother with a naughty grin and freckles. Moments after our arrival Jacky came around the corner in Kowhai and he beamed so that his face almost split.

We sat on the grass under a tree and talked with the children, who were bright and full of good questions. Their teacher and his wife were Canadian and Australian respectively. They seemed to bring the best out of their charges, so that they lacked inhibitions and told us eagerly about their own ponies and farm animals while not interrupting each other and listening intently when we talked. The schoolmaster said he was particularly thrilled that they should meet people from the outside world as not too many travellers passed that way. An author who told the children that writing books was hard work but worth the effort struck exactly the right note, he said generously. On balance, however, we gained more from the visit, seeing a side of New Zealand life which, just as in England, is disappearing. If the numbers of children drop below nine the school will close and with the farming depression that could happen anywhere. It is the same in Cornwall, where good village schools face the same threat. In New Zealand the problem is in some ways more acute, since the population is so small and the distances are so great; the transition from a rural to an urban life may be even harder and it certainly seems to make less sense to those experiencing it.

The day after we reached Gisborne the local horse show took place. We rode into town with a group of Riding for the Disabled workers in their white T-shirts, one an intrepid middle-aged blind lady who said that riding had changed her life. With Jacky driving Kowhai behind us we did a lap of honour – and then another unscheduled one at full gallop while the commentator told the crowd that we had come all the way from Invercargill and were going on to the East Cape to finish the ride. It was a great feeling to have arrived and to experience such a triumphal official ending. Although we had not ridden as much of the North Island as we had hoped, we were quite pleased with our South Island achievement. Now, we thought, just one more hard week remained and we could leave New Zealand having covered a pretty respectable distance in eight weeks. It was not to turn out that way.

# CHAPTER FOURTEEN

# *On the* marae

In Gisborne I had a chance to visit a *marae*. Thinking I was just going to be shown some carvings, I had arranged to meet someone who would take me. Louella and Jacky dropped me off at a crossroads and went off shopping.

A striking lady in a long purple dress, her dense black hair piled up on her head, greeted me.

'My name is Rose Pere,' she said. 'Do you know what to do?'

It dawned on me that I was about to be introduced formally to the *marae*, just like the Governor General at Okains Bay. I said I had a vague idea.

'Just follow me and do as I do,' she told me.

Some distance away was a pretty carved meeting house. From this and other houses around, which I now realized were part of a Maori community, figures were gathering; the *tangata whenua*, the local people, who either lived on or identified with this particular *marae*. Between us lay the open grassy space, the *marae* itself. The function of a *marae* is a place to meet, to stand and speak. It is also a place to greet visitors, *manuhiri*, and they, too, are expected to speak. Rose led me to the gate.

In a strong, confident voice she began to *karanga* and walked through the gate on to the *marae*. The *karanga* represents the first words spoken between *tangata whenua* and *manuhiri*. It is an expression of welcome that creates a pathway on to the *marae* along which a *waewae tapu* – literally a 'sacred foot', someone who is going on to a specific *marae* for the first time – can safely travel. I followed behind Rose, pausing when she paused, my eyes cast down as I had read that it is not done for *manuhiri* to look around.

'*Haeremai, haeremai, haeremai*,' she called, 'welcome, welcome visitor from afar. Bring with you the spirits of your dead that they may be greeted, that they may be mourned. Ascend on to our sacred *marae*. *Haeremai, haeremai, haeremai*.' I could not understand the words at the time but she told me later what she had said.

Slowly, pausing every few steps to *karanga*, Rose led me across the *marae*. I was carrying a briefcase in one hand and my camera case in the other. Each time we stopped I wondered if I should put them down or continue to hold them. Anyone who visits a *marae* may sleep in the meeting house, the *whare hui*. It suddenly crossed my mind that this was a bit like being led with great ceremony to the reception desk at a hotel and I began to grin. There is often a touch of farce at moving moments. Then the solemnity and enchantment of the occasion began to take me over, reality slipped and I felt myself in another world.

We reached a bench set crosswise to the meeting house out on the lawn and sat down. Rose whispered to me that I would now be greeted formally by the senior man present and then it would be my turn to speak. She suggested that as she had done, I might like to recall a loved one at the beginning. It is customary, when going on to a *marae*, to take someone who has died with one and to stand in silence for a moment in memory of all the departed.

The speaker was a bearded, fine-looking man called Freddy Maynard, who could have had little idea who I was or what I was doing there. He referred first to departed ancestors and relations, then welcomed me with flowery complements which Rose translated. Maori is a lovely sonorous language which gives significance and emphasis to all that is said. He switched to English at the end, saying that he had heard we had been riding through the country from Invercargill. This was a good way to see and understand the land and we had travelled the right way, leaving their territory until the last. I was impressed that he should wrap up an address to a total stranger so neatly.

As soon as he finished, the women seated on the carved panel along the front of the *whare hui* began to sing a *waiata*, traditional songs which come after each speech. In the silence that followed I made my way slowly out on to the *marae*. 'Just take a few steps on the grass and speak for as long as you like,' Rose had whispered to me.

Strangely, I felt no stage fright, in spite, or perhaps because of, being totally unprepared. Trying to remember what sounded so good in the bath earlier has spoiled many an after-dinner speech. To use written notes on a *marae* would run counter to the whole great Maori tradition of spontaneous oratory.

I stood alone and looked across at the row of faces below the *whare hui* waiting for me to begin and I felt a tremendous sense of privilege at being there and an urgent desire to communicate properly. It is a great honour to be invited to speak on the *marae-atea*, the area between the hosts and the guests during a welcome, and the speaking should properly be in Maori.

I began by saying how ashamed I was to be unable to use any

Maori words. I was proud to have been greeted in this unexpected and undeserved way but I would not insult their language by attempting half-learned phrases and pronouncing them wrongly. Several of the faces before me, which had been expressionless and stern, cracked at this and some shook their heads and smiled. I felt the atmosphere lift a little.

I told them I was a traveller, who had been all over the world and visited many different peoples. For the first twenty-three years of my married life I had often travelled with my much-loved wife Marika, who had died five years before, and I would like to remember her now with them.

After a short silence I said that I was now happily married again and that Louella would be coming later and hoped to meet everyone. She was sorry not to be there then, but we only had a little time in Gisborne as we planned to ride on out to the East Cape in the next day or so.

I talked about my early travels in South America and how in 1968 I had learned about the cruelty and genocide being faced by the Indians in Brazil. How they were persecuted, often to extinction, by settlers, miners and even government officials; how they had no protection under international law and no one to speak up for their rights; how a group of us had started Survival International to represent their rights until they could do so for themselves, while at the same time alerting the world to what was going on. How our organization had grown and as it grew we had discovered how large the task we had set ourselves really was. All over the world indigenous minorities faced threats to their cultures and often to their very existence from the economically and militarily more powerful societies who dominated them. Inspired by materialist philosophies, by the religious fanaticism of extreme Christian or Islamic sects or by the sheer greed of multinational companies, this domination resulted in the impoverishment of the peoples we represented and of the world itself.

I told my audience how I had learned over the years not just to regret the passing of such peoples and their cultures and to wish to mitigate their suffering, but to recognize the value of their beliefs and their approach to life, an approach which I had come to believe was in most respects preferable to those causing so many problems in the world today. If the respect for the environment which is integral to such societies had been observed by more 'civilized' cultures for the last hundred years, if development had been based on sustainable yield rather than maximum exploitation, then much of the hunger and pollution of our planet might have been avoided.

Coming closer to home, I told my audience about our involvement in the Australian Bicentennial and how this year we were successfully working with aborigine communities to point out to the world that not everyone regarded the events of 200 years ago with unqualified enthusiasm. The story of Australia's colonization by Britain is one of the most brutal records in history of the abuse of an invaded country's defenceless occupants. For the aborigines there was nothing to celebrate in '88.

Before coming to New Zealand I knew next to nothing about Maori history. I had read *The Bone People* and various papers on the Waitangi Tribunal and its implications but, like most British people, I had always thought that the relationship between Maori and *pakeha* represented one of the few success stories in the field of intercultural relations. Since being in the country I had learned differently. I had heard extreme views expressed by farmers, government officials, conservationists and human rights activists which had given me a glimmering of both sides of the argument. I had been at Okains Bay on Waitangi Day and had listened to Maori leaders and politicians hold forth. I confessed to being confused. I looked forward to learning from them what it meant to be a Maori and what they saw as the solution to bringing about racial harmony in their country.

We had ridden through their country and seen a lot from our horses. We had seen both good and bad things that had happened since the *pakeha* came. We had been impressed by much of the farming, appalled by much of the environmental destruction. *Pakeha* New Zealanders had advised us to keep off the subject of Maori affairs, but as President of Survival International, how could I possibly be expected to do so? I had been as much disturbed by the signs of extremism that I had encountered in those who feared 'black power' as I had in those who advocated it.

In the end I felt that all these problems must be solvable as New Zealand, Aotearoa, was such a superbly beautiful and plentiful land, with a long record of basic goodwill between her peoples if they could only learn to respect each other.

I concluded by saying that I would far prefer not to speak formally to them any more but, if I was permitted, to sit with them and learn from them, talking freely and informally. Then I laid a copy of my autobiography *Worlds Apart* on the ground and backed away.

It is traditional for the last, in my case the only, *manuhiri* speaker to place a *koha* (gift) on the ground at the conclusion of his speech. Originally visitors from another *marae* would have brought food, especially something rare in the hosts' district. I hoped a book was a suitable present to give.

As I returned to the bench, Freddy came forward, picked up the book, nodded his thanks and the women sang a *waiata*; I vowed to myself never to use notes again when having to give a speech – a vow which I regret I have already broken since my return through lack of courage. If there is something to be said and the speaker knows what he wants to say, then it is said much better from the heart directly to those listening. Although quite unprepared I had spoken well and confidently and I had known that I was in direct communication with the *tangata whenua*, who had listened attentively. Later Hene Sunderland, a grand Maori lady who is an expert on traditional flax weaving, told me she had been very suspicious of me before I started speaking. 'We get a lot of people coming to New Zealand who say they want to write a book about Maori issues. Frankly they are a bore. While you spoke I recognized and understood you.'

A prepared text, however eloquent, could not have achieved that, I believe. All rhetoric should, perhaps, be delivered as oratory in the Maori way, alone on the *marae*. The technique has an honourable tradition in Britain, too. Most speakers in the Oxford and Cambridge Unions, and indeed in the Houses of Parliament, are not allowed to read their speeches.

Freddy now gestured that we should cross to the front of the meeting house to *hariru* and *hongi*, that is, to shake hands and press noses. Once more I followed Rose and did as she did. Hene was first in line, a big, good-looking lady with silver hair and a black scarf knotted around her neck. It was the first time I had performed the *hongi* and I hoped I would get it right. It was easy; just two gentle direct presses, nose end to nose end, while clasping right hands and placing the left hand on each other's right shoulder – an intimate gesture, but completely lacking in embarrassing or erotic overtones; more familiar than a handshake, much less so than a kiss, except perhaps for the Russian sort politicians give each other.

All the way down the line we went and at the end I really did feel that I had been accepted into the *marae*. We sat and talked as a group. Rose dominated the conversation to begin with, telling me how she was on the Board of Education and had been on international missions concerned with indigenous rights. She said it was a hard struggle changing attitudes, even getting people to accept that such changes were necessary. As both a Maori and a woman she had constantly to combat the idea that she was just a token on committees to whom no one listened. Hearing her speak forcefully and fearlessly I doubted that. Another attack she had to counter was that she was a pagan because she was concerned with promoting Maori history and an awareness of the myths and beliefs on which *Maoritanga*, Maori culture, are based. In fact she is a practising Anglican.

The others listened and joined in with questions and comments. We all agreed that there need be no conflict between Maori beliefs and Christianity. Prejudice was largely based on ignorance and fear. For instance, one of the excuses I had heard given by *pakeha* for putting down the Maori was that they had themselves wiped out those who had settled the land before them, the very first settlers from East Polynesia, the original *tangata whenua*. These are the people often referred to as the Archaic Maori, or Moa Hunters, most of whom seem, from archaeological evidence, to have lived in the South Island where moas were most plentiful. The idea that they had simply been massacred by the later waves of Classic Maori, from whom my hosts were descended, was hotly refuted; they contended that they had intermarried with them, adopted their myths and customs and become integrated with them.

I was asked what had been my impression of race relations in their country. I had to admit that they had been very mixed. The recent surge of Maori awareness, demands for the return of land through the Waitangi Tribunal and Maori education in schools had been bitterly resented by many. Farmers feared that the land they and their predecessors had worked on would be taken from them.

'They say that land farmed by Maori is simply allowed to revert to bush,' I told them. 'Mind you, when it should never have been cleared in the first place, this might not be such a bad thing.'

'No one who acquired their land fairly need have anything to fear,' they replied. 'Land stolen should be returned, of course, but much more important is the recognition of communal title as being of equal status to individual title, so that we can pass on our land to our children.'

I spoke of the deep resentment felt by some *pakehas* at their children having to learn Maori at school. I had tried to counter this by pointing out that all education is useful in itself and learning languages perhaps especially so. I had had to learn Latin and Greek at school, which seemed pointless to many, but I have never regretted it and find they serve me well in helping me to appreciate my own language. How much more useful for all New Zealanders to understand the original language of their country, reflected in so many place names.

They told me about *Te Kohanga Reo*, The Language Nest movement, which has taken off in a big way. Under it the active teaching of their language to Maori children is promoted so that it will not die. Where speaking it used to be severely punished in schools it is now taught instead, but more is needed. Only about a quarter of Maori are fluent speakers of the language, though many more understand it. If the *marae* is to play its full and immensely valuable role in New Zealand society, a role which neither church nor state can adequately fulfil alone for the Maori people, then the language must be saved. The talk is now of 'two people in one nation', a much more healthy concept than the tired old idea of 'we are one people' which ignored and suppressed Maori identity.

I found this concept was, I confessed, the thing which had alarmed me most in New Zealand. Far too many *pakehas* seemed to emphasize only the negative manifestations of the resurgence of Maori identity and self-confidence. The media were to blame for reporting with relish every case of mugging or rape by disaffected Maori youths, who formed gangs with names like The Mongrel Mob. Although such disaffection is a familiar phenomenon in most parts of the developed world, New Zealand *pakehas* seemed stunned and terrified, perhaps through having been insulated against such things for so long. The easy-going paternalism of the past, which had allowed tolerance of and intermarriage with a demoralized and debilitated Maori society, has turned to an often savage loathing, patently based on fear.

The Maori wars between 1860 and 1872 effectively crushed any physical resistance by Maori to the loss of their land. They were brought about mainly through colonists arriving in the country having paid for land which had not yet been properly procured from the Maori. Quite apart from the different approaches to land ownership between the two cultures and the misunderstandings generated by the poor translation of the Treaty of Waitangi, the Maori, who did not see themselves as a conquered people and had in fact never been defeated in battle, resented the aggressive way in which their land was taken from them. They protested as rapacious settlers moved on to land which they had bought from the Crown for twenty times the amount that had been paid to the Maori who, denied the vote, nevertheless had to provide about half the taxation revenue. The King movement, which was formed primarily to resist the sale of Maori land, was regarded as an act of rebellion, although its original intentions were peaceful. Despite being courageous and clever fighters who won many notable battles, the Maori never stood a chance against the superior fire power of the colonists' artillery. Vast areas of ancestral land were arbitrarily confiscated to punish the 'rebels' and then either given to the soldiers so as to turn them into settlers or sold to recoup the costs of the war.

Before the wars the Maori had nearly 67,000,000 acres of tribal lands and a population which was only beginning to diminish through disease from its high level of well over 100,000 in the late eighteenth century. By 1880 it was down to little over 40,000 and the Maori spirit was, for a time, broken.

Now it was back to over 300,000, more than 10 per cent of the population and growing, supplemented by the influx of Polynesian Islanders, who have made Auckland the largest Polynesian city in the world. There were all sorts of forecasts bandied around about the date by which the majority of the New Zealand population would be 'black'. This possibility was widely regarded as a disaster.

'We really hate them,' said one couple to whom we had had to listen politely. 'They just steal things. I wouldn't have one in the house.'

'What about Liz? She's a Maori, isn't she? You like her, don't you?' asked their daughter.

'Oh, she's only a quarter Maori,' they replied smugly. 'Just enough to be cunning.'

Racist jokes were common currency in New Zealand, often fairly good-humoured in the genre of Irish or Polish jokes elsewhere, but many had a savage undercurrent.

'This country will soon be like Zimbabwe,' said another couple who were about to emigrate to South America. 'In Argentina they found the best solution to these problems. They wiped all the Indians out. And there's a big statue in the main square to the man who did it.'

These conversations, and many more, contrasted shockingly with the gentle reason and positive arguments I met on the *marae*.

During the supposed era of racial harmony when New Zealand had seen itself as a model to the world – before the Maori started getting 'uppity' – it was pointed out to me that all sorts of covert and overt discrimination did of course exist all along. Self-fulfilling prophesies about the idleness, innate stupidity and proneness to alcohol of subject peoples are a common story throughout the world. To the Maori credit, their robust approach to life and natural good humour, not to mention their prowess at rugby and their courage as soldiers, spared them the worst abuses suffered by Australian aborigines and South American Indians; the pressure just took longer to build up and it came as a great shock to the *pakeha* when it began to boil over.

Racial and sectarian problems do not go away by being swept under the carpet, nor by putting all the blame on one side. They just fester and grow wherever they occur, be it in Ireland, Cyprus, Lebanon, India or South Africa. In New Zealand there is no need for a problem. The majority of Maori are not the ugly urban gangs or disaffected louts on street corners that they are so often portrayed as. Even if they did represent a much higher proportion than I suspect, the way to rehabilitate them is not with force and calumny but by giving them an identity. This is beginning to happen today. One way is opportunity and employment within *pakeha* society; another is for them to discover their cultural heritage on the *marae* and with it a set of values at least as valid as those which they are noisily rejecting. After all, Maori culture is the only indigenous culture New Zealand has and Maori is not a foreign language but one that belongs only to New Zealand.

Most *pakeha* New Zealanders have a confused attitude to their place in the world. On the one hand there is a deep suspicion of people from Britain, a conscious rejection of any imperial connections and a recognition of New Zealand's need to make its own way in the world. No one we met referred to England as 'home' any more. At the same time there is passionate loyalty to the Queen, although this is often accompanied by an alarming and erroneous belief that it is only shared by white members of the Commonwealth. Great pride is still widely felt for the past and present links with the UK. 'We fought with you in three wars, *and* sent a frigate to the Falkland Islands. No other Commonwealth country did that,' was a common point made, albeit erroneously, as actually a New Zealand frigate was sent to the Indian Ocean to release a British one for active service in the South Atlantic. However, there is still considerable bitterness among farmers over Britain's membership of the EEC and perceived rejection of New Zealand produce, although 40 per cent of the butter still comes to Europe.

The sense of being an isolated European outpost stuck in the middle of the Pacific is very strong. Ngaio Marsh again has this to say:

The Arts in New Zealand, particularly the art of writing, have followed much the same pattern of development as the one I have tried to suggest. But whereas with the nonaesthetic New Zealander, the attitudes are instinctive and naïve, the writers have approached problems of their advance to national maturity with extreme self-consciousness, anxious analyses and an intensive and industrious taking-in of each other's washing. They are acutely sensitive to their position, greatly concerned, and rightly so, with the emergence of an indigenous genre but often disinclined to look beyond it for wider standards of comparison.

It is strange, I think, that with this fierce concentration on the New Zealand element, so few of our major writers have concerned themselves in depth with the greatest problem and surely the most interesting aspect of life in New Zealand today: the process of integration between two races and the emergence of many formidable difficulties that must be overcome before we can honestly claim to have realized the intention of our forefathers: that the Maori and Pakeha shall be as one people.

This, of course, was written long before Keri Hulme was awarded the Booker McConnell Prize in 1985 for *The Bone People*. In that savage, tender, autobiographical book she writes, 'It's very strange, but whereas by blood, flesh and inheritance, I am but an eighth Maori, by heart, spirit and inclination, I feel all Maori.'

A friend told me about her own awakening to the existence of a whole Maori world in her country. She, like many relatively isolated New Zealanders, had hardly ever met a Maori in the rural district where she grew up; but she shared a flat in Wellington with a Maori girl who worked in the same government department and one day her friend suggested she might like to visit her *marae* at the weekend.

When they arrived, they discovered that someone had just died and there was to be a *tangihanga*, a mourning ceremony and funeral. *Tangi* take precedence over all other *marae* uses and are the most important Maori cultural event.

The Maori girl explained that she was high born in that tribe and that she would have to take a leading part in the ceremony. For my *pakeha* friend it was a complete awakening. Suddenly she saw her friend wearing a ceremonial cloak and singing in a voice she had never suspected she possessed; performing rituals of which she had no understanding; laying her cloak in the open coffin; greeting all the old ladies on the *marae* with an unexpected dignity. She had followed, at first in embarrassment, then in growing reverence.

The old ladies were muttering something about *waewae tapu* and it became clear that there was a problem about her presence, being a stranger. The day was saved when her friend asked her publicly, 'Didn't you tell me that you had a Maori great aunt belonging to this tribe?' As soon as it was established that she was a relation she was accepted and thereafter she returned many times. She told me that she was beginning to understand something of which most *pakeha* in New Zealand are still totally ignorant. They are proud of how well they have treated the Maori in the past, and it is true that things were very different from Australia, where all aborigines were regarded as subhuman and good only for extermination. They are proud of the few examples of Maori culture with which they are familiar – the singing, *waiata*, and the *haka*, the posture dance sometimes performed at rugby matches. By and large, however, they still regard them as inferior, lazy and stupid blacks prone to robbery and rape and best not trusted too far.

She had begun to learn about the Maori view of the world and to see below the surface. She had learnt that a road-sweeper, an uneducated man by our western standards, might suddenly be transformed on the *marae* into a great poet and orator. 'If only people understood,' she said.

Both the Maori and the *pakeha* migrated to New Zealand. Both settled there and made the islands their home. Yet while the European considers the land belongs to him, the Maori belongs to the land. The European wants to develop the land and extract the maximum from it; the Maori wants to protect it and explore its resources. These are fundamental differences of approach and neither has a monopoly of being right. The pragmatism of conservation needs to be set against the inhumanity of hunger.

What has been lacking in the past has been mutual respect and much sign of a positive desire to work together for the common good. Perhaps the growing awareness of how disastrous the blind exploitation of this fragile land has proved in the past, combined with a

A Maori labourer may become a great poet on the *marae*.

dawning understanding of the delicate checks and balances needed to harness and sustain the whole ecosystem, may point the way to future harmony.

In New Zealand, perhaps more than anywhere else, there is an opportunity as well as a need for attitudes towards the soil and the people to coalesce so that a proper nation can grow. There is a feeling in the country that this has not happened yet.

A month after our return to England I was telephoned by the Survival International office in London to be told that a *mokomakai*, a tattooed Maori head, was about to be sold by the auctioneers Bonhams. Did I think that the Maori people, if they knew about this, would object and if so should our organization do something about it?

Although this was an issue which none of us had had to face before, I knew at once that it was something we must oppose. Even though my visits to *marae* had been very brief they had taught me that the Maori people would find such a sale deeply offensive.

We took legal advice, began proceedings for an injunction to stop the sale and sent urgent messages to contacts in New Zealand. We learnt that the sale of heads was prohibited by law in New South Wales, which at the time administered New Zealand, as early as the 1820s. There may be as many as 200 such heads around the world, mostly in museums, though out of respect for the Maori few exhibit them and none are displayed in New Zealand itself.

Tattooing, common throughout the Pacific, developed into a highly complex art in Aotearoa (New Zealand) before the arrival of Europeans and without writing or representational art the significance and beauty of the designs became very important. The heads have been likened to ancestral portraits. The Rev. Richard Taylor, writing in 1885, concluded that to have 'fine tattooed faces was the great ambition of young men, both to render themselves attractive to the ladies, and conspicuous in war: for even if killed by the enemy, whilst the heads of the untattooed were treated with indignity, and kicked on one side, those which were conspicuous by their beautiful *moko* were carefully cut off, stuck on the *turuturu*, a pole with a cross on it, and then preserved; all of which was highly gratifying to the survivors, and the spirits of their late possessors.'

Unfortunately, as whalers, traders, missionaries and settlers began to undermine and corrupt Maori culture these heads, which had in the past been treated with veneration, became trade goods in exchange for muskets or blankets.

The Maori people and the New Zealand government reacted promptly to the proposed sale, declaring their implacable opposition to it. They took over the legal proceedings and commended Survival International for 'challenging those organizations and individuals involved in a practice which can only be described as culturally insensitive'.

The affair attracted a great deal of attention in the British and New Zealand media, nearly all sympathetic to the Maori feelings, and at the last moment Bonhams withdrew the head from sale. The owner, who might have received between £6,000 and £10,000 for the head, subsequently returned it to the Maori people at a ceremony at New Zealand House and was given a fine modern greenstone club or *mere* in exchange.

Once again I found myself on a *marae*, this time the converted lobby of New Zealand House in Lower Regent Street. Rows of seats were set at an angle to each other and under the bright lights a Maori lady dressed in black and holding a frond in her hand was welcoming us with a high-pitched *karanga*.

The *manuhiri* were led by Sir Graham Latimer, Chairman of the

New Zealand Maori Council, with Archdeacon Kingi Ihaka, a leading Maori churchman. I and three other representatives of Survival International came next with Lady Latimer and we were led to our seats on the left. Opposite, the *tangata whenua* consisted of Maori living in London, with the *pakeha* High Commissioner and his wife in the centre. The head, in a box and discreetly covered with a Maori blanket, was on a table beside them.

Speeches, almost all in Maori, were made by both sides, interspersed with *waiata* sung beautifully by half a dozen Maori girls who performed confidently and professionally, accompanied by a guitar and supported by some young men and older people. It was a surprise to see so many Maori together in London. When the time came for us to join the *tangata whenua*, they formed a line and we walked across the *marae-atea* to *hariru* and *hongi* with each of them. Once again I was captured by the beauty and correctness of the ritual, but this time I found it almost unbearably moving to be meeting and greeting under such significant circumstances and in such unlikely surroundings. Each one murmured, '*Haeremai*,' or '*Kia ora*,' as we embraced, and some kissed us on both cheeks.

Mrs Weller-Poley, who had found the head in her attic, and her family now took our places on the *manuhiri* seats and there were more speeches and a short *tangi*, during which everyone expressed pleasure at the honourable outcome of the affair. Even Nicholas Bonham, representing the auction house, rose to his feet to say how glad they were that the head was being returned to join its ancestors.

Sir Graham said that he was already pretty sure that he knew which tribe the *mokomakai* came from and that it would be buried decently after he had returned with it to Aotearoa. The Archdeacon said he thought it extremely unlikely that the Maori warrior concerned had been a Christian, but he said some prayers anyway and then we all broke up and had a drink together. Talking with Sir Graham later, I was told that his people really did feel very strongly about the issue. Before he flew over he had been stopped in the street by complete strangers asking him to make sure that he did bring the *mokomakai* back with him.

The significance of the affair did not end there. Christie's had some twenty-nine heads from around the world, including Papua New Guinea and South America, due to be sold a month later. Luke Holland, our press officer, and I were invited to discuss with them which heads or other parts of tribal bodies Survival International did or did not object to them selling. The main contention of the auction houses was that such objects had acquired through time the status of historical artifacts of ethnographic interest.

At first I thought that all we would be pressing for was that when there were identifiable descendants of the society concerned and they raised objections to the sale or public display of the human remains of their ancestors, we should object on their behalf. But the publicity generated by the cancelled sale of the *mokomakai* brought an unexpected harvest of letters from around the world asking us to campaign to stop all such sales whatever their origin or age. An impassioned statement came from a Papuan tribal leader begging for the return and proper burial of all his peoples' heads, including those in the Christie's sale.

The President of the coordinating committee of all Amazon Indians, Evaristo Nugkuag, who the year before had received the alternative Nobel Peace Prize, wrote officially authorizing us to act on his peoples' behalf to secure the return of all such objects, whether they be trophies of war or ancestral relics.

We learned that an energetic organization of North American Indians had been formed with the intent 'to retrieve *all* Indian human remains from all over the world and to rebury them.'

We had to say to Christie's that we found the commercial exploitation of all ancient human remains abhorrent whatever their origins and we suggested that they set an example to all other auction houses by formally abrogating the practice. This they subsequently and courageously agreed to do. The point is not whether the heads or carved bones had completed their function within contemporary tribal ritual as objects of veneration, vilification or decoration. It is that the modern descendants of those people, already struggling against prejudice, culture shock, alien standards and at times overt racism, find it deeply offensive to learn that their ancestors are now being bought and sold. Only time will tell if one Maori *mokomakai* may be the cause of bringing this unpleasant trade to an end.

# CHAPTER FIFTEEN

# Cyclone Bola

I t rained the day we woke up at Clyde and Carol Langford's farm, Manaaki. Jacky was due with the horses in Kowhai, since there was no point in riding up the 30 miles (50 km) by road from Gisborne. A day of reorganizing ourselves lay ahead and then we planned to set off early for the last hard week out to East Cape.

When Jacky failed to turn up on time, we drove down the road to find a small mud slip had made the road impassable for the truck. Unflappable as ever, she came round the corner riding Star bareback and leading the other two. We rode back with her, little realizing that this was to be the end of the road. The day was spent ferrying all our gear up to the farm and sorting it out.

'This rain usually lasts for three days,' said Clyde. 'Why don't we delay our departure until it clears up? There's no point in getting soaked at the start and it could be quite dangerous up in the hills if we get lost.'

We agreed and so drove out of the area next morning to have some business meetings and to see the hot springs and other tourist sights of Rotorua. That night a stationary black band of cloud seemed to stretch half across the world, its edge sharp and motionless against the dark blue sky. The tail of a cyclone which had been destroying Pacific islands to the north, it was an ominous sight. Small white clouds scudded past like little express trains, there was a howling in the air and an unearthly light at dusk. We were glad not to be seeking shelter out on a high ridge with the horses. Then we thought of Carol and the children alone at Manaaki.

The news at breakfast was all of cataclysm. A state of emergency had been declared, the civil defence were in charge and all roads and flights in and out of Gisborne were closed. For 48 hours we fought to get back, driving as far as possible past landslides and floods, to sleep in a schoolhouse with others stranded by the storm. The news was all of tragedy and heroism, deaths by drowning, bridges washed out, rivers over their banks, farms cut off. Later we learned that nearly 40

Cyclone Bola caused floods which carried all before them.

inches (1 m) of rain fell in those two days, causing one of the worst
disasters of its kind ever.

As we followed a police Range Rover as part of the first convoy into
the area, we found a landscape changed beyond recognition. Where
there had been green fields, vineyards, kiwi fruit and sheep, we saw
only brown silt left behind by the height of the floodwaters, which
still surged ochre and white along new channels. Fences were buried
completely, or showed above the mud in places like First World War
barbed wire entanglements. Several cars lay on their sides in the mud
where the water had carried them and signposts pointed incongru-
ously to the sky. Trees leant sideways, waiting to fall as the water
continued to erode their roots, houses stood isolated in a sea of mud,
animals lay drowned and bloated or stood shivering on patches of
higher ground.

Stunned farmers surveyed the devastation and tried to conjure up
the phlegm and the resilience which they expected of themselves.

Like connoisseurs of wine, they compared the vintage floods of '85, '52, '48 and the formerly greatest of all, '38. Some had lived through each of them and were now finally ruined. Even those who might survive were near despair. 'Who knows when the next one will come?' asked one. 'With government help we might get straight again, but then it could all be for nothing.'

We had had no real news of Carol for two-and-a-half days and Clyde was worried. A helicopter had visited a neighbour who said he thought she was all right, but we all wanted to see for ourselves as soon as possible. We inched our way up the valley, waiting while bulldozers and farm tractors cleared a path through mud slips across the road, digging ourselves out when we became stuck. At last, at Kanakanaia, we had to abandon the car and start walking. The road, up which we had driven with relative ease three days before, rose 1,500 feet (450 m) in about 4 miles (6 km). Some of the steepest sections had even had asphalt put on recently. Now it looked as though it would never be used again. Whole hillsides had slipped across it to create heaving barriers 30 feet (10 m) high over which we had to climb. Later there was a stretch where it was hard to believe that rain had caused the damage rather than an earthquake. For over 200 yards (180 m) the whole road had dropped about 9 feet (3 m) down the hillside. I could not imagine how one began to put a problem like that right. It looked as though the whole area, with its 50,000 sheep and 10,000 head of cattle, would be cut off indefinitely. Clyde became silent and fearful as we trudged, afraid of what he might see when we reached his land, worried about his family who had had to face it all alone, sure that Carol would be in despair. However, when we finally reached their pretty house with its neat garden it looked at first as though nothing had changed. Carol greeted us cheerfully with the New Zealand panacea of a cup of tea and, in relief, we all became animated and optimistic.

Without telephone or electricity, she had been on her own except for one visit from a helicopter which, once the pilot had checked she was not desperate, had taken off again for more urgent cases. She had coped well with keeping the animals fed – not easy with their large flock of angora goats, as they dislike rain but had to go out to eat. The horses appeared unmoved by all the water that had been tipped on them. Content in their New Zealand rugs, they seemed to be enjoying the rest and the good grazing in a paddock next to the house.

It was not until the next day that we were to see the full extent of the damage. There was now no question of our riding any further. Apart from the immorality of adding to the problems faced by the rescue services if we ran into trouble, the whole landscape was now so waterlogged that progress would be impossible.

So we saddled up for a last ride together to look round the farm and

The whole road had dropped. It was hard to believe that rain had caused the damage rather than an earthquake.

see what had happened. Within 100 yards of the house we hit trouble. Halfway across a steep paddock the ground started to shake, the horses' feet sank into mud and we only just pulled back in time. A detour via the ridge above brought us to a gate. The fence, swamped by another slip, had tightened, pulling the hanging post back so that the catch was drawn tight. Since the fence was no longer stockproof anyway as the earth had rolled over and flattened it, Clyde cut the wire and we went through. Along a knife-edge ridge, from both sides of which the land had fallen away leaving an insecure spine only a few feet wide, we managed to reach the road again, but it was nearly all gone and it was hard to see on the steep hillsides where a new one could be built. For a long time the only way in and out of these isolated farms was going to be by horse.

A farmer trying to reach his property on his horse joined us and we struggled on. We passed a deer paddock in which the bodies of drowned animals could be seen. At least seventeen had been lost in the storm. One neighbour had had 1,100 sheep drowned.

Everywhere we looked there were landslips and Clyde became more and more depressed as he saw how much of his farm had simply vanished. 'Where has my land gone?' he asked. 'Down the river to Gisborne,' answered his neighbour. Indeed the problems faced by

'Where has my land gone?' asked Clyde.

the fruit and vegetable growers on the rich flats near the town were as bad as those of the farmers in the hills. Half the grapes, kiwi fruit and maize had simply vanished under silt. One man I met had started to harvest his melon crop the day the storm broke. It had cost him NZ$100,000 to plant – all borrowed money, of course – and it was a write-off. The packing factories were already laying off staff as there was clearly going to be little fruit to pack for a while. Everyone faced a grim future.

Conditions on Clyde's farm, however, were so bad that we very nearly failed to find a way across it between impassable mud slides. In all directions the green hillsides were scarred with brown gashes; an average of half the land had simply slipped into the valley and been washed away. Clyde had lost 1,000 of his 2,000 acres. The only hope of getting grass to grow again on the steep, exposed soil would be to broadcast seed at once before it dried out – but that could only be done by helicopter and all of those were still urgently needed to save lives. Not that anyone could afford to hire one in the first place.

There was a poignant moment when we reached a ridge from which there was a distant view across a deep valley to a scarred mountainside. Clyde commented that about 80 per cent of the grass cover had gone there.

'Is it yours?' I asked.

'No, that's not mine,' he replied, 'but those are.'

I looked where he was pointing and saw a line of white dots heading away from us in single file across a distant brown scree and disappearing over the ridge beyond. Some of Clyde's best angora goats had wandered across his boundary fence and were heading for the coast. It was hopeless to try to follow them; the horses would have become bogged long before we could reach them. Even if we did succeed in bringing them back, he had no secure paddocks in which to keep them. He never saw them again.

Down in the valley Jacky and Kowhai were doing rescue work, ferrying people and their stock out of danger as the flood waters rose. Jacky hugged us and we promised to come back to New Zealand.

We left. We said goodbye to Clyde and Carol, and to the horses. It was over. One Whinney was to stay with Clyde, who had taken a fancy to her. She was our thank-you present to him, the least we could do after all the trouble he had taken to make everything happen for us. Star went back to his owner, with thanks, and already there were several potential buyers for Manaaki.

Everyone agrees that the East Cape region should never have been cleared in the first place. Originally the land was covered in native forest and this held the delicate ecosystem together. Trees and scrub grew on steep slopes of mudstone and sandstone running down to the sea, highly unstable young soils bound by the vegetation. Captain Cook made his first landfall on this coast. He named the bay where he first set foot 'Poverty Bay' 'because it afforded us no one thing we wanted,' although that was the result of his first ill-fated meetings with Maori, whom his men shot when they seemed aggressive, rather than any reflection on the richness of the land. Later he traded for the sweet potatoes and yams that the Maori grew in the fertile soil and he was impressed by the 'verdure' of the surroundings. Settlement was delayed because at first it was impossible to drive roads through the soft mudstone, which even then slipped when cleared. Instead people arrived by boat, anchoring off shore and ferrying their possessions, families and foundation stock animals ashore. Basing themselves on the beaches at first, they cleared the forest inland and, finding the soil rich, then moved their sheep and cattle up the hills.

Erosion soon began and rapidly accelerated until it was recognized as some of the most severe in the world, certainly the worst in New Zealand. Gigantic slips affecting several properties scarred the landscape. At first the original landowners could afford to retire parts of their large properties, leaving them as scrub or planting trees to try to bind the soil. They grazed only where the land seemed able to take it, driving large herds of stock from place to place.

When returned soldiers were given land after both World Wars the

In the valleys crops and buildings were buried under the silt.

properties became much smaller, down to as little as 600 acres (250 hectares) from the previous 20,000 acre (8,000 hectares) holdings. At the same time the Department of Agriculture and other experts all advised the farmers to stock the land more intensively. It was inevitable that matters would deteriorate.

There is a poem by Denis Glover in the *Penguin Book of New Zealand Verse* which eloquently and crisply captures the despair so many farmers have experienced in this unforgiving land. It also catches cleverly the warbling song of the magpies, often the first sound we would hear in the mornings. They are different from the European magpie, having been imported in large numbers from Australia; less starkly black and white, bigger and more mottled, they are everywhere in the New Zealand countryside, inquisitive, invasive and faintly sinister as they watch dispassionately the farmer's efforts to tame the land.

When Tom and Elizabeth took the farm
The bracken made their bed,
And Quardle oodle ardle wardle doodle
The magpies said.

Tom's hand was strong to the plough
Elizabeth's lips were red,
And Quardle oodle ardle wardle doodle
The magpies said.

Year in year out they worked
While the pines grew overhead,
And Quardle oodle ardle wardle doodle
The magpies said.

Elizabeth is dead now (it's years ago)
Old Tom went light in the head;
And Quardle oodle ardle wardle doodle
The magpies said.

The farm's still there. Mortgage corporations
Couldn't give it away.
And Quardle oodle ardle wardle doodle
The magpies said.

Many farmers had tried planting trees to halt erosion, but with limited success. In the 1960s the Soil Conservation and Rivers Control Council – of which Carol's great uncle J. P. Hare had been the pioneering Deputy Chairman – divided the whole area into 'critical headwaters' which should be protected and 'pastoral forelands' where farming could continue. Separated by what came to be known as the 'blue line', it was hoped this solution, one of the most radical ever made in New Zealand, would stop the erosion.

Looking into the distance from the high ridges on Clyde's farm, we could see recent conifer plantations which had themselves slipped en masse down the hillside, the neat, straight rows of trees becoming wavy and broken in the process. Poplars seemed to work better. We rode through one section of scattered mature trees under which there were no slips and the land seemed firmer. There was less grass under the trees than on the open hillside and Clyde, who has himself made strenuous efforts to plant trees in recent years, said, 'Can you imagine the problems of trying to muster stock if the whole country was covered in those?' But it did seem to me a hopeful sign and a possible solution.

It is always a tragedy to see land that has been misused and it makes me angry. Mistakes are forgivable but there is an obstinacy in modern western man which seems to prevent him recognizing very simple environmental laws. Living on a small and fragile planet we simply cannot afford to waste its resources; not just the non-renewable ones such as fossil fuels but, much more importantly, the soils on which we can grow food and which nurture the whole ecosystem that preserves life in all its diversity. It is still hard for most people to imagine how the incredible richness of the rain forests could be harnessed for man's use (although those who live in them know it well enough) but we do know that there is something profoundly wrong in extinguishing so much diversity.

Too late to save what has already gone, but possibly just in time to save the planet, mankind is waking up to the danger of destroying our Eden faster than it can renew itself. Shortly after my return home, the European Parliament passed a resolution banning the importation of tropical hardwoods from Sarawak until they are produced in a sound and sustainable manner and in such a way as not to be detrimental to the interests of the forests' native inhabitants. This was a direct result of our mission to Malaysia on my way out to New Zealand, and a heartening display of concern by politicians.

In New Zealand it is easier to understand and regret the waste of productive land; to implement programmes to put things right; to form committees to monitor events and write reports on progress. Certainly there are success stories where ingenuity and hard work have made land produce well; but there are far too many failures and these have been tolerated because of the plentiful acreage and the small population, which has often been able to walk away from its mistakes. New Zealanders have tended to see land as a capital gain to be cashed in when it is time to move on. It is very noticeable that the turnover of land is far more rapid than in Europe; farmers chop and change as the mood and their finances take them and there is seldom a vision of building something long-term for the grandchildren. We even met farmers who had swapped farms. This is inconceivable in Europe where farms have often been in the same family for many generations. In New Zealand, where the attachment to the land is so new, it is all part of the process of settling down.

A proper understanding and respect for nature only comes with time. New Zealanders can hardly be blamed for failing to develop a sensitivity to their country which has changed so rapidly in the short time since their forebears arrived. The chapters of disastrous introductions, each one compounding the problems of the last, would have daunted the stoutest hearts. Yet they must learn if they are to put their house in order.

The Maori were, contrary to *pakeha* mythology, excellent farmers before the Europeans arrived. They terraced the land to prevent it slipping and observed strict taboos to prevent the overexploitation of game, fish and other resources. The early settlers would not have survived without their help, just as was the case on the east coast of North America where the Pilgrim Fathers were helped through their first hungry winters by the Indians. Maori farmers fed the settlers, their mills ground their flour, their early banking systems bailed them out; but, fatally as it turned out, they saw their land as enduring rather than making money and they were cheated out of it. Documents suppressed for more than a hundred years are today coming to light through the Waitangi Tribunal to reveal just how ruthlessly they were exploited. Once the *pakeha* are made aware of this and the current wave of racial intolerance collapses, as it must if the country is not to tear itself apart, then the basic New Zealand sense of fair play will recognize the merit of the Maori case. After all, the *pakeha* too perceive themselves as having been hard done by, first as emigrants from a country which banished them, then by an uncaring colonial administration, finally by their abandonment by that same motherland when she chose Europe as her market instead of them.

Much boils down to education on both sides, not just so that there may be equal opportunities for Maori in a *pakeha* world if that is the direction they choose to take, but also so that *pakeha* may learn to understand, respect and indeed welcome the Maori view of the world which, had it been followed, would have avoided many of the mistakes which have cost the country so dear.

New Zealand is a country of extremes in people and landscapes, attitudes and environments. The bigotry of those who have convinced themselves that different races can never exist together in harmony and so live themselves in constant fear contrasts with the sweetness and reason of life on the *marae*, where good sense and hope prevail, where everything can be resolved through discussion. The hopelessness of the East Cape, where the land is falling into the sea and should never have been exploited, is counterbalanced by the richness of the good dairy land where milk production is down to a fine art and the tended soil gives bountifully. The decent farmers, as honourable, hard working and fulfilled as any men anywhere, are a world away from the squalor of an urban Maori section where sullen youths lounge among wrecked cars, angry and aimless.

(*Opposite*) Poplars seemed to bind the soil best, preventing landslips, but most of the East Cape should never have been cleared in the first place.

Contrast is healthy, but too many in New Zealand see only their own way as right and refuse to recognize another point of view. As I write, four months after our return home, Winston Peters, a Maori member of the opposition National Party, is quoted in my English daily newspaper, the *Independent*, as speaking of 'deep and abiding loathing of all things Maori' among Europeans and 'malignant and destructive hatred' of whites by Maori radicals. 'This is the last chance we have to get race relations right,' he says. 'If we do not confront it now, in ten years there will be violence in our streets and the race riots of Watts, Toxteth and Soweto will have their New Zealand equivalent.' That would be an unnecessary tragedy in a country with so much going for it.

The souls of the Maori leave this world from the northernmost tip of the North Island, at Cape Reinga, The Leaping Place. A narrow headland juts out into the sea and on the cliff face there grows an ancient *pohutukawa* tree, said to be over 800 years old. From this the souls of the departed leap out into the water and so down to the underworld. It is an utterly beautiful spot and one which surprisingly few New Zealanders ever visit. We made the five-hour drive up from Auckland, glad that we had not arranged to ride along the straight, narrow road through Northland, nor attempted the forbidding waste of the 90-mile beach. We were overwhelmed by the views that greeted us at the end of the journey. It is a place of untamed loveliness, where scrub-covered hills drop to untouched sandy beaches battered by the waves of both the Tasman Sea and the Pacific Ocean, which meet here.

As we stood on the headland in the setting sun we could feel the whole country stretching away to the south behind us. New Zealand is a strange, restless place; the land is still unsettled and can heave or burst open at any time; the *pakeha* also are unsettled, ready to emigrate if they become dissatisfied with their government or the economy. No people have changed their landscape faster or more profoundly, carpeting some regions with the largest man-made forests on earth, denuding others to expose the bones beneath the fat of the land.

There is an energy, a life force to the country which involves all its citizens, wherever they choose to live. Whether this comes from the bounty of their homeland or from the constant knocks, many self-inflicted, to which they have been subjected over the years, I do not know. What I do know is that their problems are small compared to

(*Opposite*) Cape Reinga where the souls of the Maori leap out into the sea from the lone pohutukawa tree.

those faced by most of the world and if they cannot resolve them then there is little hope for the planet and its occupants. Three million well-educated and resourceful people occupy a potential paradise in the Pacific. They have no enemies at their borders, nor refugees crowding into camps; famines and epidemics are unknown to them; the Maori and other Polynesian immigrants some fear so much in reality pose no threat to them. They add a culture and a spice to a society which might otherwise deserve the epithet most often used by non-New Zealanders about it – boring. We did not find it boring, except in so far as the horizons of many people were limited to their own shores. This is no longer forgivable in a modern world, where distances have been shrunk by air travel, satellites and fax machines; for the business community it is all one office; for sportsmen and entertainers the whole world really is their stage.

The serpents in this Eden are all of man's own making, and man-made monsters can only be destroyed by man. Respect is the best weapon; respect for the land, which is rich and beautiful for all its fragility; respect for each other, and that includes women, intellectuals and other races, not just the good mates in the bar; above all self-respect, because New Zealanders are as worthy of it as any people, but secretly doubt their own place in the world. It is time to take down the 'Closed' sign and open up. The perfect time to do this would seem to be 1990 when, in celebrating the hundred-and-fiftieth anniversary of the Treaty of Waitangi, New Zealand will have an opportunity to show that it is possible to blend the best of North and South, and to produce racial harmony and prosperity without sacrificing independence or ruining the environment. New Zealanders should embrace their rightful role as an example to the world of everything for which other less-favoured countries strive. If they cannot do it no one can and the outlook for this planet is truly bleak.

The Lord is my Shepherd.

# *Itinerary*

| Day | Date | Route | Hours | Miles | Kms |
|---|---|---|---|---|---|
| | January | | | | |
| 1 | Sat 16 | Arrival. Mt Linton. Try out new saddles | ½ | | |
| 2 | Sun 17 | Mt Linton – Dunrobin | 9 | 30 | 50 |
| 3 | Mon 18 | Dunrobin. Exercise only | 1 | | |
| 4 | Tues 19 | Dunrobin – Centre Hill | 3½ | 15 | 25 |
| 5 | Wed 20 | Lake Mavora | 2 | 6 | 10 |
| 6 | Thurs 21 | Lake Mavora – Taipo Hut | 6 | 20 | 30 |
| 7 | Fri 22 | Taipo Hut – Mt Nicholas | 9 | 30 | 50 |
| 8 | Sat 23 | Mt Nicholas – Cecil Peak | 5½ | 15 | 25 |
| 9 | Sun 24 | Remarkables. Rest Day | | | |
| 10 | Mon 25 | ,, | | | |
| 11 | Tues 26 | ,, | | | |
| 12 | Wed 27 | Arrowtown – Roses Hut | 7½ | 26 | 42 |
| 13 | Thurs 28 | Rose's Hut – Motatapu | 3 | 15 | 25 |
| 14 | Fri 29 | Wanaka – Godley Peaks | | | |
| 15 | Sat 30 | Godley Peaks – Sutherlands Hut | 2 | 9 | 15 |
| 16 | Sun 31 | Sutherlands Hut – Mt Gerald | 3 | 13 | 22 |
| | February | | | | |
| 17 | Mon 1 | Mt Gerald – Felt Hut | 10 | 22 | 37 |
| 18 | Tues 2 | Felt Hut – Mesopotamia | 4 | 14 | 24 |
| 19 | Wed 3 | Mesopotamia – Hakatere | 5 | 19 | 32 |
| 20 | Thurs 4 | Hakatere – Glenfalloch | 6 | 30 | 50 |
| 21 | Fri 5 | Glenfalloch – Lake Coleridge | 4½ | 15 | 25 |
| 22 | Sat 6 | Hickory Bay – Okains Bay Waitangi Day | | | |
| 23 | Sun 7 | | | | |
| 24 | Mon 8 | Christchurch | | | |
| 25 | Tues 9 | Christchurch | | | |
| 26 | Wed 10 | Christchurch | | | |
| 27 | Thurs 11 | Mt White | | | |
| 28 | Fri 12 | Mt White – Deep Creek Hut | 8½ | 31 | 52 |

| | | | | | |
|---|---|---|---|---|---|
| 29 | Sat 13 | Deep Creek Hut – Esk Head – Lake Sumner | 8 | 30 | 50 |
| 30 | Sun 14 | No 2 Hut – The Poplars | 6½ | 35 | 60 |
| 31 | Mon 15 | Glenhope – St James | 7½ | 40 | 67 |
| 32 | Tues 16 | Lake Tennyson – Tarndale | 3½ | 18 | 30 |
| 33 | Wed 17 | Tarndale (Mustering) – Molesworth | 5 | 35 | 60 |
| 34 | Thurs 18 | Molesworth – Camden | 7 | 36 | 62 |
| 35 | Fri 19 | Meadowbank – Blenheim | | | |
| 36 | Sat 20 | Blenheim | | (504) | (963) |
| | | | | | |
| 37 | Sun 21 | Ferry across Cook Strait | | | |
| 38 | Mon 22 | Wellington RDA | | | |
| 39 | Tues 23 | Marton | | | |
| 40 | Wed 24 | Marton – Te Kumu | 10 | 40 | 67 |
| 41 | Thurs 25 | Marton | | | |
| 42 | Fri 26 | Kawhatau | | | |
| 43 | Sat 27 | Marton | | | |
| 44 | Sun 28 | Gentle Annie | 2 | 8 | 14 |
| 45 | Mon 29 | Kanui | 1½ | 5 | 8 |
| | March | | | | |
| 46 | Tues 1 | Napier – Mahia Peninsula | | | |
| 47 | Wed 2 | Onenui – Mahanga | 7 | 30 | 50 |
| 48 | Thurs 3 | Mahanga – Hineroa | 5 | 25 | 40 |
| 49 | Fri 4 | Hineroa – Gisborne | 3½ | 15 | 25 |
| 50 | Sat 5 | Gisborne Show | ½ | 2 | 3 |
| 51 | Sun 6 | Gisborne – Manaaki | 1 | 4 | 7 |
| 52 | Mon 7 | Cyclone Bola | | | |
| 53 | Tues 8 | ,, | | | |
| 54 | Wed 9 | Manaaki | | | |
| 55 | Thur 10 | ,, | | | |
| 56 | Fri 11 | Last ride around Manaaki | 5 | 15 | 25 |
| | | Totals | 173 | 648 | 1202 |

# A Glossary of some common New Zealand and Maori words

**Amble** A special easy gait for horses.
*Aotearoa* The Land of the Long White Cloud, the Maori for New Zealand.
*atua* ancestral gods.
**Bach** Summer holiday shack.
**Beech trees** (*Nothofagus spp.*) The evergreen Southern beech trees.
**Bellbird** (*Anthornis melanura*) An insignificant native bird with a beautiful voice.
**Billy/billycan** A tin can with a lid used for camp cooking.
**Black Swan** (*Cygnus atratus*) Introduced from Australia.
**Botflies** Flies which are parasitic to sheep, horses, man, etc.
**Bulldog/bulldogging** To throw an animal by catching its horns and twisting its neck.
**Bullockies** Bullock cart drovers.
**Bush Lawyer** (*genus Rubus*) A barbed member of the rose family, which climbs over bushes and trees often forming an impenetrable mass.
**California quail** (*Lophortyx californica*) Successful introduction which has replaced the native species.
**Chamois** Mountain antelopes from Europe released in the South Island in 1907.
**Fantail** (*Rhipidura fuliginosa*) Delightful common and tame New Zealand bird.
**Flax** (*Phormium tenax*) A valuable commercial plant with dark green leaves often six feet or more in length. Widely used by the Maori for clothing, baskets, etc, it is still used for rope production today.
**Greenstone** Nephrite jade native to New Zealand. Used by the Maori for making ornaments, war clubs, etc.
*haka* A posture dance usually performed by males.
**Hard case** Someone with the courage of his or her convictions.
*hariru* To shake hands.
*hongi* To press noses.
**Huia** (*Heteralocha acutirostris*) Almost certainly extinct bird whose feathers used to be much treasured by the Maori.
**Huntaway** Dogs which bark as they work to drive sheep.
**Hydatids** Larval tapeworms hosted by dogs and dangerous to man.
**Kaka** (*Nestor meridionalis*) A native parrot.
**Kakapo** (*Strigops habroptilus*) A ground dwelling parrot.
*karanga* The call of welcome.
**Kauri tree** (*Agathis australis*) A huge evergreen tree. The resin used to be very valuable for varnishes.

**Kea** (*Nestor notabilis*) A large green parrot, sometimes prone to attacking sheep.

**Kiwi** (*Apteryx*) New Zealand's national and most ancient bird.

***Kohanga Reo*** 'Language Nest'. A movement to foster Maori values and language.

**Kowhai** (*Sophora spp.*) Yellow-flowered native tree.

**Kumara** (*Ipomoca batatas*) The sweet potato brought to Aotearoa by the Maori as their staple diet.

*manuhiri* Guest.

**Manuka** (*Leptospermum scoparium*) The 'tea tree' – a tough, common shrub, which can grow into a small tree.

*Maoritanga* Things that relate to Maori culture.

*marae* The enclosed ground used as a Maori meeting place.

*marae-atea* The area between hosts and guests during a welcome.

**Matagouri** (*Discaria toumatou*) Wild Irishman, a very common thorn bush.

*mere* A flat weapon made of greenstone.

**Moa** (*Dinornis gigantea, et al*) Extinct flightless birds.

**Mohair** The fibre produced by angora goats. (Angora wool comes from angora rabbits.)

*moko* Tattooing.

*mokomakai* Tattooed Maori head.

**Morepork** (*Ninox novaeseelandiae*) Native owl.

**Muster/musterer** Mustering is the New Zealand word for rounding up sheep, usually, or cattle.

*nau mai* Welcome.

**New Zealand rug** An all-weather horse blanket.

**Paddock** The name for all fields, whatever their size.

*pakeha* Foreigner, usually of European descent.

**Paradise duck** (*Tadorna variegata*) New Zealand relation of the Shelduck.

*piupiu* Maori skirt made of flax.

**Pohutukawa** (*Metrosideros excelsa*) Red-flowered native tree.

**Pom/pommies** Person or people from England.

*powhiri* To welcome.

**Pukeko** (*Porphyrio melanotus*) Swamp hen.

**Rata** (*Metrosideros robusta*) Species of native hardwood tree.

**Rifleman** (*Acanthisitta chloris*) The smallest bird in New Zealand.

**Rimu** (*Dacrydium cupressinum*) Red pine.

**Robin** (*Petroica australis*) Looks quite like a European robin but is no relation.

**Run/run holder** The leaseholder of a cattle or sheep station, usually in the high country, where the government owns most of the land.

**Scree** Loose rock and stones which have slipped down a hillside.

**Section** A building lot or piece of ground.

**Skylark** (*Alauda arvenis*) Introduced from England, they have adapted to singing from a perch.

**Speargrass** (*genus Aciphylla*) The Wild Spaniard. Plants with tufts of sword-like leaves a foot or more in length.

**Station** The name for a large farm.

**Stockman** Usual name for one who musters cattle rather than sheep.

**Takahe** (*Notornis mantelli*) A very rare New Zealand bird related to the pukeko.

*taki* Dart or twig used as a challenge (*wero*).

**tangata whenua** (*People of the land*) The host people; the original inhabitants.

*tangi* Lamentation, funeral.

*tangihanga* The ceremony of mourning the dead.

*tapu* Forbidden, sacred.

**Taranaki gate** A simple wire netting gate named after the rich dairying region in the North Island.

**Tarn** A small mountain lake.

*tena koutou* Greetings.

**Thar (or Tahr)** Himalayan goats first released in the South Island in 1904.

**Ti** (*Cordyline spp.*) Cabbage tree.

**Tiki** Greenstone figure worn around the neck.

**Tomtit** (*Petroica macrocephala*) Small native flycatcher.

**Tramper** A hiker or walker.

**Tui** (*Prosthemadera novaeseelandiae*) The parson bird.

*turuturu* A pole.

**Tussock** Native grasses of various species, which grow in clumps over large areas of upland in New Zealand, creating attractive landscapes.

*waewae tapu* Forbidden footprint.

*waiata* Song; to sing.

*wero* Challenge.

*whare* House or shed.

*whare hui* Meeting house.

**Wryvel** (*Anarhynchus frontalis*) Small plover with unique bill with curve to right.

# Bibliography

Anderson, Mona. *A River Rules my Life* (A. H. and A. W. Reed, Wellington, 1963).

Ashdown, Michael and Lucas, Diane. *Tussock Grasslands, Landscape Values and Vulnerability* (New Zealand Environmental Council, 1987).

Barker, Lady. *Station Life in New Zealand* (Virago, 1984 [first published 1870]).

Bigwood, J. & K. *The New Zealand Maori in Colour*. Text by Harry Dansey (A. H. & A. W. Reed, Wellington 1963).

Bone, Robert W. *The Maverick Guide to New Zealand* (Pelican, 1986).

Buller, W. L. *A History of the Birds of New Zealand* (John van Voorst, London, 1873).

Buller, Sir Walter. *A History of the Birds of New Zealand*, 2 vols. Second Edition. Published (for the subscribers) by the author. London 1887–8. (The above, published after the author was knighted in 1886, may be considered a separate work.)

Butler, Samuel. *Erewhon* (Penguin, 1985).

Cameron, William J. *New Zealand* (Prentice-Hall, 1965).

Curnow, Allen (ed). *Penguin Book of New Zealand Verse* (Penguin, 1960).

Druett, Joan. *Exotic Intruders* (Heinemann, Auckland, 1983).

Dumas, Alexandre. *The Journal of Madame Giovanni*. Translated from the French edition (1856) by Marguerite E. Wilbur (Hammond, Hammond & Co, 1944).

Ell, Gordon. *Wildflowers and Weeds of New Zealand* (The Bush, Press, Auckland, 1983).

Fuller, Errol. *Extinct Birds* (Viking/Rainbird, 1987).

Gordon, John. *People, Places and Paddocks* (Lansdowne Press, Auckland, 1987).

Guthrie-Smith, W.H. *Tutira: The Story of a New Zealand Sheep Station*, 4th edition (A. H. and A. W Reed, 1969).

Hall, Peter and Wright, Vernon. *A Shepherd's Year* (Reed Methuen, 1987).

*Hildebrand's Travel Guide, New Zealand* (KARTO + GRAFIK, Germany, 1987).

Hulme, Keri. *The Bone People* (Pan, 1986).

Jardine, D. G. *Shadows on the Hill* (A. H. & A. W. Reed, Wellington, 1978).

McCaskill, L. W. *Molesworth* (A. H. & A. W. Reed, Wellington, 1969).

McDonald, Geoff. *Shadows over New Zealand* (Chaston, Christchurch, 1985).

McLauchlan, Gordon. *The Passionless People* (Cassell, 1977).

McLean, Denis. *The Long Pathway: Te Ara Roa* (Collins, 1986).

McLeod, David. *Many a Glorious Morning* (Whitcombe & Tombs, 1970).

Marsh, Ngaio. *Black Beech and Honeydew* (Little, Brown, 1965).
Morrell, W. P. and Hall, D. O. W. *A History of New Zealand Life* (Whitcombe and Tombs, Christchurch, 1957).
Newton, Peter. *High Country Journey* (A. H. and A. W. Reed, Wellington, 1952).
Newton, Peter. *The Boss's Story* (A. H. & A. W. Reed, Wellington, 1966).
Orange, Claudia. *The Treaty of Waitangi* (Allen & Unwin, 1987).
Orbell, Margaret. *The Natural World of the Maori* (William Collins, Auckland, 1985).
Paul, Janet and Roberts, Neil. *Evelyn Page: Seven Decades* (The Robert McDougall Art Gallery, Christchurch, 1987).
Peat, Neville. *Detours: A Journey through small-town New Zealand* (Whitcoulls, Christchurch, 1982).
Phillips, Jock (ed.) *Te Whenua, Te Iwi: The Land and the People* (Allen & Unwin, Wellington, 1987).
Poole, A. L. *Catchment Control in New Zealand* (Crown Copyright, 1983).
Pope, Diana and Jeremy. *Mobil New Zealand Travel Guides: North Island/South Island* (Reed Methuen, 1986).
Reed, A. W. *A Dictionary of Maori Place Names* (Reed Methuen, 1987).
Reed. A. W. *Concise Maori Dictionary* (Reed, Methuen, 1987).
Shadbolt, Maurice. *New Zealand, Gift of the Sea* (Whitcombe & Combs, New Zealand, 1963).
Sinclair, Keith. *The Origins of the Maori Wars* (Auckland University Press, 1980).
Tussock Grasslands & Mountain Lands Institute. Review 42, December 1984, Editor B. T. Robertson.
T.G.M.L.I. J. T. Holloway. *The Mountain Lands of New Zealand.* 1982.
T.G.M.L.I. *Proceedings of the 1987 Hill and High Country Seminar.*
Waitangi Tribunal. *Orakei Report* (Crown Copyright, 1987).
Walker, Ranginui. *Nga Tau Tohetohe: Years of Anger* (Penguin, 1987).
Wallace L. Tim and Lattimore, Ralph. *Rural New Zealand – What Next?* (Lincoln College, 1987).

# Index

Page numbers in *italics* refer to illustrations